# ECONOMIC INTEGRATION AMONG DEVELOPING NATIONS: LAW AND POLICY

Beverly May Carl

PRAEGER

PRAEGER SPECIAL STUDIES • PRAEGER SCIENTIFIC

New York • Philadelphia • Eastbourne, UK
Toronto • Hong Kong • Tokyo • Sydney

**Library of Congress Cataloging-in-Publication Data**

Carl, Beverly May.
  Economic integration among developing nations.

  "Praeger special studies. Praeger scientific."
  Includes index.
  1. Developing countries — Economic integration.
  2. International economic integration. I. Title.
HC59.7.C31418  1986  337.1′1724  85-30777
ISBN 0-03-005973-9 (alk. paper)

Published in 1986 by Praeger Publishers
CBS Educational and Professional Publishing, a Division of CBS Inc.
521 Fifth Avenue, New York, NY 10175 USA

© 1986 by Praeger Publishers

6789  052  987654321

Printed in the United States of America on acid-free paper

To my mother, Laura Payne Carl, who once superimposed a classic Portuguese dress style onto a traditional Hawaiian mumu. After suitable modifications, she produced a unique and lovely gown. So too planners are trying to fit European integration patterns onto the developing economies of the Third World. May these leaders also find the appropriate adjustments to bring forth a new design for prosperity.

# PREFACE

This book is directed toward business people, lawyers and public officials who have to deal with the complex economic structures being created by a myriad of new integration associations. Recently, *Business Latin America*[1] ran an imaginary job description for a "LAIA Coordinator," highlighting the need of multinational corporations for personnel knowledgeable about the Latin American Integration Association.

To a significant extent, the success of these integration efforts, at least in market economies, will depend on private companies taking advantage of the opportunities offered. To do so, firms and their attorneys will require information about the various markets. Likewise, effective implementation of these integration schemes will call for understanding and sympathetic government administrators. Educational institutions in turn must assume the task of training the people without whom the system cannot work.

With these concerns in mind, I began collecting materials on integration some 15 years ago. Fortunately, my work has taken me to a number of cities where integration activities have been centered: Arusha, Tanzania; Havana; Montevideo, Uruguay; Moscow; Jakarta, Indonesia; Lima, Peru; and Lagos, Nigeria. Everywhere local lawyers and public officials have been most helpful in sharing their experience and in providing useful materials. Without such assistance, this book could not have been produced.

Although the word *law* is used in the title, this is not intended as a law book exclusively for lawyers. Rather my objective has been to prepare a study easily comprehended by any layperson interested in the subject. Likewise, I have tried to write so as to minimize difficulties for readers to whom English is a second language.

Understanding the legal profession's desire to see primary sources, I have included in the appendixes many of the key provisions from the various integration agreements. Unfortunately, space limitations prevent reprinting these documents in their entirety; but in most cases citations have been given to English sources where the full text is available.

This study on economic integration hopefully will be the first in a series of books examining the role of law in economic development and wealth distribution in the Third World. Other subjects that may be covered in future volumes include private investment, mixed and planned economies, as well as foreign trade.

## NOTE

1. *Business Latin America*, January 25, 1984, p. 26.

# ACKNOWLEDGMENTS

First my gratitude goes to the Dana Foundation for its generous support, which made possible the research upon which this book is based.

Next I wish to express my appreciation to Dr. Teresa Genta Fons, my Uruguayan research assistant. In reviewing the manuscript, Dr. Genta Fons provided invaluable insights into the workings of these integration units; moreover, she even managed the tedious task of cite checking cheerfully.

Finally, I want to thank the many friends and colleagues around the world who provided so much assistance and information about these integration associations.

# CONTENTS

# APPENDIXES
## Selected Provisions from Integration Agreements

# PRINCIPAL ECONOMIC INTEGRATION UNITS AND MEMBER COUNTRIES

## COMMON MARKETS

**European Economic Community**
Belgium
Denmark
France
Germany
Greece
Ireland
Italy
Luxembourg
Netherlands
United Kingdom
Spain (due for membership 1986)
Portugal (negotiating membership)

**ANCOM (Andean) Common Market**
Bolivia
Colombia          .
Ecuador
Peru
Venezuela

**Caribbean Common Market**
Antigua
Bahamas
Barbados
Belize
Guyana
Jamaica
Trinidad/Tobago
Dominica, Grenada,
   St. Lucia, St. Vincent,
   St. Kitts-Nevis-Anguilla,
   Montserrat

**Eastern Caribbean Common Market**
Antigua and Barbuda
Dominica
Grenada
Montserrat
St. Kitts/Nevis
Saint Lucia
Saint Vincent
The Grenadines

**Economic Community of the States of Central Africa (signatories)**
Cameroon
Central African Republic
Congo
Gabon
Burundi
Rwanda
Zaire
Chad
Equatorial Guinea
Sao Tome and Principe
Angola (considering)

**Central American Common Market**
Costa Rica
El Salvador
Guatemala
Honduras
Nicaragua

## COMMON MARKETS (continued)

**Economic Community of West African States**
Benin (Dahomey)
Cape Verde
Gambia
Ghana
Guinea
Guinea-Bissau
Ivory Coast
Liberia
Mali
Mauritania
Niger
Nigeria
Senegal
Sierra Leone
Togo
Burkina Faso (Upper Volta)

**East African Common Market (defunct)**
Kenya
Tanzania
Uganda

**Arab Common Market**
Egypt
Iraq
Syria
Jordan

## FREE TRADE ASSOCIATIONS

**European Free Trade Association**
Austria
Finland
Iceland
Norway
Portugal
Sweden
Switzerland

**Latin American Free Trade Association:** now replaced by Latin American Integration Association (see below).

# TRADE PREFERENCE ASSOCIATIONS

**Association of Southeast Asian Nations**
Brunei
Indonesia
Malaysia
Philippines
Singapore
Thailand

**Latin American Integration Association**
Argentina
Bolivia
Brazil
Chile
Colombia
Ecuador
Mexico
Paraguay
Peru
Uruguay
Venezuela

**Preferential Trade Area for Eastern and Southern African States (open to membership by:)**
Angola
Botswana
Burundi
Comoros
Djibouti
Ethiopia
Kenya
Lesotho
Madagascar
Malawi
Mauritius
Mozambique
Rwanda
Seychelles
Somali Democratic Republic
Swaziland
Tanzania
Uganda
Zaire
Zambia
Zimbabwe

# OTHER INTEGRATION UNITS

**Council for Mutual Economic Assistance**
Soviet Union
Bulgaria
Czechoslovakia
East Germany
Hungary
Poland
Romania
Mongolia
Cuba
Vietnam

**Central African Customs Union (UDEAC)**
Cameroon
Central African Republic
Chad
Congo-Brazzaville
Equatorial Guinea
Gabon

**West African Economic Community**
Ivory Coast
Mali
Mauritania
Niger
Senegal
Burkina Faso (Upper Volta)

**Mano River Union**
Guinea
Liberia
Sierra Leone

**Maghreb**
Algeria
Morocco
Tunisia

# LIST OF ACRONYMS

| | |
|---|---|
| AEM | ASEAN Economic Ministers |
| AIC | ASEAN Industrial Complementation Projects |
| AIJV | ASEAN Industrial Joint Ventures |
| AIP | ASEAN Industrial Project |
| ANCOM | Andean Common Market |
| ASEAN | Association of Southeast Asian Nations |
| BLADEX | Latin America Export Bank |
| CACM | Central American Common Market |
| CAME | See COMECON |
| CARICOM | Caribbean Common Market |
| CARIFTA | Caribbean Free Trade Association |
| CFA | Communauté Financière Africaine (common currency of the West African Monetary Union) |
| CMEA | See COMECON |
| COIME | Committee on Industry, Minerals and Energy |
| COMECON | Council for Mutual Economic Assistance |
| ECCAS | Economic Community of Central African States |
| ECCM | East Caribbean Common Market |
| ECOWAS | Economic Community of West African States |
| EEC | European Economic Community |
| EFTA | European Free Trade Association |
| EMA | Andean Multinational Enterprise (Empresa Multinacional Andina) |
| FTO | Foreign Trade Organization (used in planned economies) |
| GATT | General Agreement on Tariffs and Trade |
| GSP | Generalized System of Preferences |
| IBEC | International Bank for Economic Development |
| IBRD | International Bank for Reconstruction and Development |
| IIB | International Investment Bank |
| IMF | International Monetary Fund |
| INTAL | Institute for Latin American Integration (under the Inter-American Development Bank) |
| LAFTA | Latin American Free Trade Association |
| LAIA | Latin American Integration Association |
| OPIC | Overseas Private Investment Corporation |
| PTA | Preferential Trade Area for Eastern and Southern African States |
| SDR | Special Drawing Rights |
| UAPTA | Unit of Account for the Preferential Trade Area |
| UMLA | Latin American Monetary Unit |
| UNCTAD | United Nations Conference on Trade and Development |

# 1

# THE ROLE OF INTEGRATION IN DEVELOPMENT

## INTRODUCTION: THE ECONOMIC ENVIRONMENT

Recent years have not been kind to the Third World. Hopes fueled by the 1960s' rhetoric, the "decade of development," have given way to the grim realities of the 1980s. Among nonoil developing countries, per capita economic growth declined from some 3 percent per annum during most of the 1960s and 1970s to virtually zero in 1981 and to negative figures in 1982 and 1983.[1]

The developing nations, which account for three-quarters of the earth's population, receive only one-fifth the world's income.[2] More than 2 billion people still live in countries [3] with per capita gross national products of less than $360 (the comparable figure for the United States is $13,160).[4]

Each year between 13 and 18 million humans starve to death. One half billion people do not receive enough food on a daily basis to carry out normal activities.[5] Although agricultural production increased 57 percent between 1965 and 1980, per capita food production rose a mere 6 percent due to a rapidly expanding global population.[6] Infant mortality rates per 1,000 live births are 205 for Sierra Leone, 129 for Bolivia, and 196 for Ghana, as compared to 8 for Denmark.[7] Meanwhile, of total world expenditures for public health, a mere 9 percent is spent in the Third World.[8]

The literacy rate for the United States is about 99 percent as contrasted with 10 percent for Mali, 23 percent for Haiti, and 6 percent for Somalia.[9] Yet less than one-fourth of the world's funds for public education is spent in the Third World.[10]

Moreover, the limited income earned by the Third World is often unfairly distributed within those countries. In seven developing nations, the top 10 percent of the population received more than 40 percent of the national income, while only 2 to 4.6 percent of the earnings went to the bottom 20 percent of the people. In Brazil, Kenya, Peru, and Panama, 60 percent of the national income

1

flowed to the upper 20 percent of the population, while the lowest 20 percent received approximately 2 percent.[11]

Meanwhile, public assistance from industrialized nations to the Third World has declined from an average of 0.52 percent of their GNP in 1960 to an estimated 0.37 percent in 1983. For the United States, it fell from 0.53 percent in 1960 to an estimated 0.24 percent in 1983.[12]

Rising petroleum costs, which produced a net oil bill for Third World nations of $77 billion in 1981,[13] drained foreign exchange out of these countries forcing them to resort to foreign loans. As a consequence, commercial bank lending mushroomed, and many developing nations found themselves overextended when the global recession hit in the early 1980s. By 1985 the total debt of the Third World exceeded $800 billion.[14] Although recent debt rescheduling has shored up the world financial system, some debtor nations with weak growth prospects may prove unable to make debt repayments in the future. Meanwhile, the value of the dollar rose 47 percent between 1980 and the third quarter of 1984, making repayment of dollar loans more costly.[15] To meet their debt obligations, developing countries have had to cut their imports severely.

Likewise, the terms of trade worsened for the poor countries. The cost of goods imported by the Third World nations rose more rapidly than the price of their exports, which caused their terms of trade to deteriorate by some 20 percent between 1978 and 1982. For instance, by 1983 one ton of Chilean copper could buy only one-third of the imports it could have bought ten years before.[16] At the same time a wave of protectionism has been squeezing the South out of traditional export markets in the North. Examples of U.S. restrictions against such imports include textiles, apparel, watches, certain electronic equipment, tuna fish, most footwear, and luggage.[17]

The various pressures, intensified by the global recession, produced a severe contraction in world trade. The growth rate for exports from nonoil developing nations dropped to a mere 1.7 percent in 1982.[18] Exports from Latin America to countries outside the region fell 8.3 percent in 1982; first quarter figures indicate the situation worsened in 1983.[19]

Over the next few years, Latin America will have to appropriate as much as about 30 percent of its export earnings for payment of interest on its external debt. If repayment of principal is added to this—even assuming generous rescheduling of maturities—the region will have to devote approximately one-half of its export earnings to debt service payments.[20]

These harsh realities have prompted some observers to seek new ways to decrease the Third World's dependency on the industrialized nations. One approach calls for increasing trade and investment among the developing nations themselves. As W. Arthur Lewis has pointed out:

> The fact is that the LDCs [developing countries] should not have to be producing primarily for developed country markets. In the first place, they

could trade more with each other, and be less dependent on the developed countries for trade. The LDCs have within themselves all that is required for growth. They have surpluses of fuel and of the principal minerals. They have enough land to feed themselves, if they cultivate it properly. They are capable of learning the skills of manufacturing, and of saving the capital required for modernization. Their development does not in the long run depend on the existence of the developed countries, and their potential for growth would be unaffected *even if all the developed countries were to sink under the sea. . . .* [Italics added].[21]

Recently there has been some growth in this South-South trade, which accounted for almost 8 percent of developing country exports in 1983, as contrasted with only 4 percent in 1965.[22] Still more encouraging is the nascent trend in manufactured products, with 32 percent of such industrial exports remaining in the South in 1979, as compared to 28 percent in 1973.[23]

More trade among developing nations could help ease the protectionist pressures in the industrialized countries by reducing the level of import penetration in the North. Rather than relying so exclusively on industrialized country markets, the advanced developing countries could shift sales of some of their intermediate and capital goods to lower-income developing countries. Such products often incorporate labor-intensive technology that is more appropriate to the needs of the poor nations. In turn, the lower-income countries could begin supplying industrial country markets by partially displacing the exports of more advanced developing countries. Although these shifts in trade flows would initially involve substitution, the resulting increase in total trade for the Third World could ultimately produce greater overall income and growth.

Import substitution, as a technique for saving foreign exchange, is exhausted on a national level in areas like Latin America. The import substitution process can work in the future only where the import-substituting industries will supply the regional market and not exclusively narrow domestic markets.[24]

The key to changing traditional trade patterns may well lie in the integration movements within the Third World. This thought was echoed recently by the former assistant director of the Institute for Latin American Integration (INTAL), José Maria Aragão, when he wrote that problems within that region of growing unemployment, contracting world trade, and international illiquidity can be overcome only by

> creating closer economic ties and increasing trade and investment links [among members of the regional association] as the most efficient way to reduce their difficulties and to achieve the requisite stability so that regional interdependence shall be advantageous to all members and shall constitute an effective factor in reducing their dependence on the industrialized nations and augmenting the bargaining power [of developing countries] with other nations.[25]

In the past neither regional nor global tariff preferences had much impact on trade of the Third World. Nonetheless, the potential value of these mechanisms may have been underrated. As one expert has said, "In practical terms the 1980s may be a time to press ahead" with regional preferential trade arrangements.[26]

## INTEGRATION ASSOCIATIONS

The early success of the European Economic Community (EEC) dramatized how effective economic integration can be. Between 1959 and 1971, trade among the original six member countries increased nearly sixfold;[27] by 1979 the expanded EEC accounted for 20 percent of total world trade.[28]

This stunning example prompted a number of Third World countries to seek similar gains through economic integration within their own regions. The fragmented, weak economies of these nations had posed a serious barrier to industrial growth; the need for larger markets and greater competition seemed clear.

Consequently, the last two decades have seen a proliferation of integration efforts among developing nations. Most recently spawned is the Economic Community of the States of Central Africa (ECCAS), which was formed in 1983.[29] In 1984 Bhutan, India, Maldives, Nepal, Pakistan, and Sri Lanka took the first step toward building their own common market.[30] The year before, under a pact concluded by the Persian Gulf Cooperation Council, customs duties were abolished among Bahrain, Kuwait, Oman, Qatar, Saudi Arabia, and the United Arab Emirates.[31] The newly independent country of Brunei[32] has just joined the Association of Southeast Asian Nations (ASEAN).[33]

Socialist countries also demonstrated faith in the benefits of integration by forming their own regional organization, the Council for Mutual Economic Assistance (COMECON, CAME, or CMEA) in 1949.[34] Its membership has since been enlarged to include Mongolia, Cuba, and Vietnam.

Although several of these associations have failed, they are often replaced by new arrangements. A few years ago, political and military conflict killed the East African Common Market,[35] but those same nations recently participated in creating a new Preferential Trade Area for Eastern and Southern African States (PTA).[36] Widespread violence has severely disrupted the Central American Common Market (CACM);[37] still, the organization continues functioning at some minimal level and enjoys a degree of popularity.[38]

The Caribbean Free Trade Association (CARIFTA) evolved into the Caribbean Common Market (CARICOM).[39] The members of the East Caribbean Common Market (ECCM),[40] which had already associated themselves with CARIFTA,[41] shifted their allegiance to the new CARICOM. Today, CARICOM, the larger market, is superimposed over ECCM, a smaller common market.

When a group of nations at the middle level of development decided that the Latin American Free Trade Association (LAFTA)[42] was moving too slowly, those countries were permitted to form ANCOM,[43] the Andean Common Market. Thus, ANCOM, a common market, was built inside LAFTA, a free trade association. Later, after LAFTA proved incapable of further progress, it was replaced by the more flexible Latin American Integration Association (LAIA).[44] When ANCOM failed to meet its initial tariff reduction goals, that treaty was amended to stretch out the compliance deadlines.[45] Today, ANCOM, a common market, nests within a trade preference association, LAIA.

The following analysis will focus on the economic and commercial aspects, rather than the organizational structure, of the existing integration units. Nonetheless, one might note that for Third World integration units to take substantive actions usually all members must consent, except for those projects or programs where less than unanimous participation is authorized.[46]

The writer views this study as an "interim" appraisal, since the integration process is at an interim stage. For many years—in some cases four hundred—the trade of the Third World has been directed toward the former colonial powers.[47] To redirect those trade flows to the South is exceedingly difficult. Even today, it is cheaper to ship certain products from Rio de Janeiro to New York or from Buenos Aires to Hamburg than from Buenos Aires to Rio de Janeiro, notwithstanding the shorter distance.[48] This situation is repeated in almost all developing regions.

The sheer magnitude of the integration task mitigates against a counsel of despair simply because the obstacles are thorny. Still, some 25 years have passed since developing nations began their integration efforts. Thus, it should now be possible to make a few observations and to obtain some insights that could be helpful in chartering the future course of these endeavors.

## EFFECTS OF INTEGRATION

### Trade Creation and Diversion

With integration the removal of internal trade barriers should lead to specialization or division of labor with items being produced in those nations that can do so most efficiently. Production then can be reallocated from high cost to low cost suppliers; prices can be lowered for consumers and their standard of living increased. Such effects are known as "trade creation."

On the other hand, lower cost producers outside the economic union may not be able to climb over the tariff wall to compete effectively with higher cost internal manufacturers whose goods circulate within the region duty free or at a comparatively lower duty. Consumption may thus be shifted away from lower cost external suppliers to high cost internal producers, and internal consumers can end up paying more for certain goods after integration. This negative effect is labeled "trade diversion."

The extent to which the trade creation will outweigh trade diversion depends on a number of factors, such as the degree to which the range of goods produced in the member states overlap and the degree of pre-union reliance on trade outside the region.[49]

In the case of developing nations, however, the patterns of trade seem to offer little scope for reallocation of output as the result of removal of trade barriers. Most developing nations produce similar primary commodities that they export to the industrialized nations rather than to each other. In addition, Third World nations are usually characterized by excess labor resources and a shortage of capital. Even if the capital and labor markets are pooled, these factors are unlikely to move and little reallocation of resources can be expected.[50]

## Dynamic Effects

Nonetheless, integration can offer other benefits to developing nations. The small economies in many Third World nations will not support modern industry. By reducing the trade barriers within a region, however, prospective investors can be offered larger markets. No longer are they effectively confined to one small country; rather they may sell throughout the region. Thus, economies of scale and reduced per unit cost of production can be brought into play. This permits the products to be sold at a lower price, which allows more consumers to purchase the items. With increased sales, profits can rise, thereby supplying the producer with additional funds for reinvestment. "A given level of investment for the region as a whole will yield more output after integration than before."[51] This "dynamic" effect of integration in the form of an enhanced ability to attract capital and technology is a key reason for integration among developing countries.

## TYPES OF INTEGRATION

### Free Trade Associations, Customs Unions, and Common Markets

When the earliest integration units were being formed in the Third World, their framers were limited to a few basic models. The General Agreement on Tariffs and Trade (GATT), which includes the bulk of countries with free market economies, provides in Article I that each member state shall extend most-favored nation treatment to all other member countries. Thus, if Brazil were to lower its duty on radios from Chile, Brazil would have to extend that same reduced rate to every other GATT nation.

Article 24 of the GATT, however, provided an exception to this principle for customs unions and free trade associations. Members of either of these organizations may reduce their tariffs against each other without extending such concessions to all of the remaining GATT nations. To invoke such rights, the trade group concerned had to satisfy the technical requirements of either a free trade association or a customs union.

In a free trade association, each member is to eliminate tariff and quota barriers against trade from the other member states. Each individual country within the free trade association, however, continues to charge its regular duties on products coming from outside the association.[52]

A customs union also presupposes the elimination of tariffs as between member states. For goods coming from outside the region, however, members of a customs union are obligated to replace their own individual duties with a uniform tariff applicable to the entire region.[53] This uniform duty structure may be referred to as the "common external tariff," the "common customs tariff," or, in the case of the CACM, as "equalization of duties."[54]

A common market is a customs union, plus something more. What those additional elements should be is open to discussion. Professor F. R. Root defines a common market as a customs union where "all the restrictions on the movement of productive factors—labor, capital and enterprise—" have been removed. Root maintains that "an economic union requires a single monetary system and central bank, a unified fiscal system, and a common foreign economic policy."[55]

In contrast, the legal instruments establishing Third World common markets are unlikely to provide for unlimited movement of the factors of production—at least, within the near future. In fact, such schemes often call for a good deal of directive behavior, such as devising mechanisms to channel more productive resources toward the poorer members. Capital, rather than enjoying free movement, may be subject to certain restrictions as in the case of foreign investment entering the ANCOM region.[56]

## The Trade Preference Organization Alternative

The three models described above proved a Procrustean bed for some developing regions. In conformity with the legal requirement for a free trade association, LAFTA obligated its members to reach the goal of internal free trade within 12 years. Yet LAFTA had brought together nations in very diverse stages of development (compare Mexico and Bolivia, for example), with enormous geographical separations and severe transportation obstacles. The 12-year goal soon proved unattainable, and attempts to satisfy this norm simply ceased.

The way for developing countries around this impasse opened in 1971 with the approval of the GATT Decision on Waiver[57] which authorized the waiver of the Article I most-favored nation provision when developing nations offer concessions to other developing nations. Thus, Thailand could now offer to reduce its duty on a product from the Philippines without having to extend the same lower rate to Japan. The GATT decision also meant that developing countries were free to experiment with a variety of integration models without incorporating internal free trade as a legally binding obligation.

With this new flexibility sanctioned by GATT, LAFTA could now be converted from a free trade association into a trade preference association, LAIA. ASEAN could establish a preferential trading arrangement,[58] and the nations of eastern and southern Africa could form a similar organization.

### Integrating Planned Economies

Capitalist nations have traditionally utilized tariffs as a mechanism to influence private decision making. If the duty makes the price of an imported item too high, individuals and companies will opt to buy the locally made product. The economic integration units mentioned above also use tariff structures as a means to affect purchases by private persons.

Communist nations, in contrast, do not need duties to achieve import control. In countries with planned economies, state trading organizations (foreign trade organizations, or FTOs) determine what foreign items shall and shall not be purchased. Where the FTO chooses to buy a foreign product, it is imported; if the FTO does not purchase the item, it is not imported.

Therefore, in a command economy, theoretically duties should be irrelevant and of little importance in the process of integrating socialist economies. For this reason, integration within COMECON has not meant manipulating tariffs, but rather coordinating economic plans and rationalizing resource allocation. Because of its intrinsically different nature, COMECON will be covered in a separate chapter.

### NOTES

1. International Monetary Fund, *Annual Report 1984* (Washington, D.C.: IMF, 1984), p. 9.

2. Overseas Development Council, *U.S. Foreign Policy and the Third World Agenda 1985–86*, eds. John W. Sewell, Richard E. Feinberg, and Valeriana Kellab (New Brunswick, N.J.: Transaction Books, 1985), p. 230.

3. International Bank for Reconstruction and Development, *The 1983 World Bank Atlas: Gross National Product, Population, and Growth Rates* (Washington, D.C.: IBRD, 1983), p. 8.

4. Data are based on 1982 figures. International Bank for Reconstruction and Development, *World Bank Development Report: 1984* (Washington, D.C.: IBRD, 1984), p. 219.

5. Associated Press Videotex, June 1, 1984, 4:35 EDT, APV-200, quoting Jay Levy of the United Nations Food and Agricultural Organization.

6. Overseas Development Council, *U.S. Foreign Policy and the Third World Agenda 1982*, ed. Roger D. Hansen et al. (New York: Praeger, 1982), p. 186.

7. Overseas Development Council, *Agenda 1985–86*, pp. 214–21.

8. Ibid., p. 230.

9. Ibid., pp. 214ff.

10. Ibid., p. 230.

11. International Bank for Reconstruction and Development, *Development Reports*, p. 272–73.

12. Ibid., p. 252.

13. Overseas Development Council, *Agenda 1982*, p. 193.

14. Overseas Development Council, *Agenda 1985–86*, p. 163.

15. Ibid., p. 161.

16. David Gallagher, "Chile After the Fall: Free Market Policy Gradually Vindicated," *Wall Street Journal*, May 31, 1985, p. 17; and see International Monetary Fund, *Annual Report 1984*, p. 14.

17. Excluded from the U.S. generalized system of preference (GSP). See Overseas Development Council, *Agenda 1985–86*, p. 93 nn. 16, 17.

18. International Monetary Fund, *Annual Report 1984*, p. 15.

19. José Aragão, "ALADI: Perspectivas a Partir de la Experiencia de la ALALC y de la Situación Actual de la Economía Internacional," *Integración Latinoamericana* (Buenos Aires: INTAL, December 1983), no. 86, p. 16.

20. "Editorial, La Integración Regional Como Respuesta Latinoamericana a la Crisis Económica," *Integración Latinoamericana* (Buenos Aires: INTAL, March 1984), no. 88, p. 2.

21. W. Arthur Lewis, *The Evolution of the International Economic Order* (Princeton, N.J.: Princeton University Press, 1977), p. 71.

22. United Nations, *Monthly Bulletin of Statistics* (July 1981 and June 1984), Special Table B; and United Nations Conference on Trade and Development, *Handbook of International Trade and Development Statistics* (1983), Tables 3.2B and 3.4A, as cited in Overseas Development Council, *Agenda 1985–86*, p. 192.

23. General Agreement on Tariffs and Trades, *International Trade*, 1979/80, Table A21, as cited in Overseas Development Corporation, *Agenda 1982*, p. 65.

24. "Integración Regional."

25. Aragão, "ALADI: Perspectivas," p. 16.

26. Albert Fishlow, "Making Liberal Trade Policies Work in the 1980's," in Overseas Development Council, *Agenda 1982*, p. 66.

27. Bela Balassa, *Types of Economic Integration* (Washington, D.C.: World Bank reprint series No. 69, 1976), p. 18.

28. U.S. Department of State, "The European Community," *GIST* (August 1979): 3. See also "Editorial, Importancia de la Experiencia Integracionista Europea," *Integración Latinoamericana* (Buenos Aires: INTAL, October 1984), no. 95, p. 1; and Martín Arocena, "La Experiencia de la Unión Aduanera de la Comunidad Económica Europea," ibid., p. 3.

29. "Treaty for the Establishment of the Economic Community of Central African States" (October 19, 1983), reprinted in *International Legal Materials* 23 (Washington, D.C.: American Society of International Law, 1984): 947.

30. International Monetary Fund, *Exchange Arrangements and Exchange Restrictions: Annual Report 1984* (Washington, D.C.: IMF, 1984), p. 49.

31. So long as certain minimum local content requirements are satisfied. Ibid., p. 49.

In contrast, little or no progress has been made on the Arab Common Market, established on August 13, 1964, by Egypt, Iraq, Syria, and Jordan. See Louis Henkin, Richard C. Pugh, Oscar Schachter, and Hans Smit, *International Law: Cases and Materials* (St. Paul: West Publishing, 1980), p. 1130; and Muhammad Diab, "The Arab Common Market," *Journal of Common Market Studies* 4 (1965): 238.

32. *International Herald Tribune* (Paris ed.), July 15, 1985, p. 46; and see U.S. Department of State, *Background Notes: ASEAN* (November 1983), p. 5. Papua New Guinea has also sent observers to ASEAN meetings.

33. "Agreement on ASEAN Preferential Trading Arrangements" (February 24, 1977), reprinted in *Malaya Law Review* (Kuala Lumpur), 20 (1978): 415.

34. "Consejo de Ayuda Mutua Económica, Convención Sobre Capacidad Jurídica, Privilegios, e Inmunidades" (December 14, 1959, as amended through 1979), reprinted in Junta Central de Planificación de Cuba, *Cuestiones de la Economía* Planificada (Havana, January–February 1981), no. 7, p. 218. The 1960 English version of this convention appears in United Nations Treaty Series 368 (1960): 242.

35. "Treaty for East African Co-operation," reprinted in *International Legal Materials* 6 (1967): 932; see also Philip Ndegwa, *The Common Market and Development in East Africa* (Nairobi: East African Publishing House, 1968); Philip A. Thomas, ed., *Private Enterprise and the East African Company* (Dar Es Salaam: Tanzania Publishing House, 1969); and Robert L. Birmingham, "Economic Integration in East Africa: Distribution of Gains," *Virginia Journal of International Law* 9 (1969): 408.

36. "Treaty for the Establishment of the Preferential Trade Area for Eastern and Southern African States" (December 21, 1981), reprinted in *International Legal Materials* 21 (1982): 479.

37. "General Treaty of Central American Economic Integration" (Managua, Nicaragua, 1960), reprinted in Inter-American Institute of International Legal Studies, *Instruments Relating to the Economic Integration of Latin America*, vol. 2 (Dobbs Ferry, New York: Oceana, 1975), p. 385.

38. For instance, the Kissinger report has recommended that the United States furnish additional aid to the CACM. See "Report of the President's Committee on Central America," *New York Times*, January 12, 1984, p. 7Y.

39. "Treaty Establishing the Caribbean Community (1973), Annex Establishing the Caribbean Common Market," reprinted in *International Legal Materials* 12 (1973): 1033, 1044.

40. "Treaty Establishing the Organization of East Caribbean States (1981), Annex I, Agreement Establishing the East Caribbean Common Market" (1968, as amended through 1981), reprinted in *International Legal Materials* 20 (1981): 1166, 1176.

41. For a historical background covering integration efforts in this region, see Herbert Corkran, Jr., *Patterns of International Cooperation in the Caribbean: 1942–1969* (Dallas: Southern Methodist University, 1970).

42. "Treaty Establishing a Free Trade Area and Instituting the Latin American Free Trade Association" (Montevideo Treaty, 1960), reprinted in Inter-American Institute of International Legal Studies, *Instruments Relating to the Economic Integration of Latin America*, vol. 1 (Dobbs Ferry, New York: Oceana, 1975), p. 3.

43. "Cartagena Agreement on Andean Subregional Integration" (1969), reprinted in *International Legal Materials* 8 (1969): 910.

44. "Treaty Establishing the Latin American Integration Association" (1980), reprinted in *International Legal Materials* 20 (1981): 672.

45. "Lima Protocol Amending the Cartagena Agreement on Andean Subregional Integration" (1976), reprinted in *International Legal Materials* 16 (1977): 235.

46. One commentator, however, believes that the creation of an independent secretariat in the Economic Community of West African States and in ANCOM (the "junta") was of vital importance. Since their members owe loyalty to the community rather than to a particular country, technical issues can be better isolated from the politics of national interest. Although the secretariats are merely advisory bodies and lack authoritative decision-making power, they can serve as a bridge between the national governments and the private sector. Julius E. Okolo, "Integrative and Cooperative Regionalism: the Economic Community of West African States," *International Organizations* 39 (1985): 137–38. The pertinent provision can be found for ECOWAS in the Treaty of the Economic Community of West African States (Lagos, 1975), art 8, ¶ 1, in *International Legal Materials* 14 (1975): 1200, and for ANCOM in the Cartagena Agreement on Andean Subregional Integration (1969), art. 14, supra, note 43. LAIA also has an independent secretariat. "Treaty Establishing the Latin American Integration Association" (1980), art. 40, supra, note 44. The same is true for the common market of the Central African States. Supra, note 29, art. 22(1).

47. This process is dramatically described in L. S. Stavrianos, *Global Rift: The Third World Comes of Age* (New York: William Morrow, 1981).

48. Inter-American Development Bank, *Economic and Social Progress in Latin America: Economic Integration* (Washington, D.C.: IADB, 1984), p. 176.

49. Ingo Walter and Hans C. Vitzthum, "The Central American Common Market: A Case Study on Economic Integration in Developing Regions," *The Bulletin* (New York University, Institute of Finance, May 1967), no. 44, pp. 5–7.

50. Ibid., p. 9.

51. Ibid., p. 12.

52. F. R. Root, *International Trade and Investment—Theory, Policy, and Enterprise* (1973), 378–79, as quoted in Eric Stein, Peter Hay, and Michel Waelbroeck, eds. *European Community and Institutions in Perspective: Text, Cases, and Readings* (Indianapolis: Bobbs-Merrill, 1976), p. 364.

53. Viner, "The Customs Union Issue," (1950), pp. 5, 41, 43, as reprinted in Eric Stein and Peter Hay, *Law and Institutions in the Atlantic Area: Readings, Cases and Problems* (Indianapolis: Bobbs-Merrill, 1967), p. 323.

54. Supra, note 37, art. 19.

55. Root, *International Trade*.

56. "Decision 24 of the Commission of the Cartagena Agreement, Common Regime of Treatment of Foreign Capital and of Trademarks, Patents, Licenses and Royalties, as amended (1976)," reprinted in *International Legal Materials* 16 (1977): 138. The earlier versions of Decision 24, adopted December 31, 1970, are reprinted in *International Legal Materials* 10 (1971): 152; *International Legal Materials* 10 (1971): 1065; and *International Legal Materials* 12 (1973): 349.

57. November 26, 1971 (L/3636), GATT, *Basic Instruments and Selected Documents*, 18th supp., 1972, p. 26; see also the "Group Framework Agreement" (1979), reprinted in *International Codes Agreed to in Geneva, Switzerland*, U.S. Cong., Jt. Rep. of House Comm. on Ways and Means and Sen. Fin. Comm., 96 Cong. 1st sess. (April 23, 1979), pp. 361ff.

58. "The ASEAN Declaration, Joint Communiqué, 1st Ministerial Meeting" (Bangkok, August 8, 1967), reprinted in Michael Haas, ed., *Basic Documents of Asian Regional Organizations*, vol. 6 (Dobbs Ferry, New York: Oceana, 1979), p. 1269; "Treaty on Amity and Cooperation in Southeast Asia" (February 24, 1976), reprinted in *ibid.*, p. 316; and "Agreement on ASEAN Preferential Trading Arrangements," supra, note 33. See also *Proceedings of a Conference on MNC's and ASEAN Development in the 1980's* (Singapore: Institute of Southeast Asian Studies, 1981).

# 2

# STRUCTURING TRADE PATTERNS

Perhaps the most difficult task for the developing nation integration units has been achieving the desired tariff structure. The often painful adjustments involved can produce resistance every step along the way.

## LIBERALIZING INTERNAL TRADE

To eliminate duties, basically three different approaches are available. First, internal duties may be eliminated at once. Alternatively, negotiations on tariff reductions may be conducted on a product by product basis. For instance, one nation may agree to cut its duty on widget X from 50 percent to 35 percent in exchange for the second nation's lowering its duty on widget Y from 65 to 55 percent. Finally, tariffs reduction may be done on a linear or across the board basis, which means that, apart from goods specifically excluded, duties will be cut by a specified percentage on all products. For example, members of a customs union might agree to an annual 20 percent reduction of tariffs; under such an "across the board" or linear system, intraregional duties would then end in five years.

The European Economic Community treaty adopted a system of automatic, across the board tariffs cuts, for example, a 10 percent reduction in duties the first year.[1] By the end of a fixed time period, all internal tariff and quotas barriers were to cease. In fact, the EEC accelerated its tariff reductions and was able to meet the treaty goals prior to the due dates. Developing nations, on the other hand, have opted for different approaches to this problem.

### Immediate Internal Free Trade

The conventions establishing the Central American Common Market,[2] the East African Common Market,[3] the East Caribbean Common Market,[4]

12

and the Caribbean Common Market[5] all provided that internal trade should be immediately free of duties and other tariff barriers. This method appeared feasible in these regions because no strong industrial sector, with a vested interest in protective tariffs, had developed. Moreover, these treaties usually contained exceptions for certain goods to which the free trade requirement did not apply. For instance, the Central American Treaty added an Annex A listing some 50 items on which internal duties could continue for a period of time, commonly five years. The list represented those small industries that did exist in the area—soaps, beer, paints, oils—and was intended to give those manufacturers time to adjust to the increased competition.[6]

Immediate free trade also seemed a viable alternative in those areas where goods had already been circulating freely under the previous colonial regimes. For instance, tariffs had been abolished between Tanzania, Uganda, and Kenya in 1923;[7] likewise, 85 percent of trade among CARICOM members had been exempt from duties prior to formation of the market.[8]

Nonetheless, the ideal of free movement of goods was soon eroded. Unequal distribution of benefits and serious trade diversion within the East African Common Market led to the imposition of import restrictions among the three countries as early as 1972.[9]

Although duties were, in fact, eliminated on much on the intra-CARICOM trade,[10] in the late 1970s balance of payments difficulties of some member countries made it necessary to impose quota restrictions on imports from other members.[11] Recently, CARICOM's leaders have declared their intention of removing these quotas in the near future.[12] Unfortunately, other devices are also being used to restrict the free flow of trade. Jamaica in 1982 instituted a two-tier exchange system with parallel and official rates, while Trinidad-Tobago and Antigua-Barbuda began requiring import licenses.[13] Both these devices can have the effect of restricting imports.

Between 1960 and 1978, trade among the members of the Central American Common Market increased from $32 million to over $900 million, with manufactured goods accounting for 95 percent of the total. Nevertheless, the lesser industrialized nations, Honduras and Nicaragua, complained that their more advanced neighbors were benefiting disproportionately from the reduction in tariff barriers and were flooding the markets with their manufactures.[14]

In addition, the CACM has endured a war between Honduras and El Salvador, the withdrawal of Honduras, as well as the current violence in Central America. Still, the association somehow struggles on. El Salvador and Honduras finally signed a peace treaty, and Honduras is being reintegrated back into the organization.[15]

By the start of 1982, however, all the CACM members had created barriers to intraregional trade either through restrictions on specific products or through foreign exchange controls. El Salvador, Nicaragua, and Costa Rica had imposed limitations on imports of items characterized as "luxury" goods. Honduras placed a duty of 10 percent on products from the other members. Nicaragua then imposed a similar duty on Honduran goods. In turn, Guatemala retaliated by imposing duties on items from other members that were placing duties on Guatemalan products. Costa Rica suspended trade with Guatemala, and the latter then suspended trade with the rest of the common market.[16]

This crisis was overcome not within the multilateral framework of CACM, but rather through a series of bilateral accords. In August 1982 Costa Rica and El Salvador signed separate agreements with Guatemala, reestablishing trade. Soon thereafter, Nicaragua and Honduras made similar agreements with Guatemala. As part of the peace negotiations between El Salvador and Honduras, those nations in 1981 concluded the Bilateral Free Trade Treaty, which provided for mutual free trade in some items and preferential duties for others. In 1982 a protocol was added to this treaty, placing additional items on the list for favorable treatment.[17]

While the immediate free trade obligation proved unworkable in the case of the East African unit and has certainly not been literally enforced in the Central American and Caribbean unions, it does seem that some progress has been and may still be made in the latter regions.

## Agreements to Agree in the Future

### General Considerations

At the opposite end of the spectrum are those associations whose treaties simply call for their members to agree sometime in the future about duty reductions. This, in effect, opens the way for political maneuvering by any interest group that wishes to avoid inroads on its protected markets by resisting tariff reductions.

An example of the "agreement to agree" approach can be seen in the Economic Community of West African States (ECOWAS) treaty, which provides that "Member States shall reduce and ultimately eliminate customs duties . . . " within ten years.[18] Except for a prohibition against raising existing duties or creating new ones during the first two years,[19] the treaty places no firm obligations on its members as to specific measures to achieve this goal.

Such flexibility may, however, have been essential in the case of this association because so many of ECOWAS' members already belonged to other trade organizations and had incurred certain obligations under them concerning tariffs. For example, the Ivory Coast, Mali, Mauritania, Niger, Senegal, and Upper Volta were signatories to the Treaty of Abidjan (1973), establishing the Francophone West African Economic Community. Liberia, Sierra Leone, and, since 1980, Guinea belonged to the Mano River Union (1973). A free trade area has been formed between Cape Verde and Guinea-Bissau. Obviously, time was required to work out the complex arrangements among these various organizations and ECOWAS. The executive secretary of ECOWAS in 1985 characterized this "proliferation of intraregional organizations" as "one of the greatest problems facing the community."[20]

ECOWAS' two-year duty standstill period did not become officially operative until May 1979.[21] In 1980, a program was adopted for liberalization of international trade.[22] For this purpose, goods were divided into three categories: 1) items produced by enterprises accorded "community" status; 2) those manufactured in a nation already entitled to preferences under the Mano River Union or the West African Economic Community; and 3) other merchandise. The first group of products was to be duty free. For the second category, the relatively more advanced nations (Ghana, Ivory Coast, Nigeria, and Senegal) were to begin gradually lowering their duties, starting May 1981, until they were eliminated by May 1985; less industrially advanced countries had until May 1989 to bring their tariff down to zero.

The third category, which accounts for the bulk of the ECOWAS tariff schedule, is subject to a more gradual process of intraregional reduction. For these products, the more industrialized members have six years, beginning in 1981, to reduce their duties to zero; other members have eight years. Thus, in theory, intraregional duties should be abolished by 1989.

The treaty for the Eastern and Southern African Trade Preference Association also stipulates that members shall "gradually reduce and eventually eliminate as between themselves customs duties."[23] A protocol signed at the same time, however, sets forth specific products and, as a first step, mandates preferential tariff reductions for member states thereon ranging from 10 to 70 percent.[24] After completion of this initial state, will it be possible to make future progress in the absence of concrete treaty obligations?

Likewise, the agreement creating the new Central African States common market (ECCAS) also calls for the members to "agree gradually to reduce" and "eventually eliminate customs duties between them in accordance with a programme to be determined. . . ."[25] Although 18 protocols, covering matters such as rules of origin and customs cooperation, were annexed to that treaty, no system of intraregional duty cuts was included. Hence, it remains to be seen whether these hard decisions will actually be made.

*Product by Product Negotiations*

The reader will recall that the EEC treaty made its internal tariff cuts on a linear or "across the board" basis. Thus, each year member states were obliged to reduce all their internal duties by a certain percentage. In contrast, many of the developing nation integration units have provided for the tariff reduction negotiations to be conducted on a product by product basis. This means as soon as industrialists learn that their products may be on the negotiating list, they can pressure their government to have that item removed. As a consequence, strong protectionist forces may be brought to bear against effective trade liberalization.

The Latin American Free Trade Association provided an impressive example of this truism. Under that treaty once every three years goods representing 25 percent of the aggregate value of intraregional trade were supposed to have been placed on the Common List for duty-free treatment within the region.[26] Had this obligation been fulfilled, there would have been total free internal trade in LAFTA within 12 years. At the first Common List negotiation, only 175 items out of 10,000 proposed were placed on the Common List. At the second meeting, scheduled for 1967, no agreement could be reached.[27] The last two conferences were never held.

The LAFTA treaty contained a second mechanism for tariff reduction, which, if implemented, would also have produced free trade within 12 years. Each year, every member was to offer in bilateral negotiations concessions to reduce its total duty structure by not less than 8 percent of the weighted average.[28] Labeled as the "National Schedules" negotiations, any concessions so made by a nation were to be extended to all LAFTA members under the LAFTA most-favored nation clause.[28] In practice the easy concessions were made first, permitting a total of 8,000 items to be covered in the 1962 National Schedule negotiations. After this initial stage, the offerings became more difficult, and by 1979 the total number of items on the National Schedules amounted to only 11,017.[30]

LAFTA's requirement that concessions be extended to all members was believed ultimately to constitute an obstacle to further trade liberalization. Relatively poorer countries or those with an "insufficient" markets feared that the advantages granted would benefit the richer nations like Brazil, Mexico, or Argentina. In fact, only 30 percent of the concessions granted under the LAFTA national lists were actually used.[31]

Thus, to a significant extent, LAIA replaced LAFTA's global approach to liberalization with a framework aimed at creating an area of partial economic preferences. Abandoning the "most favored nation clause," the LAIA accord authorizes "agreements of partial scope," which may be concluded among fewer than all the LAIA members; concessions granted in such pacts do not have to be extended to other LAIA members.[32] Thus, in LAIA most trade negotiations are bilateral and intended to facilitate conclusion of agreements between countries with some common interests that may not be shared by other nations in the area. In addition, it was thought that bilateral agreements could be concluded by countries in ways that will increase the potential for trade creation and minimize the risk of trade diversion.[33]

Hoping to avoid the danger of balkanization, however, the founders of LAIA included the principle of "convergence," which calls for the progressive multilaterialization of agreements of partial scope through periodic negotiations among its members.[34] Moreover, agreements of partial scope must be open to other member countries, following negotiation, and must contain provisions fostering convergence with other Latin American nations.[35]

LAIA viewed its first task as the renegotiation of its "historic patrimony," that is, renegotiating the concessions granted previously under LAFTA. This work was concluded in 1983 with the execution of 39 agreements of partial scope, most of which were bilateral. Under "Plurilateral Agreement No. 26," Argentina, Chile, Paraguay, and Uruguay did form a multilateral agreement with ANCOM. Both Brazil and Mexico, however, opted for a series of bilateral accords with each of the member states of ANCOM.[36]

ASEAN's experience with product by product negotiation is similar to that of LAFTA, but less disappointing since the ASEAN treaty scheme never promised grandiose achievements. Rather it simply says, "An effective ASEAN margin of tariff preference should be accorded on a product by product basis."[37] By the end of 1983, nearly 19,000 items had been subjected to preferential tariff cuts of 20 to 25 percent, as compared with some 6,000 items at the end of 1981. The economic ministers of the member nations, at an October 1983 meeting, agreed to increase the margin of preferences for food items, and nonfood items already subject to the arrangements, in stages to a maximum of 50 percent.[38]

Critics argue that the ASEAN tariff concessions have been of little value. In a number of cases, the concessions are on items that were already duty free, and the agreement merely made that rate binding. In other cases, the cuts made were insufficient to make the preference significant. Finally, the countries seem unwilling to give reductions in industrial sectors that could be meaningful. Likewise, little in the way of consumer goods has been offered as the members apparently wish to protect these import substitution industries.[39]

## Automatic, Linear Tariff Reductions

### Andean Common Market

The integration unit that most closely followed the EEC, with its across the board duty cuts, is ANCOM. The ANCOM treaty established four different mechanisms for achieving internal free trade. First, the agreement looked to the Common List established under LAFTA and provided that all items on the Common List would continue to circulate freely within the ANCOM region.[40]

Next the treaty called for the reservation of certain items for the "sectorial" programs; these products are to be given preferential tariff treatment.[41] Approximately 2,000 articles, amounting to one-third of all the items on the tariff schedules, were reserved for the sectorial programs.[42] Items that had been previously reserved for the sectorial program, but had not been incorporated into a specific sectorial program by the end of 1978, were to become duty free under certain conditions.[43] If such items were already produced in the ANCOM area, they were to circulate duty free after 1978.[44] Nevertheless, the ANCOM Commission could reserve certain of these items, if they were not yet produced inside the area, for manufacture by Bolivia and Ecuador and could decide whether such goods should be subject to internal duties.[45] (As relatively poorer nations within the market, Ecuador and Bolivia are frequently given special treatment.)

Third, the treaty provided that goods not produced in the region (and not reserved for the sectorial programs) would be duty free by 1971.[46] The AN-COM Commission, however, could reserve certain goods not yet produced in the region for manufacture by Bolivia or Ecuador; any internal duty structure created for such goods had to be for the benefit of Bolivia and Ecuador.[47]

Products not yet produced in the region and not allocated to the sectorial programs (see below) could also be reserved for manufacturing by Colombia, Venezuela, or Peru. Such products, however, when produced by any of these three nations were to enjoy the protection of internal tariff barriers only until the end of 1983.[48]

The bulk of the products fell within the nonscheduled goods category, subject to automatic tariff cutting provisions. As a first step, each nation had to designate, as its base rate from which the automatic cuts would be made, the lowest rate applied by that nation on the item prior to joining ANCOM.[49] Such base rate could not exceed the ad valorem, CIF, price of the item by more than 100 percent.[50]

Annual reductions of duties on nonscheduled goods were to be made by each nation. Under the original provisions of the ANCOM treaty, automatic, across the board, tariff cuts of 10 percent were to be made each year so that zero rates would be reached in 1980.[51] When this goal proved too ambitious, ANCOM adopted the Lima Protocol, which stretched out the time periods for accomplishing this end. Under the new arrangement, Colombia, Venezuela, and Peru (the relatively more developed members) were required, starting in December 1976, to make seven successive annual reductions of 6 percent each and a final reduction of 8 percent by December 31, 1983.[52] Bolivia and Ecuador were to have begun the automatic reductions with a 5 percent cut in 1979, to be followed by five cuts of 10 percent each annually from 1982 to 1986; a 15 percent cut in 1987; and a final reduction of 20 percent in 1988.[53]

Since 1969 internal tariffs have been reduced, and intraregional trade has grown from $30 million (excluding Venezuela)[54] to $1.3 billion in 1981.[55] Unfortunately, the world economic crisis produced a drop in exports for the ANCOM nations and gave rise to a wave of protectionism. Consequently, neither Venezuela nor Peru made the automatic tariff cuts scheduled for the end of 1982. Likewise, Bolivia did not fulfill certain obligations, such as those relating to products not produced in the region.[56] During the last few years, the ANCOM members have also imposed nontariff barriers, such as prior import licenses, against hundreds of items from their subregional partners.[57] Despite these shortfalls, the presidents of the five member nations have issued a declaration promising to avoid "new restrictions on trade and to eliminate the existing ones in order to advance the Andean subregional market. . . ."[58]

To increase intraregional trade further, ANCOM is studying ways to foster the use of barter or countertrade among its members.[59] (In contrast, it might be noted that the Central African States common market recognizes that barter agreements can produce trade deflection; if such is substantial, the importing state is obligated to take steps "to obviate such deflection.")[60]

### The LAIA Regional Tariff Preference

Despite LAIA's emphasis on partial scope accords, the treaty does call on its members to establish one important multilateral scheme—the regional preferential tariff.[61] Under this mechanism, LAIA nations are required to admit merchandise from other member states at lower duty rates than those applicable to goods from nonmember countries. The tariff rates on products from LAIA partners will have to be reduced by the percentage amount set in the regional preference accord.

For instance, if the regular most-favored nation rate on widget X were 90 percent and the regional preference rate were fixed at 30 percent, the duty charged for widget Xs from member states should be 63 percent,[62] calculated as follows:

$$\begin{array}{rl} & 90\% \text{ (duty applicable to item from outside nations)} \\ \times & 30\% \text{ (regional preference rate)} \\ \hline & 27\% \text{ (amount of preference)} \end{array}$$

$$\begin{array}{rl} & 90\% \text{ (duty applicable to item from outside nations)} \\ - & 27\% \text{ (amount of regional preference)} \\ \hline & 63\% \text{ (rate applicable to intraregional widget X)} \end{array}$$

It might be noted that this type of preference does not create a common lower tariff for all member countries; rather each nation maintains the level of its duties with third countries but grants a specific reduction to goods from other countries within the region.

The LAIA treaty did not stipulate the amount of such preference nor indicate the items to which it should be applied. Experts expressed concern that the percentage of preference had to be large enough to be "significant." Figures as high as 50 percent were mentioned,[63] which would have meant that goods of Latin American origin would have been subject to only one-half the duty rate payable on products from outside the region. Likewise, it was urged that such preference be accorded, not on a product by product basis, but universally with very few items excepted. To give industries time to adjust to the new arrangement, the preferential rates could be eased in gradually over a stipulated time period.[64]

Finally, on April 27, 1984, the LAIA regional preference accord was concluded[65] (see Appendix I–2). It did not provide for a 50 percent margin of preference, but for differentials ranging from 2 percent to 10 percent depending upon the degree of development of the nation levying the duty and of the country of origin.[66] Whether these small percentage cuts will be sufficient to affect trade remains to be seen. Negotiations on deeper cuts are due to begin no later than the first half of 1986.[67] Although the agreement reduces duties across the board, and not on an item by item basis, it authorizes members to submit within 60 days lists of products to be exempted from the system.[68]

### Safeguards and Escape Devices

The Central American Common Market treaty did not include safeguard clauses allowing members to derogate from a given obligation in cases of emergency. Most Third World integration associations have felt it desirable to provide such escape devices. For example, the Cartagena Agreement establishing ANCOM permitted each member to exempt a certain number of products until 1988 from the duty reductions (other than those on the Common List).[69] When Venezuela joined ANCOM, the nation was authorized to exclude a fixed number of items from tariff cutting. Moreover, this could be done on a discriminatory basis against a single member country, and that nation in turn was authorized to retaliate with comparable withholdings of duty reductions as against Venezuelan productions.[70]

Another typical escape mechanism relieves a member from its trade liberalization obligations for specified reasons, such as balance of payments difficulties. For instance, a nation within the Caribbean Common Market may impose quota restrictions on imports "for the purpose of safeguarding its balance of payments"[71] or where an "industry or a segment of an industry experiences serious difficulties. . . ."[72] The treaty for the West African common market authorizes its members to "take the necessary safeguard measures" in "the event of serious disturbances occurring in the economy."[73]

An unusual escape device was used in the now-defunct East African Common Market. Article 20 authorized the imposition of a "transfer tax," a kind of internal duty, against a partner state on manufactured goods from those nations. The tax could be imposed only on "goods of a value not exceeding the amount of the deficit in trade in manufactured goods between the State which was imposing the transfer tax and the State of origin of the goods upon which the tax was to be imposed." Such tax could not be imposed unless the acting state could show either that it also manufactured such goods or would be doing so within three months. The tax could not exceed 50 percent ad valorem and was to expire not later than eight years. All transfer taxes were to have become void 15 years after the treaty entered into force.[74]

## Privileges for the Least Developed Members

Experience has shown that integration will not work unless some compensatory mechanisms are built in to help the poorest member states. A number of different devices have been used for this purpose. For instance, standards for the "rules of origin" may be lower for the poorer members (see "Rules of Origin" below). Under the ANCOM structure, Bolivia and Ecuador are being given longer time periods to reduce their internal duties. Likewise, they are granted more time to arrive at the common external tariff. Conversely, the more developed members (Venezuela, Peru, and Colombia) had eliminated their duties against most Bolivian and Ecuadorean products by the mid-1970s.[75]

The LAIA treaty calls for its members to agree to a list of products that, when originating in the "relatively less economically developed" members, will enter the remaining nations duty free.[76] This provision refers to Bolivia, Ecuador, and Paraguay. In April 1983 a series of these so-called "Market Opening" agreements were signed, providing for nonreciprocal duty-free treatment of more than 1,000 items. Bolivia was the beneficiary of 512 such concessions, including 396 from other ANCOM nations. Ecuador received 307, which included 204 concessions from its ANCOM partners. Paraguay was the beneficiary of 242 concessions. In large part, these concessions covered so-called traditional industries, that is, foodstuffs, textiles, leather goods, ceramics, and so forth.[77] A nation granting these concessions may suspend them if such imports cause serious injury to the domestic industry in the first country; however, the safeguard clauses have a life limited to three years.[78] Bolivia has also obtained duty-free treatment for additional products in two agreements of partial scope: one with Brazil and the other with Argentina.[79]

The LAIA regional preference accord, described above, divides members into three categories: the "relatively less economically developed" members (Bolivia, Ecuador, and Paraguay); nations at the "intermediate" level of development (Chile, Peru, Colombia, Venezuela, and Uruguay); and the remainder (Brazil, Argentina, and Mexico). Different treatment is accorded to each group with the greatest benefits accruing to the poorest countries.

Although Uruguay does not qualify as "less economically developed" nation, during renegotiation of the "historic patrimony" accords it was granted slightly more favorable treatment than other countries at the same "intermediate" level. This special treatment was given because of Uruguay's small market size, its dependence on other nations for energy and raw materials, as well as its geographical location.[80]

The LAIA treaty further authorizes members to enter agreements with nations or integration units outside the region, but stipulates that any concession made by a LAIA member to an outsider must automatically be extended to Bolivia, Paraguay, and Ecuador.[81]

The first LAIA agreement with an outside nation was concluded between Mexico and Costa Rica in June 1983. In that accord Mexico unilaterally extended a preferential duty rate to a variety of Costa Rican products. Such privileges will also apply to the same items when imported from Bolivia, Paraguay, or Ecuador into Mexico.[82] Recently Mexico entered a similar pact with Guatemala,[83] while Argentina has made comparable agreements with Costa Rica, El Salvador, and Cuba.[84]

The LAIA accord also directs attention to the plight of the landlocked countries and urges they be assisted through compensatory mechanisms.[85] The Central African States common market has adopted a protocol calling for assistance to landlocked, island, "part island and semi-land locked" countries. In turn, business people from the other partner states are to be treated the same as citizens of such landlocked or island states.[86]

### Rules of Origin

Integration associations need to develop rules of origin to determine when a product is entitled to circulate within the region at the lower or zero duty rate. Such rules are usually written to regard as satisfying the origin requirements any animal, mineral, or vegetable substance that has been raised, mined, or harvested in a member state.

The difficult question arises where a good is mixed with part of its components coming from outside and part from within the region. Some associations have treated goods as "local" and entitled to regional tariff treatment if a certain percentage of the final product consists of local inputs. For instance, the East African Common Market treated an item as local if at least 30 percent of the value of the final product came from within the market region.[87]

The Economic Community of West African States has adopted a 40 percent requirement in some cases and 35 percent in others.[88] In addition, this association has specifically prohibited certain operations from qualifying for local treatment, for instance, packing, bottling, simple assembly, and labeling.[89] ECOWAS also requires a certain percent of the company's stock be held by nationals to satisfy the origin norms.[90]

The Central African States common market and the Trade Preference Association of the Eastern and Southern African States[91] have created complex rules of origin, which combine local component requirements, with percentage limitations on foreign ownership and management of the producing companies. For instance, as a general rule goods can satisfy the origin requirements in the Central African States Community only if 30 percent of the stock of the producing company is owned by regional investors, if the company is managed by a majority of regional citizens, and if components of the product imported from outside the region do not exceed 55 percent of its ex factory cost.[92] Exceptions may be made to these rules by the councils of both organizations for special cases, for example, for goods of particular importance to development.

The ASEAN Rules of Origin have set the local content requirements at 50 percent. For Indonesia, however, the amount of extra-regional input may not exceed 40 percent under Rule 3(a)(ii) [Appendix A-4].[93] Thus, the English version of this text would appear to mean that goods manufactured in Indonesia must satisfy a 60 percent local content standard. On the other hand, Professor Ralph Folsom has interpreted this clause as applying the 60 percent requirement not to items manufactured in Indonesia, but to goods produced in the other partner-states and then exported to Indonesia. His construction certainly seems more in line with the needs of this relatively lesser developed nation.[94] Still, the actual language in the rule remains unclear.

In contrast, the EEC now uses a process type of test and treats a product as "local" if the community is the place where the "last substantial and justified processing or conversion took place, effected in an enterprise equipped for that purpose and resulting in the production of a new product or a product representing a significant processing stage."[95]

The European Free Trade Association (EFTA)[96] has adopted a rule that simply provides an item will be treated as "local" if it has been worked or processed sufficiently within the region so that the finished product is now "classified under a Brussels Nomenclature tariff heading different from that of any imported third country materials or parts which are used in the processing."[97]

CARICOM originally set the local component requirement at 50 percent, unless the source was one of the poorer member countries in which case the percentage dropped to 40 percent.[98] In 1981, however, CARICOM, revised its rules of origin to follow the EFTA approach.[99] Thus, cotton imported into Jamaica from outside CARICOM and made into a shirt there would now qualify because cloth and shirts fall within different tariff classifications.

As an interim measure, the LAIA accord on the regional tariff preference uses as rules of origin the norms in effect for LAFTA in 1980.[100] The ANCOM treaties contain no rules of origin but authorize the junta to establish such norms.[101] A call was recently made for ANCOM to adopt such subregional norms.[102]

## Nontariff Barriers

During the 1970s, the industrialized nations have resorted to a variety of nontariff barriers to restrict the flow of imports. Pressures exerted on Hong

Kong and Taiwan persuaded those nations "voluntarily" to limit textile exports. Quotas on steel or on autos have become a frequent topic in newspaper headlines.

Less publicized has been the mushrooming of nontariff barriers within the developing world—even between members of the same economic integration unit. The conventions establishing ANCOM[103], CARICOM,[104] ECOWAS,[105] the CACM,[106] and the Eastern and Southern African States association[107] all call for the elimination of quotas. Some go further, as in the case of ANCOM, which mandates the elimination of "restraints of all kinds."[108] Article 28 of the CARICOM treaty does, however, authorize the use of quantitative restrictions when necessary to "safeguard its balance of payments," and, as mentioned above, some members reimposed quotas in the late 1970s. Likewise, most countries in eastern and southern Africa maintain not only high duties, but also nontariff barriers, to protect their local industry.[109]

Besides quotas, many developing nations, impelled by precarious debt positions, have resorted to a variety of other nontariff restrictions on imports as a means of reducing foreign exchange expenditures. A recent survey of Latin American nations revealed the existence some 1,300 laws and regulations that can act as a barrier to imports. Argentina, Bolivia, Brazil, Colombia, Chile, Ecuador, Mexico, Paraguay, Peru, Uruguay, and Venezuela have all created systems requiring prior import licenses. Discretionary authority to grant or deny licenses can obviously pose a formidable obstacle to imports. Brazil, Colombia, Ecuador, Mexico, and Paraguay require advance deposits for some or all imports. The amount required may be as much as 100 percent FOB of the goods, and interest may not be payable on such deposit.[110] Long delays between the date of making the deposit and receipt of the goods can mean a significant loss of earnings on those funds and thus constitute an obstacle to buying foreign goods.

All countries prohibit the import of certain goods, such as those considered dangerous to public health or safety. The Latin American nations studied likewise have lists of banned products, which, however, have been broadened to the point where they now cover, for example, refrigerators in Bolivia, cotton products in Peru, or shoes in Venezuela.[111]

Finally, there is a plethora of laws designed to protect domestic industries. Brazil will not permit the importation of machinery, parts, tools, or vehicles if a similar product is available from a national company. Many countries, for example, Argentina, require state entities to make their purchases from domestically owned firms wherever reasonably possible. Some nations have fixed prices for certain basic goods;[112] a fixed price below the world market price will clearly discourage imports. Finally exchange control restrictions may pose an insurmountable barrier to importing.

A 1983 study estimated that 40 percent of the trade within the ANCOM region was affected by these nontariff barriers.[113] Such limitations, which have been placed not only on goods from outside the Latin American region, but also on imports from other LAIA members, have seriously constrained the growth of reciprocal trade.

Although the Institute for Latin American Integration (INTAL) was understanding of the economic pressures that drove the Latin American nations to resort to these trade barriers, it has recommended that the integration process itself could be speeded up if the LAIA members would remove these nontariff measures against each other, while continuing to maintain them against goods from outside the region.[114]

Within LAIA, Article 7 of the new regional tariff preference agreement mandates the elimination of nontariff barriers.[115] For agreements of partial scope, the members agreed to freeze the status quo and abstain from imposing new nontariff barriers. Moreover, in some partial scope agreements, members have agreed to eliminate certain specific nontariff barriers. For example, Brazil, Mexico, and Colombia will waive the prior license requirement for some products under a partial scope agreement.[116]

If regional integration units are to reduce or abolish nontariff barriers among themselves, more careful thought must be given to exactly which kinds of limitations are to be eliminated. Laws directed toward protection of public health and safety are likely to be kept. Politically sensitive industries and those related to national security will probably continue to be privileged. Likewise, it does not seem unreasonable for a poor nation simply to ban the importation of certain luxury items, such as a Rolls Royce. On the other hand, blanket requirements for import licenses and advance deposits could well be modified for the benefit of partner nations within a trade unit.

Such an approach has already been started within the Eastern and Southern African Trade Preference Association. That organization has adopted a protocol that selects a common list of products entitled to regional trade preferences. In addition to preferential duty rates, such goods, when originating from a member state, must be given preferential treatment in allocating any quotas, in issuing import and export licenses, in granting foreign exchange licenses, and in requiring advance import deposits.[117]

Quotas may be imposed in the Central African States common market when required by balance of trade difficulties[118] or when needed to protect an infant or strategic industry.[119] A protocol on "Non-Tariff Hindrances to Trade" also prohibits dumping, as well as export subsidies, by regional partners and provides that goods so affected may be banned by other members.[120]

## ESTABLISHING A COMMON EXTERNAL TARIFF

### Customs Unions and Common Markets

For those integration units that style themselves a "common market" or customs union, a common external tariff must be constructed. This task can also prove difficult since purchasers within the region face the prospect of being cut off from cheaper outside goods in favor of higher cost regional producers.

To achieve common external rates, the EEC again took a linear approach. The rates for individual items were set at the "arithmetical average of the duties" applicable in the six original members.[121] Members' own duties were to be adjusted by fixed percentage amounts according to a set timetable to arrive at the common external tariff by a certain date.[122] (The EEC was also able to accelerate this procedure and reach this goal prior to the treaty deadline).

Treaties establishing integration units in the developing world have not followed the EEC on this matter. Rather, the right to set the common tariffs has been delegated to various decision-making bodies that are supposed to agree on acceptable schemes. Once again this opens the way for discussions on an item by item basis with the consequent maneuvering from various interest groups.

Still some progress has been achieved. A series of protocols to the 1960 Central American Agreement on the Equalization of Import Duties and Charges established tariff schedules and duty rates.[123] These protocols were to have equalized all but about 2 percent of the total tariff classifications. Nevertheless, in recent years these arrangements have proved less than satisfactory. In December 1984, the CACM members concluded a convention establishing a new framework under which the common external tariffs will be negotiated for inclusion in an annex to that agreement. In addition, the convention provides rules on valuation of goods for duty purposes and envisions a Central American Uniform Customs Code. By February 1985, Guatemala, El Salvador, and Nicaragua had already ratified this pact.[124]

In building the common external tariff, the ANCOM treaty provides for a two-step procedure.[125] The first step called for the creation of a minimum common external tariff for each item within the Brussels Nomenclature. For goods with duty rates below those established by the minimum common external tariff, the member states were required to have raised their tariffs up to the level of this minimum common external tariff by 1975.[126] For products with duty rates above those minimum common external tariff levels, the individual nations could temporarily retain their existing duties. A special hardship clause in the Cartagena Agreement makes it possible for a country to seek temporary suspension of the minimum common external tariff.[127] The ANCOM commission was to have set the rates for the final common external tariff by the end of 1978, and Venezuela, Peru, and Colombia were to have brought their duties in line with the final common tariff by the end of 1983. Bolivia and Ecuador had until the end of 1988 to accomplish this.[128] (Sectorial programs are governed by special rules, and neither the minimum nor the final external tariff is applicable.)

Economic difficulties have prevented the ANCOM members from living up to their obligations under the common external tariff. An external tariff—a barrier to outside goods—amounts to an implicit subsidy of domestic producers. Thus, in the absence of a comprehensive compensation policy, the level and coverage of the common external tariff become very difficult to implement. As of 1983 Peru still had 137 items below the minimum common external tariff, Venezuela 132 items, and Colombia 67 items.[129]

The Caribbean Common Market treaty directed the member states to agree to a plan and schedule for a common external tariff. To a large extent, the common tariffs already set for the East Caribbean Common Market (ECCM) were deemed to satisfy the CARICOM obligation for the ECCM nations.[130] As of 1982, however, only four of the more developed members of CARICOM (Trinidad-Tobago, Guyana, Jamaica, and Barbados) had agreed to a common external tariff. The poorer members, whose duties are substantially lower, have not adopted the CARICOM external tariffs. Because imported raw materials, equipment, and parts are subject to only minimal duties, companies within CARICOM have not been compelled to utilize local materials and technology. The entire common external tariff of CARICOM is now undergoing revision;[131] of particular concern in this process is the impact of such structure on the poorest members of the Organization of Eastern Caribbean States.[132]

The Economic Community of West African States treaty postponed this problem. Article 14 of that agreement provides that a common external tariff should be erected and in place within five years after completion of the eight-year internal tariff liberalization.[133] On the basis of the present internal program, the common external tariff should be finished by May 1994. The intracommunity trade liberalization, however, is already behind schedule. Thus, the Lagos Plan of Action now envisions that duty structure as being in place by the year 2000.[134]

The need to mesh the ECOWAS common external tariff with those of the Mano River Union and the West African Economic Community further complicates this process. During the 1984 annual ECOWAS summit meeting, a resolution was adopted urging these two subgroups to merge their aims with those of ECOWAS to facilitate achievement of a single customs union.[135]

The states of the Central African common market simply "agree to the gradual" establishment of a common external tariff. No schedule of obligations is included in the treaty.[136]

## Free Trade Associations and Trade Preference Organizations

Free trade associations, such as LAFTA, can avoid these problem since they do not have to establish a common external tariff. Likewise, a trade preference organization is not required to create a common external tariff. Nevertheless, the treaty for the Eastern and Southern African States Trade Preference Association does call for the gradual evolution of a common external tariff.[137] This agreement, however, envisions the conversion of the unit into a common market after ten years.[138]

## COMPENSATION FOR LOSSES RESULTING
## FROM TRADE LIBERALIZATION

Traditionally, Third World countries have relied heavily upon indirect taxes for revenue. Customs duties have accounted for as much as 50 percent of governmental revenues for the Comoros, Seychelles, and Somalia.[139] A similar situation existed in West Africa. Customs receipts made up 48 percent of the government's revenue in Upper Volta, 49 percent in Benin, and 53 percent in Gambia.[140] Hence, relinquishing customs revenue on goods from partner states could impose a hardship on these nations, which are already very poor.

To confront this problem, the ECOWAS convention created the Fund for Co-operation, Compensation and Development,[141] whose resources may be used to compensate member states that have suffered loss of import duties from the application of the trade liberalizing provisions of the treaty.[142] A subsequent implementing protocol obligates each member nation exporting to another ECOWAS country to pay into this fund a sum of money equivalent to the "losses occasioned by her exports."[143] The amount of such compensation is to be measured by the difference between what would have been collected on the goods at the most-favored nation's rate for outside countries and what was actually collected as the result of the liberalizing provisions of the ECOWAS treaty. These monies may in turn be used by the fund to compensate other members for their losses.[144]

The Central African States common market also established a compensation fund for this purpose. Members are entitled to receive from the fund convertible currency equal to the difference between the compensation due for its imports and the compensation it owes for exports.[145]

The Francophone West African Economic Community had created a similar compensation system. In 1980, however, as trade decreased, the amounts of compensation due the weaker members from the Ivory Coast and Senegal increased to the point where the latter nations felt compelled to reduce these resource transfers. Thus, the efficacy of this mechanism was jeopardized.[146]

## GOODS IN TRANSIT

If an area is integrated, goods from one nation should be able to flow freely to a third member through the territory of a second member. Such in-transit merchandise should be subject neither to duties nor other trade barriers by the second country. Provisions must also be made for landlocked states; otherwise, products imported from outside the region would be dutiable by the port of entry country and then again subject to the tariff of the landlocked nation.

A number of mechanisms have been designed to deal with these problems. For instance, all three African integration units exempt goods in transit from import duties.[147] An annex to the Central African common market treaty sets forth a form for a "PTA (TIA) Carnet" to be used with regional goods in transit.[148]

Where duties on extraregional products have already been paid at the state of entry, the African associations have established reimbursement systems under which the importer may seek a refund of the duty paid the "collecting state," less a small administrative charge.[149] (As poorer nations, the Comoros and Djibouti are only required to refund 50 percent of the duties paid.) The state of destination then charges its regular extraregional duty on the goods.

## NOTES

1. "Treaty Establishing the European Economic Community," (March 25, 1957), art. 14, United Nations Treaty Series, vol. 298, p. 3.

2. "General Treaty of Central American Economic Integration" (Managua, Nicaragua, 1960), art. 3, reprinted in Inter-American Institute of Legal Studies, *Instruments Relating to the Economic Integration of Latin America*, vol. 2 (Dobbs Ferry, New York: Oceana, 1975), p. 385.

3. "Treaty for East African Co-operation" (1967), art. 11, reprinted in *International Legal Materials* 6 (Washington, D.C.: American Society of International Law, 1967): 932.

4. "Treaty Establishing the Organization of East Caribbean States (1981), Annex I, Agreement Establishing the East Caribbean Common Market," art. 6 (1968, as amended through 1981), reprinted in *International Legal Materials* 20 (1981): 1166.

5. "Treaty Establishing the Caribbean Community (1973), Annex Establishing the Caribbean Common Market," art. 15, reprinted in *International Legal Materials* 12 (1973): 1033, 1044.

6. Ingo Walter and Hans C. Vitzthum, "The Central American Common Market: A Case Study on Economic Integration in Developing Regions," *The Bulletin* (New York University, Institute of Finance, May 1967), no. 44, p. 30.

7. Sena Eken, "Breakup of the East African Community," *Finance and Development* (Washington, D.C.: International Monetary Fund, December 1979), p. 36.

8. Inter-American Development Bank, *Economic and Social Progress in Latin America: Economic Integration* (Washington, D.C.: IADB, 1984), p. 50.

9. Eken, "East African Community."

10. Bela Balassa, *Types of Economic Integration* (Washington, D.C.: World Bank reprint series No. 69, 1976), p. 27.

11. Inter-American Development Bank 1980–81 Report, *Economic and Social Progress in Latin America* (Washington, D.C.: IADB, 1982), p. 120.

12. Instituto para la Integración de América Latina, *El Proceso de Integración en América Latina en 1982* (Buenos Aires, 1983), p. 191.

13. Instituto para la Integración de América Latina, *El Proceso de Integración in América Latina en 1983* (Buenos Aires, 1984), p. 196.

14. Richard Feinberg and Robert Pastor, "Far from Hopeless: An Economic Program for Post-War Central America," in *Central America: Anatomy of Conflict*, ed. Robert S. Leiken (New York: Pergamon Press, 1984), pp. 193, 195–97.

15. Supra, note 11, p. 112.

16. Supra, note 12, pp. 172–73.

17. Ibid., p. 173.

18. "Treaty of the Economic Community of West African States" (Lagos, 1975), art. 13, ¶ 1, reprinted in *International Legal Materials* 14 (1975): 1200; and see Bruce Zagaris, "The Economic

Community of West African States (ECOWAS): An Analysis and Prospects," *Case Western Reserve Journal of International Law* 10 (Cleveland, 1978): vol. 39, p. 93.

19. "Treaty," supra, note 18, art. 13, ¶ 2.

20. Report of Momodu Munu to the ministerial delegation attending the 1985 ECOWAS summit, as cited in Howard French, "Organizational Overlaps Slows Regional Unity," *International Herald Tribune* (Paris ed.), July 27-28, 1985, p. 12; and John B. McLenaghan, Saleh Nsouli, and Klaus-Walter Riechel, *Currency Convertibility in the Economic Community of West African States* (International Monetary Fund, 1982), p. 14.

21. "Treaty," supra, note 18, art. 13(2) and see McLenaghan, Nsouli, and Riechel, *Currency Convertibility*, p. 15.

22. "Decision of the Authority of Heads of State and Government of ECOWAS relating to Trade Liberalization in Industrial Products, May 18, 1980," *ECOWAS Official Journal* 2 (June 1980): 6; and see Julius Emeka Okolo, "Integrative and Cooperative Regionalism, the Economic Community of West African States," *International Organization* (1985): 121.

23. "Treaty for the Establishment of the Preferential Trade Area for Eastern and Southern African States" (December 21, 1981), art. 3(4)(a)(i), reprinted in *International Legal Materials* 21 (1982): 479.

24. "Protocol on the Reduction and Elimination of Trade Barriers on Selected Commodities to Be Traded within the Preferential Trade Area," art. 4, Annex I, reprinted in *International Legal Materials* 21 (1982): 498.

25. "Treaty for the Establishment of the Economic Community of Central African States" (October 19, 1983), art. 27, reprinted in *International Legal Materials* 23 (1984): 947.

26. "Treaty Establishing a Free Trade Area and Instituting the Latin American Free Trade Association" (Montevideo Treaty, 1960), art. 7, reprinted in Inter-American Institute of International Legal Studies, *Instruments Relating to the Economic Integration of Latin America*, vol. 1 (Dobbs Ferry, New York: Oceana, 1975), p. 3.

27. Michael J. McDermott and William H. Weiland, "Latin American Experience with Economic Integration," *Virginia Journal of International Law* 10 (1969): 153.

28. Supra, note 26, art. 5.

29. Ibid., art. 18.

30. José Aragão, "ALADI: Perspectivas a Partir de la Experiencia de la ALALC y de la Situación Actual de la Economía Internacional," *Integración Latinoamericana* (Buenos Aires: INTAL, December 1983), no. 86, p. 5; see also Diana Tussie, "Latin American Integration: From LAFTA to LAIA," *Journal of World Trade Law* 16 (1982): 399.

31. "A Comparative Analysis of the 1960 and 1980 Montevideo Treaties," *Latin American Integration* (Buenos Aires: INTAL, June 1982), p. 75.

32. "Treaty Establishing the Latin American Integration Association" (1980), art. 7, reprinted in *International Legal Materials* 20 (1981): 672.

33. Inter-American Development Bank, *Economic and Social Progress in Latin America: Economic Integration* (Washington, D.C.: IADB, 1984), p. 25.

34. Supra, note 32, art. 3(b).

35. Ibid., art. 9(b). See also Teresa Genta Fons and Nelida Susana Rivero, *Proceso de Reestructuración de A.L.A.L.C. Y Creación de A.L.A.D.I.* (Montevideo, Universidad de la República Uruguaya, 1981), p. 23; Alberto Zelada Castedo, "Derecho de la Integración—Estudios: Convergencia y Multilateralismo en la ALADI," *Integración Latinoamericana* (Buenos Aires: INTAL, August 1984), p. 48; and Robert Carcano, "Investment and the Andean Pact: From Political Response to Legal Structures in Safe Harbors," *Dickenson International Law Annual* 2 (1983): 96.

36. Instituto para la Integración de América Latina, *El Proceso de la Integración en América Latina en 1983* (Buenos Aires, 1984), pp. 32-34; and José Aragão, "ALADI: Perspectivas," p. 12; and "Comentarios—ALADI: Culminación de una Etapa en la Renegociación del Patrimonio Histórico," *Integración Latinoamericana* (Buenos Aires: INTAL, October 1983), no. 84, pp. 44-45.

37. "Agreement on ASEAN Preferential Trading Arrangements" (February 24, 1977), art. 8, par. 1, reprinted in *Malaya Law Review* (Kuala Lumpur) 20 (1978): 415.

38. International Monetary Fund, *Exchange Arrangements and Exchange Restrictions: Annual Report 1984* (Washington, D.C.: IMF, 1984), pp. 48–49.

39. See, for example, Gerald Tan, "Intra-ASEAN Trade Liberalisation: An Empirical Analysis," *Journal of Common Market Studies* 20 (1982):321; Purificacion Valera-Quisumbing, "Can ASEAN Forge a Viable Legal Regime for Regional Cooperation?" *Philippine Law Journal* 56 (1981):209; Yasuba, "The Impact of ASEAN on the Asia-Pacific Region," in *ASEAN in a Changing Pacific and World Economy*, ed. Ross Garnaut, (Canberra: A.N.U. Press, 1980), p. 73; H. W. Arndt and Ross Garnaut, "ASEAN and the Industrialization of East Asia," *Journal of Common Market Studies* 17 (1979):191; and Stuart Drummond, "Fifteen Years of ASEAN," *Journal of Common Market Studies* 20 (1982): 301, 309.

40. "Cartagena Agreement on Andean Subregional Integration" (1969), arts. 45(b), 49; and see art. 100(d), reprinted in *International Legal Materials* 8 (1969):910; and "Lima Protocol Amending the Cartagena Agreement" (1976), reprinted in *International Legal Materials* 16 (1977): 235.

41. "Cartagena Agreement," supra, note 40, arts. 34(e), 45(a).

42. Robert Fulmer, "The Andean Common Market: Implications for U.S. Business," *Andean Pact: Definition, Design, and Analysis* (Council of the Americas ed., 1973), pp. 1, 7.

43. "Cartagena Agreement," supra, note 40, arts. 47, 53.

44. "Lima Protocol Amending the Cartagena Agreement on Andean Subregional Integration" (1976), art. 4(b), reprinted in *International Legal Materials* 16 (1977): 235.

45. Ibid., art. 4(a).

46. "Cartagena Agreement," supra, note 40, arts. 50, 52.

47. Ibid.

48. Ibid. and "Lima Protocol," supra, note 44, art. 3.

49. "Cartagena Agreement," supra, note 40, art. 52(a) and "Lima Protocol," supra, note 44, art. 3.

50. "Cartagena Agreement," supra, note 40, art. 52(a).

51. Ibid., art. 52(c).

52. "Lima Protocol," supra, note 44, art. 8.

53. Ibid., art. 9; and see Beverly May Carl and Lawrence Johnson, "Venezuela and the Andean Common Market," *Denver Journal of International Law & Policy* 7 (1978): 151.

54. Junta del Acuerdo de Cartagena, Grupo Andino: *Evaluación del Progreso de Integración: 1969-1979* (1979), p. 89.

55. Supra, note 32, p. 87.

56. Ibid., pp. 97–98.

57. Reinaldo Figueredo P., "El Comercio Internacional y las Políticas para el Establecimiento del Mercado Subregional Andino," *Integración Latinoamericana* (Buenos Aires: INTAL, January–February 1985), no. 98, p. 20.

58. "Plan de Emergencia para Reorientar la Integración," *Integración Latinoamericana* (Buenos Aires: INTAL, September 1983), no. 83, p. 63.

59. "Plantean la Alternativa del Trueque en la Subregión, *Integración Latinoamericana* (Buenos Aires: INTAL, June 1984), no. 91. p. 46.

60. Supra, note 25, art. 38.

61. Supra, note 32, art. 5.

62. ALADI [LAIA], Secretaría General, "Estudio Sobre Puesta en Vigencia de la Preferencia Arancelaria Regional" (Montevideo, ALADI/SEC/Estudio 2, September 8, 1982). p. 23.

63. César Peñaranda, "Estrategia Para la Integración Económica en América Latina," *Integración Latinoamericana* (Buenos Aires: INTAL, March 1984), no. 88, pp. 22, 26–27; and "Editorial, La Integración Regional Como Respuesta Latinoamericana a la Crisis Económica," ibid. p. 3.

64. "Editorial," supra, note 63, p. 3.

65. "Acuerdo Regional Relativo a La Preferencia Arancelaria Regional," ALADI/AR.PAR./4, April 27, 1984, reprinted in *Integración Latinoamericana* (Buenos Aires: INTAL, May 1984), no. 90, p. 77.

66. Ibid., art. 5.

67. Ibid., chap. 12, art. A.

68. Ibid., arts. 3, 8.

69. "Cartagena Agreement," supra, note 40, art. 55; and "Lima Protocol," supra, note 44, art. 1.

70. Carl and Johnson, "Andean Common Market," nn. 52–55 and accompanying text.

71. Supra, note 5, art. 28.

72. Ibid., art. 29; see also Joseph F. O'Connell, "The Caribbean Community: Economic Integration in the Commonwealth Caribbean," *Journal of International Law & Economics* 11 (1976): 35. Similar clauses appear in the Cartagena Agreement, supra, note 40, arts. 78–81 and the LAFTA agreement, supra, note 26, arts. 23–26.

73. Supra, note 18, art. 26.

74. Supra, note 3.

75. "Cartagena Agreement," supra, note 40, art. 97 and Inter-American Development Bank, *Economic and Social Progress in Latin America: Economic Integration—1984 Report* (Washington, D.C.: IADB, 1984), p. 53.

76. Supra, note 32, art. 18.

77. Instituto para la Integración de América Latina, *El Proceso de Integración en América Latina en 1983* (Buenos Aires: INTAL, 1984), p. 53.

78. Ibid., p. 54; see also Enrique Sabatté, "Sistema de Apoyo a Los Paises de Menor Desarrollo," *Síntesis ALADI: 1982 Plena Vigencia del Nuevo Tratado de Montevideo* (Buenos Aires: INTAL, 1982), p. 9.

79. Instituto para la Integración de América Latina, *El Proceso de Integración en América Latina en 1983* (Buenos Aires: INTAL, 1984) pp. 50–51.

80. "Los Acuerdos de Alcance Regional de Apertura de Mercados en Favor de los Países de Menor Desarrollo Económico Relativo," *Integración Latinoamericana* (Buenos Aires: INTAL, October 1984), no. 95, p. 40 n. 23.

81. Supra, note 32, arts. 25(a), 27(a).

82. "Información Latinoamericana," *Integración Latinoamericana* (Buenos Aires: INTAL, October 1983), no. 84, p. 51.

83. Inter-American Development Bank, *News*, November 1984, p. 2.

84. Supra, note 77, pp. 52–53 and "Legislacón Nacional: Argentina," *Integración Latinoamericana* (Buenos Aires: INTAL, January–February 1985), no. 98, p. 85.

85. Supra, note 32, art. 18.

86. "Protocol on the Situation of Land-Locked, Island, Part-Island, Semi-Land-Locked and/or Least Developed Countries," arts. 3, 4, ECCAS treaty, supra, note 25, Annex XVIII, *International Legal Materials* 23 (1984): 1008.

87. Supra, note 3, art. 11, par. 3(b).

88. "Protocol Relating to the Definition of the Concept of Products Originating from Member States of the Economic Community of West African States" (November 5, 1976, as amended May 29, 1979), art. 2, par. 1(b).

89. Ibid., art. 4.

90. Ibid., art. 2(2); and "Decision of the Authority of Heads of State and Government of ECOWAS Relating to the Fixing of the Desirable Level of National Participation in the Equity Capital of the Industrial Enterprises Whose Products Benefit from Preferential Duty," May 28, 1980, *ECOWAS Official Journal* (June 1980): 5.

91. "Protocol on the Rules of Origin for Products to Be Traded Between the Member States of the Preferential Trade Area," Rule 2, PTA, Annex III, supra, note 23, *International Legal Materials* 21 (1982): 505.

92. "Protocol on the Rules of Origin for Products to be Treated [Traded] Between the Member States of the Economic Community of Central African States," Rule 2, ECCAS, Annex I, supra, note 25, *International Legal Materials* 23 (1984): 966.

93. Supra, note 37, Annex I, Rule 3(a)(i) and (ii).

94. Ralph H. Folsom, "ASEAN as a Regional Economic Group—A Comparative Lawyer's Perspective," *Malaya Law Review* (Kuala Lumpur) 25 (1983):203.

95. "Council Regulation 802/68 on the Common Definition of Origin of Goods," art. 5, (1968) J.O. L148/1, CCH Comm. Mkt. Rep. Par. 3821, reprinted in Eric Stein, Peter Hay, and Michel Waelbroeck, *European Community and Institutions in Perspective: Text, Cases, and Readings* (Indianapolis: Bobbs-Merrill, 1976), p. 984.

96. "Convention Establishing the European Free Trade Association" (January 4, 1960), reprinted in ibid., Doc. Supp. 360.

97. "Protocol No. 3: Rules of Origin," *EFTA Bulletin* 3 (1972): 19, reprinted in ibid., p. 989.

98. Supra, note 5, art. 14.

99. Supra, note 12, p. 195.

100. Supra, note 65, art. 9; see also Resolutions No. 49(II), 83(III), and 84(III).

101. "Cartagena Agreement," supra, note 40, art. 83.

102. Figueredo, supra, note 57, p. 25.

103. Supra, note 40, art. 46.

104. Supra, note 5, art. 21.

105. Supra, note 18, art. 12.

106. Supra, note 2, art. 3.

107. Supra, note 23, art. 16.

108. Supra, note 40, art. 46.

109. Shailendra Anjaria, Sena Eken, and John F. Laker, *Payments Arrangements and the Expansion of Trade in Eastern and Southern Africa* (International Monetary Fund, Washington, D.C., 1982), p. 10.

110. Juan Guillermo Valenzuela, "Restricciones No Arancelarias en Los Países de la ALADI," *Integración Latinoamericana* (Buenos Aires: INTAL, January–February 1984), no. 87, pp. 7–10.

111. Ibid., pp. 8–9.

112. Ibid., pp. 10–12. This article contains a detailed country by country analysis of the different types of nontariff barriers to trade.

113. Ibid., p. 13.

114. "Editorial: La Integración por la Vía de la Eliminación de las Restricciones No Arancelarias al Comercio Recíproco," ibid., pp. 1, 2.

115. Supra, note 65; and Resolución 5 as cited in Valenzuela, "Restricciones No Arancelarias," p. 12.

116. Valenzuela, "Restricciones No Arancelarias," p. 12.

117. "Protocol on the Reduction and Elimination of Trade Barriers on Selected Commodities To Be Traded Within the Preferential Trade Area," art. 5, supra, note 23, reprinted in *International Legal Materials* 21 (1982): 499.

118. "Protocol on Non-Tariff Hindrances to Trade," art. 2, Annex II of the ECCAS treaty, supra, note 25, *International Legal Materials* 23 (1984): 971ff.

119. Supra, note 25, art. 34(4).

120. "Protocol on Non-Tariff Hindrances to Trade," art. 3, supra, note 118.

121. Supra, note 1, art. 19.

122. Ibid., art. 23.

123. (San Jose, Costa Rica, September 1, 1959), reprinted in Inter-American Institute of International Legal Studies, *Instruments Relating to the Economic Integration of Latin America*, vol. 2 (Dobbs Ferry, New York: Oceana, 1975), p. 441 and see summaries of various protocols, pp. 448–50.

124. "Convenio sobre el Régimen Arancelario y Aduanero Centroamericano," (December 14, 1984), reprinted in *Integración Latinoamericana* (Buenos Aires: INTAL, May 1985), no. 101, p. 76–83, and Instituto para la Integración de América Latina, *El Proceso de Integración en América Latina en 1980* (Buenos Aires, 1981), p. 138.

125. Supra, note 40, arts. 60, 61.

126. Ibid., art. 64.

127. Ibid.

128. "Lima Protocol," supra, note 44, art. 2.

129. Supra, note 13, p. 97.

130. Supra, note 5, art. 31.

131. Lawrence Mann, "Una Evaluación de la Comunidad del Caribe: Perspectivas y Problemas en 1983," *Integración Latinoamericana* (Buenos Aires: INTAL, July 1984), no. 92, p. 29.

132. Supra, note 12, p. 196.

133. Supra, note 18.

134. International Monetary Fund, *Exchange Arrangements & Exchange Restrictions: Annual Report 1984* (Washington, D.C.: IMF, 1984), p. 47.

135. Ibid.

136. Supra, note 25, art. 29.

137. Supra, note 23, art. 12(b).

138. Ibid., art. 29.

139. Anjaria, Eken, and Laker, *Payments Arrangements*, p. 10.

140. McLenaghan, Nsouli, and Riechel, *Currency Convertibility*, p. 15.

141. Supra, note 18, art. 50.

142. Supra, note 18, art. 52(c).

143. "Decision of the Authority of Heads of State and Government of ECOWAS Relating to the Application of the Compensation Procedures for the Loss of Revenue Suffered by ECOWAS Member States as a Result of the Trade Liberalization Programme" (May 19, 1980), art. II (1)(a), *ECOWAS Official Journal* 2 (June 1980): 7–8.

144. "Protocol Relating to the Fund for Cooperation, Compensation and Development of the Economic Community of West African States" (November 5, 1976), art. 2(a) and (b).

145. "Protocol Relating to the Compensation Fund for Loss of Revenue," arts. 4, 5, Annex VI of the ECCAS treaty, supra, note 25, *International Legal Materials* 23 (1984): 988.

146. Howard French, "Organizational Overlap Slows Regional Unity," *International Herald Tribune* (Paris ed.), July 27–28, 1985: 12, 14.

147. "Protocol on Transit and Transit Facilities," art. 2(3), Annex IV of the ECCAS treaty, supra, note 25, *International Legal Materials* 23 (1984): 974; "Protocol on Transit Trade and Transit Facilities," art. 2(3), Annex V of the PTA treaty, supra, note 23, *International Legal Materials* 21 (1982): 513; ECOWAS treaty, supra, note 18, art. 22(3).

148. "Protocol on Transit and Transit Facilities, Appendixes I, II, supra, note 25, *International Legal Materials* 23 (1984): 977–82.

149. "Protocol on the Re-Export of Goods," art. 3, Annex III of the ECCAS treaty, supra, note 25, *International Legal Materials* 23 (1984): 972; "Protocol on the Re-Export of Goods within the Preferential Trade Area," art. 4, Annex IV of the PTA treaty, supra, note 23, *International Legal Materials* 21 (1982): 511; "Protocol Relating to the Re-Exportation Within the Economic Community of West African States of Goods Imported from Third Countries" (November 5, 1976), art. 2.

# 3

# INVESTMENT POLICY

If an integration unit is to be more than a mere customs union or mutual duty reduction club, it will have a number of additional features. For instance, the East African common market created a group of corporations to operate the railroads, harbors, post offices, and telecommunications systems.[1] In the early 1970s, I flew from London to Uganda on a plane of the East African Airways and a few days later discussed air law in Arusha, Tanzania, with the General Counsel of the East African Community. Unfortunately, those same aircraft subsequently formed the subject of a bitter dispute between the member nations when the East African Community broke up.

The nontariff elements brought into the integration process will differ from one unit to another. The objectives sought through these supplemental mechanism are diverse and, on occasion, appear inconsistent. At times, the desire to attract foreign investment, foster entrepreneurial capitalism, and ensure free competition seems to have been paramount. Other times the pendulum swings toward reining in the foreign investor, insuring local control of industrial development, as well as maximizing use of indigenous resources and technology. The balance struck by a particular integration unit depends not only on the political attitudes of its leaders, but also on the prevailing intellectual climate and the economic conditions existent at the time a specific measure is adopted.

## COMPETITION

Some units have adopted provisions inspired by the antitrust norms of the EEC convention. For example, CARICOM authorizes its council to investigate restrictive business practices or the abuse of a dominant position when such a case is reported to it.[2]

ANCOM has promulgated Decision 45, which provides for measures to prevent distortion of competition. Practices distorting competition are defined as "dumping," "improper manipulation of prices," "practices intended to disturb the normal supply of raw materials," or other practices "having similar effects."[3] If a member state believes it has been so injured, such nation may ask the "junta" of ANCOM for permission to impose a discriminatory tariff against goods produced as a result of such practices. The junta is also directed to request the member countries in whose territory such practices are occurring to adopt the measures necessary to eliminate the distortion.[4] In addition, the technology transfer rules of the Andean Foreign Investment Code[5] forbid the inclusion in licensing or investment contracts of many clauses that amount to restrictive business practices. Examples of prohibited provisions are clauses mandating tied purchases or imposing export restrictions.

## LIMITATIONS ON TAX INCENTIVES

A readily observed phenomenon in the Third World is competition among developing countries to offer increasingly larger tax incentives to private investors, especially foreign companies. Such competition can take a heavy toll on public revenues in poor nations. Although tax incentives seldom have much real influence on the actual investment decision, developing countries fear that another nation's incentives may artificially affect the direction of the investment flow. Thus, the members of both the Central American Common Market[6] and CARICOM[7] have adopted treaties establishing the maximum fiscal incentives that any member might grant to private investors. The member nations may offer lesser incentives, but not more. In fact, the CACM nations in writing their domestic legislation have tended to track the treaty provisions.

In contrast, ANCOM has not yet issued any similar rules but has adopted an interim provision prohibiting members from increasing or adding new incentives.[8]

## CONTROLS ON FOREIGN INVESTMENT:
## THE ANDEAN FOREIGN INVESTMENT CODE

Perhaps the most important legislative act of ANCOM was the enactment of Decision 24 in 1970, known as the Andean Foreign Investment Code.[9] This law covers direct foreign investments, foreign private loans, and technology transfers from abroad. The code established a minimum level of restrictions that each member state must impose on foreign inputs; the individual nations, however, remain free to impose other more restrictive limitations in addition to those contained in the code.[10]

All new and existing foreign investments are required to be registered with and approved by the appropriate national government.[11] Loans from foreign sources to private companies inside the region must also receive prior governmental approval.[12] All contracts to import technology, as well as those to use patents or trademarks, must likewise be approved and registered.[13] Failure to comply with these registration requirements will result in loss of the right to remit earnings[14] or capital,[15] to make payments on principal or interest,[16] as well as to transfer royalties abroad.[17]

## The Divestment Provisions

Inspired by Professor Albert Hirschman's thesis that foreign companies should gradually begin divesting themselves of equity investments in Latin America,[18] the decision makers of ANCOM built into the Andean Foreign Investment Code provisions to compel periodic sales of foreign-held shares to nationals within the subregion. Foreign enterprises[19] making new investments in the region after enactment of Decision 24 must agree to transform themselves into "mixed" or "national" companies within a time period not to exceed 15 years for investments in Peru, Venezuela, or Colombia or 20 years for those in Ecuador or Bolivia.[20] Expansion of an existing enterprise is considered new for this purpose.[21]

A "mixed" enterprise is one in which foreign investors hold less than 50 percent of the stock.[22] A firm in which foreigners own less than 20 percent of the shares is a "national" company.[23] A citizen of any ANCOM member state may be treated as a national when computing these percentages.[24] For example, Peruvian shareholders in a Venezuelan company would be considered "Venezuelan." When so required by the law of their home nation, however, subregional investors must receive the consent of their own government to make such an investment.

Under these transformation agreements, at least 15 percent of the shares must be held by local investors at the time that production begins if the investment site is in Venezuela, Peru, or Colombia. Local investors must own 30 percent of the stock by the time that one-third of the 15–year time period has passed; upon expiration of two-thirds of this time period, 45 percent of the stock must be in the hands of local persons. At the end of not more than 15 years, at least 51 percent of the stock must be owned by locals. The longer stretchout period for Ecuador and Bolivia reduces the requisite percentage amounts at each stage; for example, only 5 percent of the shares must be held by local investors at the time that production begins.[25]

Subject to certain exceptions, foreign-owned companies existing within the ANCOM region prior to the effective date of Decision 24 did not have to satisfy these divestment requirements. If, however, such companies wished to receive the advantages of the reduced internal ANCOM tariff rates on shipping their products into other member states, they too had to transform themselves into national or mixed enterprises not later than 1989.[26]

The Andean Foreign Investment Code provides for some major exceptions to these divestment requirements. Article 34 of the code exempts foreign enterprises that export more than 80 percent of their production outside the ANCOM region; such firms, however, will not qualify for the reduced internal tariffs when they sell to other ANCOM nations, unless they do agree to divest. This article also exempts investments in the tourism sector from the fadeout provisions. Article 36 of the code stipulates that a company shall be considered "mixed" if the state owns a portion of its shares, even if that percentage is less than 51 percent, so long as the state has a "determining capacity" in the decision of the enterprise. Finally, the recent ANCOM Decision 124 provides that investments by public international lending institutions (e.g., the World Bank) or by foreign government developmental assistance programs shall be treated as "neutral" capital and excluded in computing the percentages required to qualify as a "mixed" or "national" company.[27]

The code also stipulates that divestment provisions do not have to be applied to investments in the basic products sector.[28] The term *basic products* includes exploitation of minerals, oil, gas, or forests, as well as pipelines. For Bolivia and Ecuador, this also includes primary agriculture and livestock activities. In fact, Ecuador is not currently imposing any share ownership requirements on investors in petroleum, agricultural, agroindustry, or tourism projects.[29] In these "basic products" sectors, concession contracts not in excess of 20 years are allowed during the first ten years of the code.[30]

Certain sectors of the economy are reserved for "national" companies only. Included in this category are all public services.[31] New investments in insurance, commercial banking, or financing institutions are limited national companies. Existing banks had to convert to national companies (80 percent local) within three years or lose the right to accept deposits.[32]

New investments were also restricted to national companies for the following industries: domestic transportation services, advertising, television, newspapers, and magazines. Existing enterprises operating in these fields were to have undergone transformation into national enterprises by the end of 1977.[33]

The code did, nevertheless, permit a member state to waive the requirement that certain economic sectors be reserved for national companies,[34] but, unless the firms operating in these fields qualify as either "mixed" or "national," they will be denied the privilege of selling to other ANCOM nations at the reduced internal duty rates.[35] Finally, the code reserves domestic marketing services for national companies[36] but allows member states to make exceptions to this rule in special circumstances.[37]

To implement these various ownership requirements, the code had to require that all member states revise their domestic laws to mandate the change of bearer shares into nominative shares.[38] Finally, the code had to provide for a system of certificates of origin to be issued to those firms that have complied with the transformation requirements and thus are entitled to sell to other ANCOM nations at the reduced internal duty rates.[39]

## Remittance of Earnings

Originally, the Andean Foreign Investment Code prohibited foreign investors from remitting abroad yearly profits in excess of an amount equal to 14 percent of the investment.[40] Likewise, member states could not authorize foreign investors to reinvest annually profits in excess of the equivalent of 5 percent of the company's capital.[41] ANCOM, displaying its flexibility, responded to complaints by foreign investors that these ceilings were too restrictive. In 1976 the code was revised to increase the ceiling on remittances to 20 percent of the investment base. Moreover, the member states could even authorize a larger amount so long as they reported it to the ANCOM Commission.[42] The ceiling on the amount of profit that the foreign investor has an automatic right to reinvest was increased from 5 percent to 7 percent and may be added to the capital base upon which the 20 percent remittance and 7 percent reinvestment limits are computed to the future.[43]

## Foreign Loans

For foreign source loans between related companies, the interest rate may not exceed three percentage points above the market rate for first-class securities in the country of origin of the funds. This rule applies to parents, subsidiaries, and affiliates. The code also calls on its member states to deny long-term credit from the domestic market to foreign enterprises.[44] Finally, Article 15 provides that member governments shall refrain from guaranteeing foreign private loans, unless the state is a participant in the project involved.

## Forum Selection Clauses and Subrogation Rights

Foreign investors often wish to insert a choice of court or "forum selection" clause in their contracts. For instance, an investment agreement might provide that any disputes arising thereunder will be submitted to a court in New York. Alternatively, the parties may provide for submission of controversies to an international arbitral tribunal. In addition, foreign companies have traditionally asserted the right to invoke diplomatic protection of their home government to represent them in disputes with the local state.

Most Latin American nations, in contrast, adhere to the Calvo Doctrine. Named for an Argentine jurist, this doctrine asserts that foreign investors should be treated no differently from local investors. Thus, foreign investors should renounce recourse to diplomatic protection of their home government and confine litigation of differences to the local courts. These concepts are reflected in the Andean Foreign Investment Code. Article 51 prohibits both contractual clauses that remove controversies from national courts and those that allow subrogation by the home nation to the rights of the investor.

Meanwhile, within the United States, a governmental agency, the Overseas Private Investment Corporation (OPIC), was providing political risk insurance and financial guaranties to U.S. businesses investing in the developing world. The statute creating OPIC had been interpreted to mean that such programs would be available only if the foreign host nation had agreed to arbitrate investment disputes that could not otherwise be settled. Normally, such international arbitration would entail OPIC's pressing claims on behalf of the U.S. investor and thus run counter to the prohibition against subrogation in Article 51 of the Andean Foreign Investment Code. Consequently, for a 13-year period, the OPIC insurance and guaranty programs were suspended for investments in the ANCOM region.

In 1984, a compromise was reached that permits OPIC to resume operations in at least some ANCOM countries. Under this agreement, Ecuador has consented to international arbitration of investment disputes so long as local remedies inside Ecuador are first exhausted. Thus, Ecuadorean concern for retention of initial juristiction of investment disputes was satisfied. Since prior exhaustion of local remedies is a standard requirement of international law, this term posed no difficulty for the United States. In addition, however, OPIC also agreed to assign its rights to a "fiduciary agent" to represent OPIC in any Ecuadorean litigation. By using a legal representative to pursue litigation, OPIC has thereby avoided direct confrontation between the Ecuadorean state and a U.S. government entity before the Ecuadorean courts. A similar accord with Colombia was concluded in April 1985.[45]

## Results

Because of domestic political changes in Chile, this nation became dissatisfied with the Andean Foreign Investment Code and ultimately in 1976 negotiated a withdrawal from ANCOM.[46] (However, since Venezuela, which was not an original member, decided to join ANCOM, the number of members remained at five.)

When the Andean code was first promulgated, its provisions were denounced as unacceptable, and dire predictions were made that foreign investment in the region would cease. The furor now seems to have died down, and statistics indicate that investment capital is still flowing in. From 1971 (the year Decision 24 became fully effective) to 1977, direct foreign investment in the region grew at an average rate of 7.6 percent annually to increase the total accumulation thereof from approximately $5 billion in 1971 to $8 billion in 1977. The number of foreign subsidiaries and affiliates within the region rose from 663 in 1968 to 1,228 in 1976.[47]

This should not really be surprising. First, investment decisions are based on considerations, such as the presence of natural resources, size of the market, stability of government, availability of skilled labor, access to credit, transportation facilities, and infrastructure facilities, such as water and electricity.[48] Neither tax incentives nor percentage limitations on ownership are normally decisive factors.

In addition, the notion that retention of majority ownership in local hands secures effective control is illusory. Developing nations suffer from a shortage of capital equipment, managerial talent, and technical skill; they also lack global distribution networks for their manufactures. Frequently, the local partner needs access to overseas financing or technology available to the foreign company. Thus, studies have concluded that if a multinational company owns as much as 25 percent of the equity it will have effective control over a developing nation enterprise.[49]

Hence, most foreign companies wishing to invest in ANCOM could conform to the requirements of the code and still be in charge. Decision 24 attempted to deal with this problem by requiring that the percentage of national ownership be reflected in the "technical, administrative, financial and commercial management of the enterprise."[50] How such a provision is to be implemented is unclear. In any event, although local persons may constitute a formal majority on the board, commercial realities can still vest the real authority in the foreign partner because of its financial and technical resource base.

Finally, ANCOM has taken a flexible approach to Decision 24. For example, increasing the allowable profit remittances from 14 to 20 percent probably meant little in practice since historically most companies had remitted well under 14 percent. This move, however, achieved psychological benefits by displaying a receptive attitude toward foreign investment.[51] In 1984, Colombia proposed that Decision 24 be modified to increase the number of situations in which foreign capital could be invested in "national" companies.[52]

Although investment in the region has not recently grown as much as hoped, this is probably attributable less to the restrictive provisions of the code than to the global recession with its contraction of markets and foreign exchange shortages.[53] These disincentives have dampened investors' enthusiasm and caused U.S. foreign investment flows to *all* developing nations to fall from $6.1 billion in 1981 to $2.4 billion in 1983.[54]

## RESTRICTIONS ON TECHNOLOGY TRANSFERS FROM ABROAD

The Andean Foreign Investment Code also imposes limitations on the transfer of technology. Contracts to license foreign patents, know-how, or trademarks must be approved by an appropriate agency of the member nation.

### Patent and Know-how Licenses

An agreement to transfer technology may not be approved if it contains any of the following clauses: those allowing the supplier to fix the sale or resale price of the goods produced thereunder; those giving a purchase option to the technology supplier; those obligating the licensee (without compensation) to transfer back to the supplier inventions or improvements arising out of such technology; those restricting the volume or structure of production; or those requiring the purchaser to pay royalties on patents that are not used. Save in exceptional circumstances, these contracts may not include clauses limiting or prohibiting exports of the goods manufactured thereunder. Likewise proscribed are clauses that require the licensee to employ permanently personnel selected by the supplier as well as clauses that limit the licensee to procuring capital goods, raw materials, intermediate products, or other technology from a particular source. This procurement prohibition may be waived in exceptional cases, so long as the cost of the item does not exceed the world market price.[55]

ANCOM also promulgated the Andean Industrial Property Code,[56] Decision 85. As of 1978, it was in effect only in Ecuador because of controversies resulting from some of its provisions. Article 5(c) excludes from patentability, "pharmaceutical products, medicines, active therapeutic substances, and beverages and foods for human, animal and vegetable use." Patentability may also be denied by member governments to inventions that "affect the development of the" country.[57]

More serious could be Article 5(d), which excludes "foreign inventions" if the patent request is filed in the ANCOM nation more than one year after a patent registration request was submitted in the first nation in which registration was sought. This could place a great burden on transnational enterprises, which would be obligated to apply for patent protection almost simultaneously with their application in any other nation. Once, however, a patent application is filed in one member nation, the clock is stopped and the applicant has an additional year to file for patent protection in any other member country.[58]

Rights granted under a patent may be conditional.[59] Patents may be granted for a period of ten years, renewable twice for five-year periods upon proof of adequate utilization.[60]

Most unusual of the provisions in this code are those on obligatory licensing. First, the patent holder must notify the appropriate authorities within three years that the technology covered by the patent is being adequately "worked."[61] Upon expiration of that initial three-year period, any person may request the government for a license to use such technology if one of the following situations exists: (1) the patented invention has not been used within the ANCOM country; (2) the use of such invention has been suspended for more than one year; (3) the use of the invention does not satisfy reasonable conditions of quantity, quality, or price as needed by the national market; or (4) the holder has failed to license another holder who can satisfy the needs of the national market under reasonable conditions of quantity, quality, and price.[62] The holder of a compulsory license is required to pay compensation to the patent owner.[63] In the case of patents related to public health or national development needs, the member governments may demand a compulsory license at any time.[64]

## Trademarks

Licensing agreements for foreign trademarks may not incorporate clauses that limit or forbid exports of the goods produced under the trademark, that fix the sale or resale price of the product, that obligate the licensee to pay for an unused trademark, or that require the user to employ permanently personnel selected by the licensor. Also, the agreements may not compel the licensee to use raw materials, intermediate goods, or equipment supplied by the licensor or its affiliate companies; in exceptional cases, the recipient nation may permit such a clause, if the cost of the item does not exceed the world market price.[65]

Provisions of the Andean Industrial Property Code on trademarks are more standard, but the code does forbid a trademark owner from objecting to the importation of goods bearing the same trademark if the item comes from another ANCOM country and if the nation is clearly identified.[66] A trademark applicant in one ANCOM nation has a priority right for six months to make a similar application in other member states.[67] Trademark registrations are valid for only five years, but they may be renewed upon proof of use in a member country.[68]

## Royalties and Choice of Court Clauses

The Andean Foreign Investment Code prohibits the payment of royalties between a majority foreign-owned subsidiary and its parent or affiliates. Moreover, such payments may not be deducted from taxable income.[69] Finally, technology contributions may not be capitalized.[70] And, once again, clauses removing jurisdiction from the local courts are forbidden.[71]

## INDIGENOUS MULTINATIONAL ENTERPRISES

Developing nations are interested not only in attracting and/or controlling transnational enterprises from the industrialized world, but also in fostering the growth of their own indigenous firms. Moreover, there is a pressing need for the local companies to begin thinking in terms of the larger integrated market instead of merely their own small market. To accomplish this goal, both ANCOM and ASEAN are endeavoring to promote the formation of region-wide private companies with shareholders from more than one ANCOM nation.

## The ANCOM EMAs

To encourage formation of such regional companies, ANCOM issued Decision 169 on Andean Multinational Enterprises.[72] Although such a company is created under the national law of the country in which its principal domicile is located, it must add to its name the words "Andean Multinational Enterprise" or the letters "EMA" (Empresa Multinacional Andina).[73] To qualify as an EMA, 80 percent of the shares must be held by nationals of two or more ANCOM countries;[74] if, however, the place of principal domicile is Bolivia or Ecuador, this requirement, for at least ten years, is reduced to 60 percent.[75] When an EMA is formed by investors from only two countries, the amount of investment from each nation may not be less than 15 percent of the total capital.[76] At least one director must be selected for each member country whose nationals have an equity participation of not less than 15 percent.[77]

EMAs have the right to establish branches in the member countries that are distinct from the nation of their principal domicile.[78] EMAs may also transfer earnings back to the country of principal domicile in freely convertible currency.[79] They are entitled to national treatment with regard to taxation[80] and internal credit.[81] This decision also includes provisions to avoid double taxation of income earned by a regional branch of an EMA.[82]

In 1982 the Mixed Chambers of Commerce of Venezuela and Colombia announced plans for 18 EMAs, with a total Venezuelan investment of $42 million in Colombian firms and Colombian investments in Venezuelan companies of $28 million. Likewise, that year a group of Peruvian and Bolivian business people stated that it would jointly invest $50 million in projects to develop the Lake Titicaca area.[83]

The first Andean multinational enterprise, Ozalid, S.A. EMA, started production in 1984. Based in Bogota, the firm will produce photosensitive paper and was capitalized as follows: $620 million from a Venezuelan company, $200 million from a U.S. concern, and $150 million from a Colombian businessman.[84]

## ASEAN Local Joint Ventures

ASEAN too has demonstrated an interest in promoting indigenous "multinational" enterprises. In 1983 ASEAN concluded an agreement on joint ventures under which eligible private companies are entitled to preferential tariff treatment and to some degree of protection against competition. The requirements for such a company are share ownership by nationals of at least two participating countries within ASEAN[85] and a minimum of 51 percent of the stock held by ASEAN nationals.[86] The latter requirement may be waived in certain circumstances, for example, where the 50 percent of the production will be exported outside the ASEAN region, or where the participating nations consent to a higher percentage of foreign ownership, and so on.[87] (See "ASEAN Industrial Joint Ventures" below for more details.)

## INDUSTRIAL PLANNING

As indicated above, some of the associations did not choose to leave investment decisions exclusively to market forces, but rather took a more managerial or planned approach (in Spanish called "dirigismo"). Their leaders believed it essential to direct resources toward particular industrial sectors or geographic regions in order to achieve some balance in the distribution of benefits among members. For example, allocation of regional industries among its member states is a major feature of the East Caribbean Common Market.[88] Financial institutions, like the Central American Bank for Economic Integration, often contribute to this goal through their lending policies.

As mentioned in Chapter 2, the Economic Community of West African States will provide immediate internal duty-free treatment for enterprises accorded "community" status. Thus far, ECOWAS has placed its industrial planning emphasis on gathering information about the region's industrialization. Eventually, this data will be used to formulate a legal framework that, hopefully, will ensure equitable allocation of such "community" ventures among all members.[89]

Planners may also wish to "rationalize" production by dividing up various stages of the process and assigning them to different countries. Critics of this approach contend that this amounts to a division of markets and thus violates concepts of free enterprise and free competition. Advocates of such complementation or sectorial planning reply that developing nations are too short of resources to engage in inefficient duplication. Not every country can make every item. Nor is it efficient for several small nations to try to manufacture the same widget; the resulting competition may lead to losses for everyone. It is better to ensure the success of one country (or firm) by manipulating the legal structure to limit production to specified nations. Thus, rational division and allocation of the production process are seen as an eminently desirable objective.

Several integration associations have established fairly complex schemes for this purpose. Below is a brief description of some of them.

### The CACM Integrated Industries Approach

In 1959, the Central American Common Market adopted the Agreement on the System of Central American Integrated Industries.[90] This mechanism was intended to attract new industries by giving them certain benefits on an exclusive basis and by denying competitors equal rights for a period up to ten years.

To achieve the status of an "integrated" industry, the company had to negotiate a protocol that would be approved by all five member nations.[91] Once a plant was so designated, its products were to be immediately duty free throughout the region, whereas its competitors' goods would be subject to internal duties for a period of time. In planning for the common external tariff, the integrated industry was to be protected against outside competitors.[92] In addition, such an industry was to enjoy priority in government purchases.[93] CACM was prohibited from granting integrated status to a second plant in a country that already had one integrated project until every other member nation had an integrated plant.[94]

In practice, this technique was unsuccessful. As of 1967, only two industries had been designated as integrated: a tire factory in Guatemala and a caustic soda and insecticide plant in Nicaragua. Moreover, the value of the status was blunted when the Executive Council of the CACM approved the establishment of a competing tire plan in Costa Rica. The administrative procedures required for securing this status discouraged many from even trying. The program was also criticized as being monopolistic.[95] With virtual free trade having been achieved a few years later, the focus shifted away from this program to tax incentives and bank financing.

### LAFTA/LAIA Complementarity Agreements

Under Article 16 of the LAFTA accord, members were encouraged to conclude complementation agreements among themselves under which they might allocate different segments of production of a specific good among several members and then create an appropriate tariff structure to protect the nation that had been assigned a particular component.

For example, the glass-making industry might have an agreement whereby one type of glass is produced in country A and another type in country B. Country A would agree to liberalize imports of the type of glass to be produced in country B, and country B would liberalize imports of the type of glass produced in country A. Where horizontal specialization is involved, various stages of the particular industrial process are located in different nations.[96]

The first LAFTA complementarity accord was concluded in 1962 between Argentina, Brazil, Uruguay, and Chile. Based on a plan submitted by IBM, the agreement divided up production of data-processing equipment so that

Argentina was to have a plant to produce electronic sorters, collators, and accounting machines while Brazil was to receive a factory for punchers, verifiers, and auxiliary machinery. Another U.S. company was to license a Chilean firm to manufacture card stock for the machines. Then the member nations of the complementary agreement were to eliminate within 30 days all tariff and trade restrictions on the specified product from the assigned nation. After implementation of the agreement, zonal trade in these machines did increase from $164,000 in 1962 to $2.5 million in 1965.[97]

A variety of other complementary agreements followed over the years covering industries such as household electrical appliances, air conditioners, radio tubes, and lamps.

The new LAIA pact divides these industry allocation accords into two categories: commercial agreements and complementation pacts. Commercial agreements are defined by Article 10 as those exclusively intended to promote trade among the member countries. One of the first tasks undertaken by LAIA was to review the complementation agreements previously concluded under the LAFTA treaty. By the end of 1982, 22 LAFTA complementation agreements had been updated and converted in to LAIA commercial agreements.[98] During the renegotiations, only one signatory, Colombia, withdrew from an agreement (No. 5 on chemicals). In accord with the theory of convergence, new signatories are to be welcomed to these agreements, and, in fact, Venezuela chose to join accord No. 13 (photography).[99]

These earlier arrangements have, however, been criticized as stemming mainly from the subsidiaries of multinational corporations and thus amounting to little more than intra-enterprise specialization. Moreover, with but one exception, no use was made of this mechanism to program or induce new investment.[100]

The LAIA treaty now provides two devices that can be developed to encourage new investments in priority sectors. Article 11 redefines the term *complementation agreements* as those that promote "maximum utilization of factors of production, stimulate economic complementation, assure equitable conditions of competition, facilitate the exports of the products to the international market, and promote the balanced and harmonious development of member countries." Moreover, agreements of "partial scope," described in the previous chapter, could be used to protect the favored industries by creating an external tariff barrier against competing imports.

## The ANCOM Sectorial Program

Under the Sectorial Program ANCOM decides which products contained in a particular industry, such as the metalworking industry, will be reserved for the sectorial program. Then those items are divided up and assigned among the five member nations. Some assignments are to one member exclusively; in other cases, an assignment may be shared among several members.[101] Bolivia and Ecuador, as the poorest members, are to be given special consideration in this process. Once a product has been assigned to a nation, ANCOM creates a special preferential tariffs structure to provide an advantage to the producers in the favored nation.[102] For example, the item from the assigned nation may circulate duty free through the region, while competing manufacturers in other members would be subject to an internal duty.

Technically, such assignments do not create a monopoly because companies in nonfavored countries are not prohibited from producing and selling the item throughout the region although they are not supposed to expand. Typically, the law establishing the sectorial program will, prohibit nonfavored member states from extending government credit or tax incentives[103] to such competing firms. Moreover, such nations may not authorize direct foreign investment to produce that good.[104]

Thus far, four sectorial programs have been established: metalworking, iron and steel, petrochemicals, and automotive. The results have not been as dramatic as the drafters of these schemes had hoped. Still production has begun in 45 percent of the items assigned. It is estimated that $185 million in investments have been made under the programs and 4,500 new jobs created.[105] Consideration is now being given to revising these programs, which could involve elimination of assignments of products to Colombia, Peru, and Venezuela.[106]

## ASEAN Complementation Programs

### ASEAN Industrial Projects

ASEAN has developed several different schemes for achieving industrial cooperation. The ASEAN Industrial Projects (AIP) program comprises large-scale projects intended to cover the needs of the whole region. They are supposed to be sponsored by all ASEAN governments, and special care has been taken to allow equity participation by all member countries. At least one of these projects should be located in each nation. The host country is expected to hold 60 percent of the equity, and the balance is to be shared, not necessarily equally, by other ASEAN countries. The shareholder agency of the host country is to be designated by the respective government, which, in turn, is required to own at least one-third of the shares of such agency.[107]

Four AIP projects have been approved: ammonia/urea fertilizer plants in Indonesia and Malaysia, a copper fabrication facility in the Philippines, and a Thai soda ash project.[108] The Indonesian urea factory will belong to a holding company formed by Indonesia and the other ASEAN governments. ASEAN collectively will be responsible for repayment of the loan capital to be raised. Since, however, none of the member nations impose, nor wish to impose, tariffs on urea from third countries, preferences can only take the form of assured access to the domestic markets of the partner countries. Both the Malaysian and Indonesia plants are near completion.[109]

The Thai soda ash project is to be 60 percent owned by the Thai government, while Malaysia, Indonesia, and the Philippines are to take 13 percent each and Singapore, 1 percent. This $400 million plus project is to be financed through a soft loan pledged by Japan in 1977.[110]

## ASEAN Industrial Complementation Projects

In 1971 the ASEAN Chambers of Commerce and Industry were established to involve private industry more directly in the planning process. ASEAN then asked these chambers to organize industrial clubs in the economic sectors believed to be most feasible for complementarity arrangements. Each corporation was thereafter to restrict its manufacture to certain items. Industrial clubs have emerged in the automotive, pulp, paper, and steel industries.[111]

This scheme was formalized in the 1981 Basic Agreement on ASEAN Industrial Complementation, which is directed toward private small and medium-sized industries located in the region.[112] ASEAN Chambers of Commerce and Industry, as well as member governments, are to identify and recommend products for inclusion in "ASEAN Industrial Complementation" (AIC) packages.[113] After final approval by the ASEAN economic ministers of an AIC package, the products therein are allocated among the member states that wish to participate in the particular AIC program. As a general rule, at least four nations must participate in an AIC package.[114]

Once selected, an AIC product is entitled to the privilege of "exclusivity." Exclusivity means that participating countries, other than the one to whom the product was assigned, may not set up new facilities nor expand existing ones to manufacture that product, unless 75 percent of the production of that good is to be exported outside the ASEAN region. An exception to the exclusivity rule also exists for projects that have already been "firmly planned" in another participating nation that has not been assigned that particular item. During the period of exclusivity, special preferences such as mandatory sourcing and local content requirements may also be applied.

The privileges of exclusivity are available for two years for a product that is already being produced within the region at the time of the AIC allocation. For a product not being manufactured at that time, exclusivity shall be enjoyed for three years from the date of start-up of the factory or from the target date of such start-up, whichever comes first.[115]

The ASEAN Automotive Federation took the lead in complementation proposals. Two such packages have now been approved, and specified products from eligible member-states will enjoy preferential tariffs within the region. Among products receiving these benefits, are diesel engines for Indonesia, seat belts and headlights for Malaysia, passenger auto body panels for the Philippines, universal joints for Singapore, and body panels for commercial vehicles for Thailand. A number of foreign investors are involved in this complementation scheme. Ford, through its subsidiary, Ensite Inc., will operate the Philippine body plant. Nissan Ltd. owns the body panel factory in Thailand, while the West German firm, Kloeckner-Humboldt-Deutz, has licensed the technology for the Indonesian diesel plant.[116]

Whether the auto complementation plan will succeed is yet unknown. The scheme could be defeated by differences in quality among the complemented Asian auto parts and by the desire to produce a "national" car. These complementation plans also run into the problems of achieving an equitable division of benefits and of meshing with national investment decisions.[117]

### ASEAN Industrial Joint Ventures

In addition, the ASEAN Chambers of Commerce and Industry recommended the promotion of regional joint ventures.[118] This suggestion was recently incorporated into a formal accord. As explained above,[119] the benefits of this status are available only to companies that are owned by shareholders from more than one ASEAN nation and in which extraregional persons do not hold more than a stipulated percentage of shares.

Once again the ASEAN Chambers of Commerce and Industry, together with member governments, are to propose products for inclusion in the AIJV lists. If at least two member nations indicate their intention to "participate" in a particular AIJV product, then that item is included on the final list, which must be approved by the ASEAN economic ministers. After such approval, interested parties have six months to obtain approval from the appropriate national government agencies to produce such products.[120]

An AIJV product manufactured in the country or countries to which it was allocated is entitled to enter other participating nations at a preferential duty at least 50 percent lower than the rate otherwise applicable. Such preferential tariff shall become available within 90 days after commercial production has started in the assigned nation(s).[121] For existing products, the reduced rate will be applicable within 90 days from the date the ASEAN economic ministers approved the item for the AIJV list.[122]

This preferential duty treatment will continue for four years from the date of the implementation of the tariff preference.[123] Companies that produce the same product in a participating nation but have not received the AIJV designation are not entitled to the AIJV preferential duty rates for the first four years.[124] Moreover, nonparticipating nations are not required to extend a preferential duty to AIJV products from the country or countries to which the item was assigned.[125] Once the four-year period has expired, all AIJV products, whether made in a participating or nonparticipating ASEAN nation, shall be treated equally and will be entitled to the same tariff preference as against extraregional competitors.[126]

If by the end of a stipulated six-month period, there is only one approved project for an AIJV product, participating nations shall grant that project exclusivity which means that the participating countries may not set up new production facilities for the same product for a period of three years.[127] This rule does not apply if 75 percent of the production of the new facility is for export to non-ASEAN nations.[128] The exclusivity privilege is not available for products existing before creation of the AIJV lists[129] nor for items for which more than one project has been approved.[130]

The reader will note that the ASEAN AIJV scheme has many similarities to the ANCOM Sectorial Program. Both plans provide a temporary tariff advantage to induce private investment in the selected industrial sector. ASEAN, however, offers the favored nation (or company) only lower duty rates than its competitors, whereas in ANCOM the favored goods will circulate throughout the common market duty free. The ASEAN exclusivity privileges, when available, are broader than the protection offered by ANCOM since the latter is usually limited to proscribing the extension of government credits, granting tax incentives, or authorizing foreign investment in the competing facilities. Finally, ASEAN has linked the preferential tariff structure to a requirement of an obligatory joint venture between citizens of two or more ASEAN nations. Such linkage with the EMA is absent in ANCOM.

## FREE MOVEMENT

As explained above, technically economic integration should eventually provide for free movement of all factors of production, including labor. Nonetheless, developing nations plagued by severe unemployment and underemployment—with estimates ranging as high as 60 percent in some countries—could not be expected to open their doors freely to outside workers. Such concern prompted the drafters of the CARICOM treaty to include the following provision: "Nothing in this Treaty shall be construed as requiring, or imposing any obligation on, a Member State to grant freedom of movement to persons into its territory whether or not such persons are nationals of other Member States of the Common Market."[131]

Other associations have preferred, at least, to retain free movement as an ideal. For example, the East Caribbean Common Market Convention directs the Council of Ministers to submit to member states proposals "for the phased removal of obstacles to the freedom of movement of persons within the Common Market."[132]

The ECOWAS adopted a protocol recognizing the right of citizens of its members to enter, to reside, and to establish a business in the territory of other partner states and sets forth stages for the gradual implementation of these rights over a 15-year period. As the first step, the protocol provides that citizens of member nations may enter each other's territory without visas for a period of 90 days, subject to an additional 90-day renewal.[133] When Nigeria in 1982 expelled an estimated 2 million Ghanaian workers,[134] it argued that this action was consistent with the protocol on the ground that these individuals had overstayed the limit and were no longer legally in the country. Again claiming the 90-day visiting period had expired, Nigeria in the spring of 1985 was attempting to expel another 700,000 alien workers.[135]

During the 1985 ECOWAS summit, the Nigerian expulsions were challenged by the other member states which pointed out that under the second phase of the free movement protocol, ECOWAS citizens should enjoy the right to reside anywhere in the region.[136] Finally, a compromise was worked out whereby implementation of the second phase would be delayed until 1986, at which time its application would become mandatory. In turn, Major General Muhammadu Buhari, then the Nigerian head of state, promised that during the interim, victims of natural disasters, such as drought and famine, would not be treated as illegal aliens.[137] The current status of this promise is unknown.

The Central African States common market has adopted a rather liberal protocol authorizing free movement of citizens of the region to hold a job, to exercise a craft, or to establish an enterprise in other member countries.[138] It seems likely that these rights will be circumscribed by domestic legislation in the partner nations.

## AVOIDANCE OF DOUBLE TAXATION

CARICOM has concluded a convention to prevent double taxation of companies located in more than one partner nation.[139] ANCOM has prepared two model conventions on avoidance of double taxation: one for use between member states and the other for utilization between an ANCOM nation and an outside country.[140]

## NOTES

1. The Secretariat, *The East African Community Handbook* (Arusha, Tanzania:), pp. 28–37.

2. "Treaty Establishing the Caribbean Community (1973), Annex Establishing the Caribbean Common Market," art. 30, reprinted in *International Legal Materials* 12 (1973): 1033, 1044.

3. "Decisión 45, Normas para Prevenir o Corregir las Prácticas que Puedan Distorsionar la Competencia dentro de la Subregión" (December 18, 1971), art. 2, reprinted in *Ordenamiento Jurídico del Acuerdo de Cartagena*, vol. 1 (Lima: Junta del Acuerdo de Cartagena, 1982), p. 140; an

English translation of this decision appears in F. V. Garcia-Amador, *The Andean Legal Order: A New Community Law* (Dobbs Ferry, New York: Oceana, 1978), p. 406.

4. "Decisión 45," supra, note 3, art. 8.

5. "Decision 24 of the Commission of the Cartagena Agreement, Common Regime of Treatment of Foreign Capital and of Trademarks, Patents, Licenses and Royalties, as amended (1976)," arts. 20, 21, reprinted in *International Legal Materials* 16 (Washington, D.C.: American Society of International Law 1977): 138. The earlier versions of Decision 24, adopted December 31, 1970, are reprinted in *International Legal Materials* 10 (1971): 152; *International Legal Materials* 10 (1971): 1065; and *International Legal Materials* 12 (1973): 349.

6. "Central American Agreement on Fiscal Incentives to Industrial Development" (July 31, 1962), reprinted in Inter-American Institute of International Legal Studies, *Instruments Relating to the Economic Integration of Latin America*, vol. 2 (Dobbs Ferry, New York: Oceana, 1975), p. 479. On November 7, 1983, plenipotentiaries of the governments of Guatemala, El Salvador, Nicaragua, and Costa Rica signed a protocol to this convention. *Integración Latinoamericana* (Buenos Aires: INTAL, January–February 1984), no. 87, p. 58. See also D. Gantz, "Uniform Tax Incentives Legislation in Central America," *International Lawyer* 4 (1970): 467.

7. "Agreement on the Harmonization of Fiscal Incentives to Industry" (Georgetown, Guyana, June 1, 1973), reprinted in Inter-American Institute of International Legal Studies, *Instruments of Economic Integration in Latin America and the Caribbean*, vol. 2 (Dobbs Ferry, New York: Oceana, 1975), p. 569; and see supra, note 2, art. 40; and Rachelle L. Cherol and Susana Zalduendo, "El Marco Legal de la Inversión Extranjera en el Caribe y Centroamérica," *Integración Latinoamericana* (Buenos Aires: INTAL, December 1984), no. 97, p. 32.

8. "Temporary Provisions Attached to Decision 13 and 109 of the Andean Foreign Investment Code (Decision 24)," reprinted in *International Legal Materials* 16 (1977): 155.

9. Supra, note 5.

10. For a detailed description of the implementation of Decision 24 by the courts and legislatures of the member nations, see F. V. Garcia-Amador, *The Andean Legal Order* (Dobbs Ferry, New York: Oceana, 1978), pp. 175–88.

11. Supra, note 5, arts. 2, 5.

12. Ibid., art. 14.

13. Ibid., art. 18.

14. Ibid., arts. 1, 37.

15. Ibid., arts. 1, 8.

16. Ibid., art. 16.

17. Ibid., art. 21.

18. A. Hirshman, "How To Divest in Latin American and Why," *Essays in International Finance*, no. 76 (Princeton, N.J.: Department of Economics, Princeton University, 1969.

19. Supra, note 5, art. 1.

20. Ibid., art. 30.

21. Ibid., art. 1.

22. Ibid.

23. Ibid.

24. Ibid.

25. Ibid., art. 30.

26. Ibid., art. 28.

27. Ibid., temporary provision, p. 155.

28. Ibid., arts. 39, 40.

29. *Latin American Weekly Report* (London), August 2, 1985, p. 4; and U.S. Overseas Private Investment Corporation, "Ecuador Relying Heavily on Free Market Orientation," *Topics* (Washington, D.C.: OPIC, spring 1985), p. 4.

30. Supra, note 5, art. 40.

31. Ibid., art. 41.

32. Ibid., art. 42.

33. Ibid., art. 43.

34. Ibid., art. 44. Ecuador reportedly is permitting banks to be 49 percent owned by foreigners. Supra, *Topics*, note 29.

35. Supra, note 5, art. 44.

36. Ibid., art. 43.

37. Ibid., art. 44.

38. Ibid., art. 45.

39. Ibid., arts. 29, 32.

40. See earlier version of code in *International Legal Materials* 10 (1971): 152, 1065, supra, note 5, art. 37.

41. Supra, note 5, art. 13.

42. See 1976 version of code, ibid., art. 37.

43. Supra, note 5, art. 13.

44. Ibid., art. 16, and 17.

45. "Introductory Note: Investment Guaranty Agreements with Ecuador and Colombia," *International Legal Materials* 24 (1985):556. The United States-Ecuador Agreement is set forth on pp. 567–70, ibid.

46. See *International Legal Materials* 15 (1976): 1446.

47. *Junta del Acuerdo de Cartagena, Evaluación de Proceso de Integración: 1969–1979* (Lima: Junta del Acuerdo de Cartagena, 1979), pp. 48–52, 172.

48. Juan Sourrouille, Francisco Gatto, and Bernardo Kosacoff, "Comportamiento Económico de las Filiales de Empresas Transnacionales en América Latina," *Integración Latinoamericana* (Buenos Aires: INTAL, December 1984), no. 97, p. 3.

49. Sunaryati Hartono, *In Search of New Legal Principles* (Bangdung, Indonesia: University of Padjadjaran, 1979), p. 73.

50. Supra, note 5, art. 1.

51. Carlos M. Correa, "Características y Tendencias de la Regulación de las Inversiones Extranjeras en América Latina y el Caribe," *Integración Latinoamericana* (Buenos Aires: INTAL, December 1984), no. 97, p. 31.

52. "Colombia Plantea un Cambio en la Estrategia del Pacto Andino Frente a las Inversiones Extranjeras," *Integración Latinoamericana* (Buenos Aires: INTAL, August 1984), no. 93, p. 102.

53. Sergio Bitar, "La Inversión Estadounidense en el Grupo Andino," *Integración Latinoamericana* (Buenos Aires: INTAL, January–February 1985), no. 98, p. 48.

54. Overseas Development Council, *U.S. Foreign Policy and the Third World Agenda 1985–86*, eds. John W. Sewell, Richard E. Feinberg, and Valeriana Kellab (New Brunswick, N.J.: Transaction Books, 1985), p. 65.

55. Supra, note 5, art. 20; see also John Pate,"The Andean Common Market," in *Technology Transfer: Laws and Practise in Latin America*, ed. Beverly M. Carl (Chicago, American Bar Association, 1980 rev.), p. 59; and Roberto Danino, "Peru," ibid., p. 115.

56. "ANCOM Decision No. 85, Regulations for the Application of Rules on Industrial Property" (June 5, 1974), reprinted in F. V. Garcia-Amador, *The Andean Legal Order: A New Community Law* (Dobbs Ferry, Oceana, 1978), p. 368; see also Pate, "Andean Common Market," pp. 77–80.

57. "Decision No. 85," supra, note 56, art. 5(e).

58. Ibid., art. 10.

59. Ibid., art. 24.

60. Ibid., art. 29.

61. Ibid., art. 30(a).

62. Ibid., art. 34.

63. Ibid.

64. Ibid., art. 39.

65. Supra, note 5, art. 25.

66. "Decision no. 85," supra, note 56, art. 75.

67. Ibid., art. 73.

68. Ibid., arts. 69, 70.

69. Supra, note 5, art. 21.

70. Ibid.

71. Ibid., art. 51.

72. "Decision 169 on Andean Multinational Enterprises" (1982), reprinted in *International Legal Materials* 21 (1982): 542. An earlier version of this law is Decision 46, reprinted in *International Legal Materials* 11 (1972): 357; and see Francesc Vendrell, "Derecho de la Integración—Estúdios: El Nuevo Régimen Jurídico de las Empresas Multinacionales Andinas," *Integración Latinoamericana* (Buenos Aires: INTAL, June 1983), no. 80, p. 23; and Rachelle L. Cherol and José Núñez del Arco, "Derecho de la Integración—Estudíos: Empresas Multinacionales Andinas: Un Nuevo Enfoque de la Inversión Multinacional en el Grupo Andino," *Integracíon Latinoamericana* (Buenos Aires: INTAL, October 1982), no. 73, p. 42.

73. "Decision 169," supra, note 72, art. 9.

74. Ibid., art. 1(b).

75. Ibid., art. 2.

76. Ibid., art. 1(c).

77. Ibid., art. 16(3).

78. Ibid., art. 23.

79. Ibid., art. 24.

80. Ibid., art. 19.

81. Ibid., art. 20.

82. Ibid., art. 26.

83. Instituto para la Integración de América Latina, *El Proceso de Integración en América Latina en 1983* (Buenos Aires: INTAL, 1984), p. 140.

84. "Surge la Primera Empresa Multinacional Andina," *Integración Latinoamericana* (Buenos Aires: INTAL, December 1984), no. 97, p. 59.

85. "Basic Agreement on ASEAN Industrial Joint Ventures," (Jakarta, November 7, 1983), art. I, ¶ 3(b), reprinted in *International Legal Materials* 22 (1983): 1233.

86. Ibid., art. I, ¶ 5.

87. Ibid., art. I, ¶ 5(b).

88. Kevin P. Power, *Caribbean Basin Trade and Investment Guide* (Washington, D.C.: Washington International Press, 1984), p. 265.

89. Julius Emeka Okolo, "Integrative and Cooperative Regionalism: The Economic Community of West African States," *International Organization* 39 (1985): 145.

90. Reprinted in Inter-American Institute of International Legal Studies, *Instruments Relating to the Economic Integration of Latin America*, vol. 2 (Dobbs Ferry, New York: Oceana 1975), p. 451; and see subsequent protocols amending that agreement, pp. 456–79.

91. "Protocol to the Agreement on the System of Central American Integrated Industries" (January 29, 1963), art. 3, reprinted in ibid., p. 456.

92. "Agreement on the System of Integrated Industries" (June 10, 1958), art. 7, reprinted in ibid., p. 451.

93. Ibid., art. 7.

94. Ibid., transitional article.

95. Ingo Walter and Hans C. Vitzthum, "The Central American Common Market: A Case Study on Economic Integration in Developing Regions," *The Bulletin* (New York University, Institute of Finance, May 1967), no. 44, p. 43.

96. Ann Tonjes, U.S. Department of Commerce, *Overseas Business Reports: The Role of 'Complementarity' Agreements in LAFTA* (OBR 68–11, March 1968), p. 2.

97. Ibid., pp. 6–7.

98. Supra, note 83, pp. 49–51.

99. "Companies Focus on LAIA As Deadline Nears For Tariff Revisions," *Business Latin America*, March 9, 1983, p. 76.

100. Inter-American Development Bank, *Economic and Social Progress in Latin America: Economic Integration* (Washington, D.C.: IADB, 1984), p. 63.

101. "Cartagena Agreement on Andean Subregional Integration" (1969), arts. 47, 50, reprinted in *International Legal Materials* 8 (1969): 910; and "Lima Protocol Amending the Cartagena Agreement" (1976), reprinted in *International Legal Materials* 16 (1977): 235.

102. "Cartagena Agreement," supra, note 101, arts. 34(f), 45(b), 49; and see Dale Furnish and W. Atkin, "The Andean Group's Program for Industrial Development of the Metalworking Sector: Integration with Due and Deliberate Spid*," *Lawyer of the Americas* (University of Miami) 7 (1975): 29.

103. ANCOM, "Decision 146, Reestructuración del Programa del la Industria Metalmecánica e Incorporación de Venezuela al Mismo" (June 16–23, 1979), art. 30, reprinted in Junta del Acuerdo de Cartagena, *Ordenamiento Jurídico del Acuerdo de Cartagena* 4 (1982): 1.

104. Ibid., art. 32.

105. Instituto para la Integración de América Latina, *El Proceso de Integración en América Latina en 1982* (Buenos Aires, 1983), p. 111.

106. *El Proceso de Integración en América Latina en 1983* (Buenos Aires: INTAL, 1984), p. 110.

107. Enrique Sabatté, *Selection of Technological Families for Complementary Industrial Cooperation in ASEAN Countries: Project Findings and Recommendations* (Unpublished report for U.N. Industrial Development Organization, February 8, 1979), p. 46.

108. U.S. Department of State, *Background Notes: ASEAN*, November 1983, p. 5.

109. U.S. Department of Commerce, *A Business Guide to the Association of Southeast Asian Nations* (Washington, D.C., 1980), p. 11.

110. Raphael Pura, "Joint Projects in Thailand, Philippines, Get Go-Ahead from ASEAN Ministers," *Asian Wall Street Journal*, January 25, 1982, p. 16.

111. Micheal Haas, ed., *Basic Documents of Asian Regional Organizations*, vol. 8 (Dobbs Ferry, New York: Oceana, 1980), p. 197.

112. Sabatté, *Technological Families*, p. 46.

113. "ASEAN Industrial Complementation," (Manila, June 18, 1981), art. II, reprinted in *International Legal Materials* 22 (1983): 1229.

114. Ibid., art. I.

115. Ibid., art. IV.

116. Ralph H. Folsom, "ASEAN as a Regional Economic Group: A Comparative Lawyer's Perspective," *Malaya Law Review* 25 (1983):213.

117. Ibid.

118. See introductory clauses to the "Basic Agreement on ASEAN Industrial Joint Ventures," supra, note 85.

119. See text accompanying notes 85–87.

120. Supra, note 85, art. II(1)–(4).

121. Ibid., art. III(1).

122. Ibid., art. III(6).

123. "Supplementary Agreement to Amend the Basic Agreement of ASEAN Industrial Joint Ventures" (November 7, 1983), *International Legal Materials* 22 (1983): 1243, ¶ 1.

124. Supra, note 85, art. III(3).

125. Supra, note 123, ¶ 2.

126. Supra, note 85, art. III(8).

127. Ibid., art. III(4)–(5).

128. Ibid., art. III.

129. Ibid., art. III(9).

130. Ibid., art. III(4).

131. Supra, note 2, art. 38.

132. "Agreement Establishing the East Caribbean Common Market (1968, as amended through 1981), art. 12(2), Annex I to the Treaty Establishing the Organization of East Caribbean States" (1981), reprinted in *International Legal Materials* 20 (1981): 1166, 1176.

133. "Protocol Relating to Free Movement of Persons, Residence, and Establishment" (May 29, 1979), Part II, art. 2, and Part III, art. 3, *ECOWAS Official Journal* 1 (June 1979): 3.

134. *Wall Street Journal*, February 4, 1983, p. 18; *Dallas Times Herald*, January 5, 1983, p. A-15.

135. "Nigeria Orders Illegal Aliens Out," *Dallas Times Herald*, May 4, 1985, p. 24A.

136. "Protocol Relating to Free Movement," supra, note 133, art. 2(3).

137. Howard French, "Summit Compromises on Nigerian Expulsions," *International Herald Tribune* (Paris ed.), July 27-28, 1985, p. 9.

138. "Protocol Relating to the Freedom of Movement and Right of Establishment of Nationals of Member States, articles. 3 & 4, Treaty for the Establishment of the Economic Community of Central African States" (October 19, 1983), Annex VII, reprinted in *International Legal Materials* 23 (1984): 989-90.

139. "Agreement for the Avoidance of Double Taxation and the Prevention of Fiscal Evasion with Respect To Taxes on Income and for the Encouragement of International Trade and Investment" (Georgetown, Guyana, June 1, 1973), Inter-American Institute of International Legal Studies, *Instruments of Economic Integration in Latin America and the Caribbean*, vol. 2 (Dobbs Ferry, New York: Oceana, 1975), p. 587; and see supra, note 2, art. 41.

140. "Decision 40, Aprobación del Convenio para Evitar la Doble Tributación entre los Países Miembros y del Convenio Tipo para la Celebración de Acuerdos Sobre Doble Tributación Entre los Países Miembros y Otros Estados Ajenos a la Subregión" (November 8-16, 1971), reprinted in Junta del Acuerdo de Cartagena, *Ordenamiento Jurídico del Acuerdo de Cartagena: Decisiones*, vol. 1 (Lima, 1982), pp. 110ff. For a detailed analysis of these models, see Honey Lynn Goldberg, "Conventions for the Elimination of International Double Taxation: Toward a Developing Country Model," *Law & Policy in International Business* 15 (Washington, D.C.: Georgetown University Law School, 1983), p. 833. See also International Bureau of Fiscal Documentation, *International Fiscal Harmonization, No. 3: Fiscal Harmonization in the Andean Countries* (Amsterdam: IBFD, 1985).

# FINANCIAL AND LEGAL ASPECTS

In addition to trade and investment concerns, true economic integration demands coordination of financial and legal policies. The sophisticated European Economic Community is engaged in the complex process of "harmonizing" laws in many economic and commercial areas. Such harmonization includes, for instance, agreeing upon standards for company law and then directing its members to bring their national legislation into accord.[1] Although such unification of law may be a bit ambitious for many developing countries at present, typically the treaties of these associations envision harmonization as an eventual goal.[2] A supranational tribunal of the EEC, the Court of Justice has also produced a multitude of decisions regulating a vast variety of community concerns.

Likewise, the prosperous EEC has created financial institutions to assist its own weaker members, as well as former colonies in the Third World. Finally, the EEC seems to be evolving gradually into a full monetary union.

One would not expect integration associations in the South to have progressed as far along these lines as the EEC. Nonetheless, an analysis of what has been accomplished does show an embryonic promise.

## FINANCIAL INTEGRATION

### Development Lending Institutions

Establishing a regional financial institution to help direct the flow of capital into poorer areas can be an effective tool for achieving a more equitable distribution of the benefits of integration. A relatively successful example of this approach is the Central American Bank for Economic Integration.[3] This bank makes loans to governments and governmental agencies, as well as to private enterprise. Although the bank may take equity shares in a project, it will try later to sell these shares to the public. In 1980–81, the bank's loans totalled slightly over $200 million.[4] For similar purposes, the Eastern and Southern African Trade and Development Bank has been established by that trade preference association.[5]

The Andean Development Corporation,[6] with an authorized capital of $400 million, has proved to be the most important channel in ANCOM for community investments. Lending in 1983 included a $10 million credit to Bolivia for small and medium-size mining ventures as well as a $15 million emergency loan to Ecuador for restoration of farmlands.[7]

As directed by Article 50 of the ECOWAS treaty,[8] a protocol was concluded in 1976 on the Fund for Cooperation, Compensation and Development to promote development in the less developed areas of the community. By 1985, the fund was earning enough from its investments to cover operating expenses and to finance some substantial project work out of its own resources. Equally important, the organization had succeeded in attracting significant aid sources, including $8 million from the European Investment Bank. The fund's first endeavor in telecommunications to improve links in West Africa has been described as "quite successful."[9]

## Monetary Integration

### Currency Convertibility and Monetary Unions

As a long-range goal, an economic integration unit may also envision a monetary union. A full monetary union would involve issuance of a single currency for all participating countries. Stages along the way to such goal include an agreement establishing free convertibility of members' currencies; next, the extension of convertibility to outside currencies; and then a partial monetary union, where the union would establish the exchange rates between members' currencies. The European Economic Community is moving along this path.

In 1979, the Committee of the Central Bank Governors of the Economic Community of West African States region requested the International Monetary Fund (IMF) to develop recommendations for a program to achieve convertibility within the region as an intial step toward monetary union. Six nations within ECOWAS (Benin, Ivory Coast, Niger, Senegal, Togo and Upper Volta) had already formed the West African Monetary Union and now share a common currency—the CFA (Communauté Financière Africaine) franc. The CFA franc, backed by France, is freely convertible; consequently, these six states seem less than enthusiastic about building a functioning ECOWAS monetary union with other members whose currencies are not convertible.[10] In contrast, the East Caribbean Community already has a common currency and its own central bank.[11]

A 1964 agreement established a Central American Monetary Council composed of the heads of the central banks of the member nations. The group was charged with taking gradual, progressive steps toward the creation of a Central American Monetary Union.[12] Although unable to fulfill this ultimate goal, the Monetary Council has played a useful role in other less ambitious fields.[13]

## Multilateral Clearing Arrangements

*Purpose.*    Regional clearing arrangements are often considered a desirable adjunct for economic integration units. Where such an arrangement exists, a company that has exported a product to a partner nation is paid in its national currency by its own commercial bank upon presentation of the appropriate documents. In turn, the exporter's commercial bank is reimbursed in national currency by the central bank of the exporting nation, which in turn receives a credit from the clearing facility. The account of the importing nation's central bank (comparable to the U.S. Federal Reserve Bank) is debited in the same amount. The latter bank is then reimbursed in currency of the importing nation by the importer's commercial bank, which in turn is paid by the importer.

At the end of an agreed settlement period, the debit and credit positions of each of the participating countries are offset, and the clearing facility computes the net position of each member nation vis-à-vis the others. At that point countries with negative balances must pay the creditor nations the amounts of the balances in hard currency.[14]

Such arrangements can help developing nations because the working amounts of convertible currencies that each nation must hold can be reduced, since convertible currencies are used only to settle the net balances at the end of each settlement period. Thus, a savings in foreign exchange may be effected. With the reciprocal payments facilities available in the LAIA region, it has been estimated that imports into Latin American nations from other members of the association require only 20 to 25 percent as much foreign exchange as imports form outside the region.[15]

On the other hand, the possible savings may be exaggerated. The above argument is valid to the extent that deficits within one country or group of countries offset surpluses of others. Within a particular integration unit, however, the trade may be unbalanced, with certain nations having substantial trade surpluses not just with one or a few of their regional partners, but with nearly all of them. For example, in the eastern and southern African region, roughly two-thirds of the intraregional trade could not be compensated under a clearing facility because of unbalanced trade patterns. Such accounts would continue to be settled in hard currencies.[16]

Under a clearing arrangement, each nation remains free to set its own exchange rate. Likewise, pegging policies are established by individual countries.

One nation may opt to peg its currency to the U.S. dollar, another to the special drawing rights (SDR) of the IMF, while a third chooses to let its currency float freely on the market.[17]

*Facilities Connected with Integration Units.* As early as 1961, a Central American clearing house was established for that region,[18] and soon some 80 percent of the payments resulting from intrazonal trade were channeled through that organization.[19] A few years later, these Central American countries made a clearing house agreement with Mexico, a nonmember of CACM.[20]

In 1965 the central banks of the countries within the Latin American Free Trade Association also created a mechanism for multilateral liquidation of balances and reciprocal extension of credit.[21] In addition to the 11 LAIA nations, the Dominican Republic now participates in this arrangement.[22] The convention establishing the Caribbean Common Market likewise obligated its members to develop "clearing arrangements by their Central Monetary Authorities,"[23] and CARICOM now has facilities for full multilateral clearances and settlements.[24]

The ECOWAS treaty called for creation of "a multilateral system for the settlement of . . . accounts."[25] In 1975 the Articles of Agreement for the Establishment of the West African Clearing House was signed, and the clearing house became operative the next year. Today all members of ECOWAS, except Cape Verde, belong to this clearing house.[26] Finally, both the Eastern and Southern African Trade Preference Association[27] and the Central African States common market[28] have adopted protocols establishing such facilities.

*Mandatory versus Optional Utilization* A question currently being raised is whether use of the clearing facility should be obligatory. Some experts have argued that the Latin American Convention should be revised to make channeling through the facility mandatory, especially since so many member nations are encountering difficulties in their external liquidity. It is pointed out that the percentage of LAIA and Dominican Republic trade channeled through the facility dropped from 79 percent in 1980 to 64 percent in 1982. A number of central banks within the LAIA region are now compelling use of the multilateral channel.[29]

On the other hand, some authorities contend that traders should be permitted to continue using alternative bilateral or private arrangements, such as direct settlement at the commercial bank level. In this way, the multinational facility will be forced to become efficient in order to attract business.[30]

*Unit of Account.* A clearing facility must keep its books in a unit of account acceptable to all members. CARICOM and the Latin American Integration Association both use the U.S. dollar, to which their participants' currencies are also pegged. The Central American Clearing House employs the Central American peso, which is tied to the U.S. dollar ($CA)=US$1. The unit of account of the West African Clearing House is based on the SDR, an approach which seems appropriate for this diverse group of nations whose currencies are pegged to different currencies or baskets of currencies.[31] ANCOM has recently created the "peso andino" to which member's currencies will be tied. The initial issue of these peso andinos amounted to US $80 million.[32]

*Period of Settlement*    Net creditors in a multilateral system do not wish to accept long settlement periods. At the same time, it is in the interest of the debtors to seek to extend the settlement period. Some clearing arrangements are associated with credit facilities to help finance net debtor positions (see below).

The Central American Clearing House and the CARICOM facility settle accounts every six months; LAIA every four months;[33] and the West African Clearing House, one a month.[34] Two Latin American writers have urged that LAIA time periods be increased to six or eight months. Since Mexico and Venezuela, which are both petroleum exporters, enjoy apparently permanent credit balances, they should accept a slightly longer delay in reimbursement.[35] Conversely, some central banks in a creditor position claim that even the one-month period in the West African Clearing House is too long and should be reduced to two weeks. Moreover, even that one-month period often stretches to between four and six months due to administrative delays.[36]

*Credits and Swing Balances*    The Caribbean Community Multilateral Clearing Facility permits a member to defer settlement of up to 50 percent of its net debtor position to the next settlement period.[37] The amount of net credit to be granted by any one participating nation in the Central American Clearing House is limited to $6 million; in theory, a member country could receive as much as $24 million in credits.[38] The West African Clearing House provides that, as general rule, the amount of credit a participating country shall provide will be limited to 20 percent of the value of the imports (CIF) from, and exports (FOB) to, the other participating countries. The amount of credit automatically available to a member is limited to 10 percent of the combined annual value of imports from and exports to other participating nations.[39]

*Results*    For years the clearinghouses in Latin America functioned remarkably effectively, except for a few situations where there was a need to resort to balance financing. Unfortunately, this situation changed drastically in 1979 due to the debt crisis that eroded the countries' reserves. By the end of 1982 one central bank had excluded itself from the clearing arrangement and others did not use the clearinghouse mechanism for channeling results of their bilateral accounts. This produced a crisis in the LAIA system.[40]

The Central American Clearing House is still functioning, although with serious difficulties. Between 1979 and 1983, the balances outstanding rose from nil to $300 million. That figure, nonetheless, represented only 5.4 percent of the total transactions channeled through the system in the previous six years. Of the $5.4 billion that passed through the clearinghouse during that time, 80 percent of the transactions were cleared automatically, and the remaining 20 percent were paid in dollars.[41]

The situation was similar in the CARICOM region. Between 1977 and 1983, 85 percent of the transactions automatically cleared; less than 15 percent had to be settled in dollars. Even so, the facility reached the limit of its allowable credit and had to suspend operations in March 1983. The CARICOM facility has now consolidated its debit balances through medium-term financing up to $100 million.[42]

To deal with these problems, the Latin American institutions took the following steps: limiting transactions to those that could be cleared 100 percent automatically; seeking additional financing; or temporarily ceasing operations. Such measures often compel certain countries to balance their trade flows bilaterally; to do so, they have to cut back on their own imports, and consequently intraregional trade as a whole shrinks. LAIA has gone to considerable lengths to preserve these mechanisms, even to the extent of temporarily excluding certain banks from the system.[43]

*Financing Regional Trade Deficits*

To complement the clearinghouses in the financing of regional trade balances, two specific mechanisms are in effect between the central banks of the countries belonging to the Ibero-American integration units: the Central American Common Market Fund (CACM Fund) and the Santo Domingo Agreement. The CACM Fund was formed to finance debit balances resulting from settlements made by the Central American Clearing House. The fund's resources include $50 million obtained from the Latin American Export Bank (BLADEX) and $100 million contributions paid in local currencies by the member states. Although this fund had made $50 million in loans by 1984, such a sum represented merely a modest contribution when compared to the massive balance of payments disequilibria and lack of liquidity besetting the region.[44]

The Santo Domingo Pact was concluded in 1969 between the members of LAFTA (LAIA) and the Dominican Republic to provide interim financing for multilateral clearing of reciprocal trade balances. This mechanism distributed among the members lines of credit in proportion to their quotas in the IMF.[45] In August 1982 two additional facilities were created: one to help members suffering from lack of liquidity in their overall balance of payments and the other to aid nations incurring liquidity shortfall because of natural disasters. These three lines of credit reached $700 million by the end of 1982. As of April 1983, the first mechanism had been used 23 times, the second 2 times, and the third only once.[46]

In addition to participating in the LAIA clearinghouse arrangements, central banks of the ANCOM countries in 1976 created the Andean Reserve Fund to provide members with balance of payments assistance through loans and guaranties. The fund may secure resources from the capital markets, as well as from governmental bodies. By the end of FY 1983, the fund had assets equivalent to almost $600 million[47] and had loaned $52 million to the Central Bank of Bolivia, $195 million to the Peruvian Central Bank, and $122 million to Ecuador's Central Bank.[48]

Besides short-term loans for temporary liquidity problems, nonrenewable credits for up to four years are available.[49] The amount of credit extended by the fund cannot exceed the lesser of the following limits: (1) 2.5 times the paid in capital by Colombia, Peru, and Venezuela; (2) the total balance of payments deficit of the applicant nation during the preceding 12 months; or (3) a percentage, to be fixed by the fund's directors, of the imports made by the applicant nation during the preceding 12 months.[50]

The immense needs of the Latin American and the Caribbean region for trade financing far exceed the capacity of the above mechanisms. Still a high degree of regional cooperation did help ease the situation temporarily, while more permanent solutions are sought.[51] A number of proposals are now being studied for revision of the Latin American system. Except for the Andean Reserve Fund, none of the above Latin American institutions is a separate legal entity.

The LAIA Advisory Committee for Financial and Monetary Affairs has prepared a draft "LAIA Monetary Accord." In additions to a multilateral clearing facility, this proposal would create as a reserve currency, the UMLA ("Unidad Monetaria Latinoamericana" or Latin American Monetary Unit). The UMLA, which is similar to the Special Drawing Rights of the International Monetary Fund, would be intended to help alleviate liquidity problems. Each member state would be assigned a quota of UMLAs, and they could be used by the clearinghouse in settling accounts. Finally, the agreement would formalize the Santo Domingo arrangement by creating the Fund for Financial Co-operation to carry out the three types of credit operations authorized under the Santo Domingo Agreement, described above.[52]

## JURIDICAL INTEGRATION

### Supranational Tribunals

The Court of Justice of the EEC has played a vital role in enforcing the trade liberalization norms, in promoting vigorous competition, and in determining whether national or community law prevails.[53] Even though the original six members of the EEC were civil law nations and technically did not follow the theory of stare decisis, in fact, the existence of the supranational tribunal in the EEC has been highly effective in achieving a consistent pattern of regulation in that market.

Several of the Third World integration associations did not follow this EEC example. Only after considerable delay did ANCOM finally create a supranational court for its market.[54] An early exception to this indifference to the judicial branch was the Treaty of the East African Community, which did include a Common Market Tribunal for East Africa.[55] In the case of *Okunda v. Republic of Kenya*,[56] it was claimed that a legislative act of the common market was inconsistent with a provision of the Constitution of Kenya. Although the case was decided on other grounds, the court stated:

> it is quite clear that the Constitution of Kenya is paramount and any law, whether it be of Kenya or of the Community . . . which is in conflict with the Constitution is void to the extent of the conflict. . . . The provisions of a treaty entered into by the Government of Kenya do not become part of the municipal law of Kenya save in so far as they are made such by the law of Kenya. If the provisions of any treaty, having been made part of the municipal law of Kenya, are in conflict with the Constitution, then to the extent of such conflict, such provisions are void. . . .[57]

Although this language is dicta, rather than decisional, it illustrates the importance of establishing a decision-making body to resolve such disputes. Suppose, for instance, that in reference to an integration matter the decisions of the highest court within one nation conflict with those of the supreme court in another member country. Or assume a member state passes a statute inconsistent with the legislation of the integration association? What if the officials within a partner nation insist on charging their private importers an incorrect duty rate on a product? If their own administrative or judicial organs are not enforcing the integration units rules, to whom is the business person to look for a remedy?

The newer organizations seem to recognize the importance of this ECOWAS,[58] the Eastern and Southern African PTA,[59] and the Central African States[60] common market all establish a supranational tribunal. The 1980 LAIA, however, does not. Although the CARICOM treaty provides for setting up an ad hoc tribunal for disputes involving a member state, it does not create a permanent court.[61] Organizations like LAIA and CARICOM, which lack a strong judicial intermediary, need to consider establishing a regional tribunal.

The most elaborate judicial structure is found in the new ANCOM Treaty Creating the Court of Justice of the Cartagena Agreement.[62] That document permits member states to sue on claims that legislative "decisions" of the commission and "resolutions" of the junta are contrary to the basic Cartagena Agreement.[63] (This is analogous to charging that a statute is "unconstitutional.") Moreover, individuals and companies may challenge legislation and regulations of ANCOM before the Court.[64] Either the junta[65] or another member state[66] may sue a partner state for noncompliance with its ANCOM obligations. In cases where an issue related to the ANCOM structure arises, national courts may ask the Court of Justice for a ruling on that point.[67] Once rendered, the ruling of the Court of Justice is binding on the national court.[68]

Ratification of the pact on the ANCOM tribunal has not been easy. Although that treaty requires adherence by all ANCOM states and prohibits any reservations, strong political forces in the Venezuelan Congress insisted upon the autonomy of the national judges and the Venezuelan Supreme Court. Thus, the Venezuelan ratification legislation added the requirements that ANCOM decisions (i.e., legislation) that modified Venezuelan law be approved by the national Congress and that interpretation of Andean Pact norms must conform to certain specified articles of the Venezuelan Constitution.[69] Although this political compromise forestalled congressional opposition in that nation, it creates doubt concerning the supremacy of the common market and its institutions.

In April 1983 an Ecuadorean minister indicated that his nation might bring suit against Venezuela for noncompliance with its treaty obligations. Venezuela, pointing out that other members also were in default, indicated it would enter bilateral negotiations to seek a reciprocal trade agreement.[70]

Nonetheless, in August 1983 a Statute for the Court was signed, laying down detailed procedural rules concerning complaints, answers, evidence, hearings, judgments, and enforcements.[71] Hopefully, economic conditions will soon improve and ANCOM members become more amenable to accepting supranational authority.

## The Right of Withdrawal

The Central American Common Market treaty did not grant a right to withdraw, yet Honduras did so for a period of years. Chile withdrew from ANCOM, but its withdrawal was negotiated, and it agreed to continue abiding by certain obligations.[72] For example, Chile did not renounce the group's double taxation treaty.[73]

ECOWAS,[74] CARICOM,[75] LAIA,[76] the Central African states common market,[77] and the Eastern and Southern African trade preference association[78] all give members the right of withdrawal. At the early stages of integration, such withdrawals may not be particularly important. Nevertheless, after a certain degree of integration has been achieved, the cost of withdrawal could become prohibitive. As the European Court of Justice pointed out in Costa v. ENEL:

> As opposed to other international treaties, the Treaty instituting the EEC has created its own [legal system] . . .
> By transferring to the Community legal orders [functions] which hitherto were part of their internal legal orders, the Member States have thus brought about a final limitation of their sovereign rights which cannot be revoked by means of subsequent unilateral measures which are incompatible with the concept of community. . . .[79]

This recognition that some restrictions on sovereignty is essential to the integration process represents a mature reaction that could well be emulated by integration associations in the Third World.

# NOTES

1. Eric Stein, Peter Hay, and Michel Waelbroeck, *European Community and Institutions in Perspective: Text, Cases, and Readings* (Indianapolis: Bobbs-Merrill, 1976), pp. 591ff.

2. See, for example, "Treaty Establishing the Caribbean Community (1973), Annex Establishing the Caribbean Common Market," art. 42, reprinted in *International Legal Materials* 12 (Washington, D.C.: American Society of International Law, 1973): 1033, 1044; and "Treaty of the Economic Community of West African States" (Lagos, 1975), art. 30, reprinted in *International Legal Materials* 14 (1975): 1200.

3. "Agreement Establishing the Central American Bank for Economic Integration" (December 13, 1960), reprinted in Inter-American Institute of International Legal Studies, *Instruments Relating to the Economic Integration of Latin America,* vol. 2 (Dobbs Ferry, New York: Oceana, 1975), p. 505.

4. Instituto para la Integración de América Latina, *El Proceso de Integración en América Latina en 1982* (Buenos Aires, 1983), p. 181.

5. "Treaty for the Establishment of the Preferential Trade Area for Eastern and Southern African States" (December 21, 1981), arts. 32–35, reprinted in *International Legal Materials* 21 (1982): 479.

6. "Agreement Establishing the Andean Development Corporation" (1968), reprinted in *International Legal Materials* 8 (1969): 940.

7. Instituto para la Integración de América Latina en 1983, *El Proceso de Integración en América Latina en 1983* (Buenos Aires, INTAL, 1984), p. 140.

8. "Treaty of the Economic Community of West African States" (Lagos, 1975), reprinted in *International Legal Materials* 14 (1975): 1200; Olusegun Yerokun, "The Economic Community of West Africa: Its Evolution and Scope," *Indian Law Journal* 20 (1980): 284.

9. Ad'Obe Obe, "West Africa Struggles to Overcome Division," *South* (London), August 1982, p. 65; and Richard Synge, "Regional Fund Is Polishing Financial Image," *International Herald Tribune* (Paris ed.), July 28–29, 1985, p. 11.

10. Howard French, "Organizational Overlap Slows Regional Unity," *International Herald Tribune* (Paris ed.), July 27–28, 1985, p. 12; and John B. McLenaghan, Saleh Nsouli, and Klaus-Walter Riechel, *Currency Convertibility in the Economic Community of West African States,* vol. 1 (International Monetary Fund, 1982).

11. Inter-American Development Bank, *Economic and Social Progress in Latin America: Economic Integration* (Washington, D.C.: 1984), p. 47.

12. "Agreement for the Establishment of the Central American Monetary Union" (San Salvador, February 25, 1964), arts. I, V, reprinted in Inter-American Institute of International Legal Studies, *Instruments of Economic Integration in Latin America and in the Caribbean,* vol. 2 (Dobbs Ferry, New York: Oceana, 1975), p. 523.

13. Dada Hirezi, "Evaluación de la Integración Centroamericana," *Integración Latinoamericana* (Buenos Aires: INTAL, December 1983), no. 86, pp. 23, 31.

14. Shailendra Anjaria, Sena Eken, and John F. Laker, *Payments Arrangements and the Expansion of Trade in Eastern and Southern Africa* (International Monetary Fund, 1982) p. 24.

15. "Editorial, La Integración Regional Como Respuesta Latinoamericana a la Crisis Económica," *Integración Latinoamericana* (Buenos Aires: INTAL, March 1984), no. 88, p. 32.

16. Anjaria, Eken, and Laker, *Payment Arrangements,* p. 21.

17. Ibid., p. 24.

18. "Agreement Establishing the Central American Clearing House" (Tegucigalpa, July 28, 1961), reprinted in Inter-American Institute of International Legal Studies, *Instruments of Economic Integration in Latin America and in the Caribbean,* vol. 2 (Dobbs Ferry, New York: Oceana, 1975), p. 151.

19. Ibid., p. 521.

20. "Agreement on Clearance and Reciprocal Credits Between the Central Banks Members of the Central American Clearance House and the Bank of Mexico" (Mexico City, August 27, 1963), ibid, p. 124.

21. "Agreement Between the Central Banks of the Member Countries of LAFTA" (September 1965), reprinted in Inter-American Institute of International Legal Studies, *Instruments of Economic Integration in Latin America and in the Caribbean*, vol. 1 (Dobbs Ferry, Oceana, 1975) p. 121; and "Regulations for the System of Multilateral Clearance of Balances Between the Central Banks of the Countries of LAFTA" ibid, p. 124.

22. José Aragão, "ALADI: Perspectivas a Partir de la Experiencia de la ALALC y de la Situación Actual de la Economía Internacional," *Integración Latinoamericana* (Buenos Aires: INTAL, December 1983), no. 86, p. 11; and Echegaray Simonet, "El Proceso de Revisión de los Mecanismos Financieros de la ALADI," *Integración Latinoamericana* (Buenos Aires: INTAL, September 1983), no. 83, p. 19.

23. Supra, note 2, art. 43(3)(b).

24. Anjaria, Eken, and Laker, *Payment Arrangements*, p. 48.

25. "Treaty of the Economic Community of West African States" (Lagos, 1975), art. 37, ¶ 1, reprinted in *International Legal Materials* 14 (1975): 1200.

26. McLanaghan, Nsouli, and Riechel, *Currency Convertibility*, pp. 23–24.

27. "Protocol on Clearing and Payments Arrangements, Annex VI, Treaty for the Establishment of the Preferential Trade Area for Eastern and Southern African States" (December 21, 1981), reprinted in *International Legal Materials* 21 (1982): 528. For a description of the clearing arrangements available in the Far East under the Asian Clearing Union, see Anjaria, Eken, and Lakev, *Payments Arrangements*, p. 49.

28. "Protocol on the Clearing House for the Economic Community, Treaty for the Establishment of the Economic Community of Central African States" (October 19, 1983), Annex VIII, reprinted in *International Legal Materials* 23 (1984): 990.

29. Simonet, "Proceso de Revisión," p. 24; and Aragão, "ALADI: Perspectivas," p. 17.

30. Anjaria, Eken, and Laker, *Payments Arrangements*, p. 23.

31. Ibid., pp. 24, 48–49.

32. "Entra en Vigencia el Peso Andino," *Integración Latinoamericana* (Buenos Aires: INTAL, January–February 1985), no. 98, pp. 56–57.

33. Anjaria, Eken, and Laker, *Payments Arrangements*, p. 48.

34. "Articles of Agreement of the West African Clearing House," (Lagos, March 14, 1975), art. VIII, §9, as cited in McLenaghan, Nsouli, and Riechel, *Currency Convertibility*, p. 24.

35. Simonet, "Proceso de Revisión," p. 24; and Aragão, "ALADI: Perspectivas," p.17.

36. McLenaghan, Nsouli, and Riechel, *Currency Convertibility*, pp. 227–28.

37. Anjaria, Eken, and Lakev, *Payments Arrangements*, p. 23.

38. Ibid., p. 48.

39. Ibid., p. 49.

40. Supra, note 11, p. 59.

41. Ibid.

42. Ibid., pp. 59–60.

43. Ibid., p. 59.

44. Ibid., p. 58.

45. "Multilateral Accord on Reciprocal Assistance to Confront Temporary Liquidity Deficits" (September 1969), as cited in Simonet, "Proceso de Revisión," p. 19; and Aragão, "ALADI: Perspectivas," p. 11.

46. Aragão, "ALADI: Perspectivas," p. 12.

47. Supra, note 7, p. 143. "Treaty for the Creation of the Andean Reserve Fund" (November 12, 1976), reprinted in *International Legal Materials* 18 (1979): 1191.

48. José Maria Aragão, "Los Sistemas de Pagos Latinoamericanos," *Integración Latinoamerica* (Buenos Aires: INTAL, September 1984), no. 94, pp. 9–10.

49. Supra, note 7, p. 142.

50. Aragão, "Sistemas de Pagos," p. 9.

51. Supra, note 11, p. 60.

52. Carlos V. Kesman and Aldo A. Dadone, "Una Reformulación de la Propuesta de 'Convenio Monetario de ALADI' " *Integración Latinoamericana* (Buenos Aires: INTAL, March 1985), no. 99, p. 39; and see Alfredo Echegaray, "El Sistema Monetario Internacional y los Fondos Comunes Latinoamericanos," *Integración Latinoamericana* (Buenos Aires: INTAL, March 1985), no. 96, p. 14.

53. See, for example, "Costa v. Ente Nazionale Energia electtrica impresa gia della Edison Volta, 10 Recueil 1141" (July 15, 1964), [1961–66 Transfer Binder] *Common Market Reporter.* (CCH), ¶ 8023 (1965).

54. ANCOM, "Treaty Creating the Court of Justice of the Cartegena Agreement" (May 28, 1979), *International Legal Materials* 18 (1979): 1203.

55. "Treaty for East African Co-operation," (1967), arts. 80, 81, reprinted in *International Legal Materials* 6 (1967): 932.

56. The decision of the High Court of Kenya (1969) is printed in *East African Law Report* (1970): 453.

57. The decision of the community court is *East African Commission v. Republic of Kenya*; printed in *East African Law Reports* (1970): 457.

58. "Treaty of the Economic Community of West African States" (Lagos, 1975), art. 11, reprinted in *International Legal Materials* 14 (1975): 1200.

59. "Treaty for the Establishment of the Preferential Trade Area for Eastern and Southern African States" (December 21, 1981), art. 10, reprinted in *International Legal Materials* 21 (1982): 479.

60. "Treaty for the Establishment of the Economic Community of Central African States" (October 19, 1983), arts. 16–22, reprinted in *International Legal Materials* 23 (1984): 947.

61. Supra, note 2, arts. 11, 12; and Nicholas Liverpool, "La Ley Como Instrumento Armonizador en el Proceso de Integración en el Caribe," *Integración Latinoamericana* (Buenos Aires: INTAL, July 1984), no. 92, p. 45.

62. Supra, note 54 and see "Decision 184, Estatuto del Tribunal de Justicia del Acuerdo de Cartagena" (1983), reprinted in *Integración Latinoamericana* (Buenos Aires: INTAL, November 1983), no. 85, pp. 76ff.

63. "Decision 184," supra, note 62, arts. 17, 18.

64. Ibid., art. 19.

65. Ibid., art. 23.

66. Ibid., art. 24.

67. Ibid., art. 29.

68. Ibid., art. 31.

69. Ven. Law of May 19, 1983, arts. 2 and 3, *Gaceta Oficial*, no. 3216 Extraordinario, July 7, 1983.

70. John Pate, "Introductory Note," *International Legal Materials* 23 (1984): 422.

71. "Decision 184, Statute of the Court of Justice of the Cartagena Agreement," reprinted in ibid, p. 425.

72. Under Decision 102 of October 30, 1976, all Chile's rights and obligations under ANCOM ceased except for those emanating from certain specified decisions. A mixed commission of Chile and the ANCOM members was created to administer the decisions to which Chile remained bound. "Recent Actions Regarding Treaties to Which the United States Is Not a Party," *International Legal Materials* 15 (1976): 1446.

73. Honey Lynn Goldgerg, "Conventions for the Elimination of International Double Taxation: Toward a Developing Country Model," *Law & Policy in International Business* 15 (Washington, D.C.: Georgetown University Law School, 1983), p. 857, no. 84. "Decisión 40, Aprobación del Convenio para Evitar la Doble Tributación entre los Países Miembros y del

Convenio Tipo para la Celebración de Acuerdos Sobre Doble Tributación Entre los Países Miembros y Otros Estados Ajenos a la Subregión" (November 8–16, 1971), reprinted in Junta del Aceurdo de Cartagena, *Ordenamiento Júridico del Acuerdo de Cartagena*, vol. 1 (Lima, 1982), pp. 110ff.

74. Supra, note 58, art. 64.

75. Supra, note 2, art. 27.

76. "Treaty Establishing the Latin American Integration Association" (1980), art. 63, reprinted in *International Legal Materials* 20 (1981): 672.

77. Supra, note 60, art. 91.

78. Supra, note 59, art. 48.

79. Supra, note 53.

# 5

# HYPOTHETICAL TRANSACTIONS

To help the reader understand how the mechanisms described above work, a group of hypothetical cases will now be given. The suggested solutions follow at the end of this chapter.

A word of caution is necessary. Exercises such as these can be helpful as a background, but, in practice, anyone planning a commercial endeavor in these countries must do an additional on-site investigation to update information.

Particular care must be taken where a country belongs to more than one integration unit—such as ANCOM/LAIA, ECCM/CARICOM, or ECOWAS and the Mano Union. Before making any decisions, one must determine whether a benefit available from an association may have been eroded by a prior concession made in the other organization.

The consequences of overlooking the legal impact of the second integration unit can be grave. Under the metalworking sectorial program, ANCOM had set the common external tariff at 55 percent on a particular product and exclusively assigned it to Bolivia. Relying on that arrangement, a U.S. company had invested in Bolivia to manufacture that item only to find itself undersold in other ANCOM nations by competing products from Argentina and Brazil. Because of prior LAFTA concessions made by some ANCOM states, these goods could enter those nations from Argentina and Brazil without paying the 55 percent ANCOM common external tariff rate. The LAFTA concessions were legally binding exceptions to the ANCOM common external tariff. The Bolivian venture finally had to shut down.

The problem of meshing rules from different integration units may be compounded in the case of LAIA. Not only will the planner have to check the various ANCOM laws and the LAIA regional preferences, but also one will need to ascertain whether there are any relevant agreements of partial scope or accords providing special benefits to the less developed members.

In approaching these problems, the reader should first check the country list at the beginning of this book to determine whether the nations concerned are members of an integration unit. If the answer is yes, then one should study the relevant appendixes at the end of this book to determine what provisions would affect the proposed transaction.

## PROBLEMS

### No. 1

Alpha Company, a 30-year old Colombian corporation, is 75 percent owned by Beta, Inc., a Texas corporation owned in turn by U.S. citizens. The remaining 25 percent of Alpha's shares is owned by Colombian citizens. Alpha's factory in Colombia is worth $1 million book value. It manufactures agricultural tools. The managers of Beta are considering several alternatives.

a. The first possibility is that they will do nothing and just leave the situation as it is. Alpha sells its products only within Colombia.

b. The second alternative is for Beta to sell its shares in Alpha to Salvage, Inc., a New York corporation owned by U.S. citizens. Salvage has offered $700,000 for the Alpha shares owned by Beta.

c. The third alternative is to expand Alpha's operation and produce a new line of agricultural tools. The proposed expansion would call for $2.7 million in additional investment funds. The total value of the expanded plant would be $3.7 million, consisting of the following: $1 million representing Alpha's existing assets; $2 million in a new equity investment from the Zed company, an Ohio corporation owned by U.S. citizens. The remaining $700,000 would come from Mr. Omega, a Venezuelan citizen.

Discuss any problems involved with these alternatives.

### No. 2

Delta, a West German company, wishes to establish a Bolivian subsidiary to produce handmade shawls, ponchos, and stoles. Delta expects to sell these goods in the industrialized world where such handmade products are so expensive. Delta plans to own 100 percent of the Bolivian company. Are there any obstacles to this proposal?

### No. 3

Cue, a Georgia firm, would like to buy Zita, a company wholly owned by Peruvian nationals. Any problems?

### No. 4

Epsilon, a U.S. company, is considering a possible fishing investment in

Peru. Epsilon would own one-third of the project. Soki, a Japanese firm, would take another third. The remaining third of the shares would be held by Pescados, S.A., a Peruvian corporation wholly owned by the Peruvian government. Will Epsilon and Soki have to divest?

## No. 5

The Mu corporation is a Venezuelan company that is 60 percent owned by Se, a Californian company, and 40 percent by Olé, a Venezuelan company. Mu has signed an agreement to transform itself into a national enterprise at the end of the prescribed period. Se is thinking about transferring its patented knowledge on how to produce widget A to Mu. In lieu of a licensing agreement, Se is considering having Mu increase its capital by another million dollars. Olé would invest an additional $400,000 in Venezuelan currency in Mu and receive shares of stock in exchange. Se would grant Mu the right to use this patented knowledge and take back 60 percent of the new stock.

If this stock arrangement cannot be worked out, Se would alternatively be willing to license the technology in exchange for royalties. Se's standard licensing contract contains the following provisions:

(a) The licensee (Mu) will purchase the motors for widget A only from the licensor (Se).
(b) The licensee will grant back to the licensor any inventions or improvements discovered through the use of the licensed technology.
(c) The licensor reserves the right to fix the resale price of products manufactured with the technology.
(d) The licensor will not export the products made with the licensed technology to Latin American countries outside ANCOM nor to Europe. (Se has previously given an exclusive license to a French company to manufacture this widget for the European market.)
(e) Any disputes arising under this contract will be submitted to a court in California.

That contract would also authorize the licensee to use Se's trademark on the goods produced under the license in exchange for 1 percent of the net sales. Such royalty payments must be made to Se, even if the licensee decides not to use the Se trademark.

## No. 6

Assume that under ANCOM Decision 146 production of electric circuit breakers is exclusively assigned to Ecuador under the metalworking sectorial program. Assume further that the Annex VI (common external tariff rate) is set at 60 percent and Annex V (duties applicable between countries with a shared assignment) is 29 percent.

Prior to decisions 57 and 146, the member countries had the following duty rates on circuit breakers: Bolivia, 95 percent; Colombia, 85 percent; Peru, 25 percent; Ecuador, 110 percent; and Venezuela, 10 percent.

　　a. What duty will circuit breakers from Bolivia going into Colombia, Peru, or Venezuela pay?

　　b. Assume that production had already started in Ecuador at date of Decision 146. What duty would this item be charged if made in Colombia and sent to Peru, or Venezuela? For how long?

　　c. Assume that production had not started in Ecuador as of the date of Decision 146. What duty would be charged on this item if made in Venezuela and sent to Peru or Colombia? For how long?

　　d. Assume that production of this item had begun in Ecuador as of the date of Decision 146. What duty will this item be charged on entering Ecuador if it were made in Bolivia, Colombia, Peru, or Venezuela? For how long?

　　e. If production has not started in Ecuador as of the date of Decision 146, what duty may Ecuador charge upon such an item coming from any of the other four member countries? For how long?

　　f. What is the duty on a circuit breaker coming into Venezuela from South Korea?

　　g. What is the duty for circuit breakers made in Ecuador and sent to Colombia, Peru, or Venezuela?

## No. 7

Use the same duty structure as given in question number six, but assume that production of circuit breakers has been assigned to both Ecuador and Bolivia.

　　a. What will the duty on this product be if it is made in Ecuador or Bolivia and sent to Colombia, Peru, or Venezuela?

　　b. What will the duty be if it is made in Colombia and sent to Peru or Venezuela? For how long?

　　c. What will the duty be if it is made in Ecuador and sent to Bolivia? For how long?

## No. 8

Use the same duty structure as given in question number six, but assume that production of circuit breakers has been assigned to Ecuador and Venezuela.

　　a. What will the duty be if it is made in either Ecuador or Venezuela and sent to Peru, Colombia, or Bolivia?

　　b. What will the duty be if it is made in Bolivia and sent to Colombia or Peru?

c. What will the duty be if it is made in Ecuador and sent to Venezuela?

d. What will the duty be if it is made in Venezuela and sent into Ecuador? For how long?

## No. 9

Use the same duty structure as given in question number six, but assume that production of circuit breakers has been assigned to Venezuela and Peru.

a. What will the duty be if it is made in Venezuela and sent into Peru and if production had already begun as of the date of Decision 146?

b. What will the duty be if it is made in Peru and sent into Venezuela and if production had not begun as of the date of Decision 146?

## No. 10

Assume that Paraguay has a duty on electronic typewriters of 105 percent. Chile's duty on electronic typewriters is 85 percent. In a LAIA agreement of partial scope among Argentina, Chile, and Paraguay, Argentina agrees to lower its regular 66 percent duty on electronic typewriter ribbons to 40 percent for ribbons from Paraguay. In the same accord Argentina agrees also to reduce its duty on print heads from 77 percent to 55 percent for print heads from Chile. In exchange, Paraguay agrees to reduce its duty on Argentine electronic typewriters to 49 percent, and Chile agrees to lower its duty on Argentine electronic typewriters to 15 percent. This partial scope agreement contains a most-favored nation clause applicable only to members of this particular agreement. (Assume all these goods are excluded from the regional tariff preferences.)

What duty rate will electronic typewriters entering Paraguay pay if from:

a. Chile?

b. Argentina?

c. Brazil?

d. Japan?

What duty will electronic typewriter ribbons pay on entering Argentina from:

e. Brazil?

f. United States?

g. Paraguay?

h. Chile?

i. Venezuela?

What duty will print heads pay on entering Argentina from:

j. Mexico?

k. Taiwan?

l. Chile?

m. Paraguay?

## No. 11

Assume that the duties on widget Z are as follows: Argentina, 85 percent; Brazil, 65 percent; Mexico, 45 percent; ANCOM, 40 percent; and Chile, 55 percent. The LAIA countries all agree that widget Z will be placed on a list of products that, if originating in the relatively less economically developed members, will be duty free in the remaining countries. (Assume that widget Z was excluded from the regional tariff preference agreement.)

What duty will be imposed on a widget Z entering Mexico from:

a. Venezuela?
b. Ecuador?
c. Brazil?
d. Taiwan?
e. Bolivia?

What duty is applicable is widget Z enters Brazil from:

f. Argentina?
g. Mexico?
h. Ecuador?
i. Paraguay?

## No. 12.

Assume that Mexico concludes an agreement of partial scope with the Central American Common Market under which Mexico agrees to reduce its 35 percent duty on tires to 25 percent for those from the CACM. In return, the CACM agrees to lower its 38 percent tariff on automobiles to 28 percent for Mexican cars. (Assume both items were excluded from the LAIA regional tariff preferences.)

What duty will be paid on cars entering Guatemala from:

a. Brazil?
b. United States?
c. Ecuador?
d. Mexico?

What duty will be levied on tires entering Mexico from:

e. Honduras?
f. Panama?
g. Argentina?
h. W. Germany?
i. Bolivia?
j. Paraguay?

## No. 13

Assume that Brazil enters an agreement of partial scope with ASEAN under which ASEAN nations agree to give Brazilian oil well drilling equipment a 30 percent preferential rate in exchange for Brazil's granting a 10 percent preferential rate on petroleum products from ASEAN nations. Assume that Indonesia charges a 100 percent duty rate on imported oil well drilling bits. Assume that Brazil's regular duty on imported kerosene is 50 percent. (Assume both items were excluded from the LAIA regional tariff preferences.)

What duty will be charged on drill bits entering Indonesia from:

a. Brazil?
b. Mexico?
c. Japan?
d. Bolivia?

What duty rates will be charged on kerosene imported into Brazil from:

e. Indonesia?
f. Mexico?
g. Ecuador?
h. Venezuela?
i. United States?

## No. 14

Assume that widget X was not excluded from the products included within the LAIA regional preference accord and that these countries normally impose the following duties rates on widget Xs: Colombia, 50 percent; Mexico, 100 percent; Paraguay, 200 percent.

What duty will widget X pay on entering Mexico from:

a. United States?
b. Argentina?
c. Bolivia?
d. Peru?

What duty rate will widget X pay on entering Colombia from:

e. Thailand?
f. Paraguay?
g. Brazil?
h. Chile?

What duty rate will widget X pay on entering Paraguay from:

i. Italy?
j. Mexico?
k. Venezuela?
l. Bolivia?

## No. 15

Omega, a French company, manufactures widget Xs in France. Omega is thinking about an investment in Latin America to manufacture widget Xs. Omega is considering Panama, Brazil, or Colombia as a site.

During renegotiation of the "historic patrimony" in LAIA, Colombia agreed to lower duties on Brazilian widget Xs from 75 percent to 25 percent. ANCOM has set the minimum common external tariff on widget Xs at 40 percent and the final common external tariff at 60 percent. Assume that widget X falls under the residual automatic tariff cutting provisions of the ANCOM treaties. The Central American Common Market equalized the duty on widget Xs at 44 percent. (Assume this item was excluded from the LAIA regional tariff preferences.)

If Omega invests in Panama, what will the duty on widget Xs be on entering:

    a.   Colombia?
    b.   Costa Rica?
    c.   Bolivia?

What duty rate will be applicable to the widget X on entering Colombia if Omega places its investment in:

    d.   Brazil?
    e.   Mexico?
    f.   Peru?
    g.   Bolivia?

## No. 16

John Smith, president of Smith, Ltd., a United Kingdom company, has been favorably impressed by a kind of motorized rickshaw used to provide very cheap public transportation in South Asia. He believes there is a need for a similar vehicle in the big cities of Africa. Thus, to manufacture such a vehicle he is considering an investment in Brazzaville, Congo; Accra, Ghana; or Lusaka, Zambia.

The motors for this venture would be imported from Raj, Ltd., an Indian company. The gears, pedals, and wheels would be supplied by British firms. The wooden chassis and padded seats would be made locally. Likewise, the assembling and painting would be done locally. Imported components will account for about 65 percent of the value of the finished vehicle.

Smith believes the domestic market of any of the three nations under consideration is too small to support this venture; to be profitable, he would need access to the markets in a number of additional African countries. Assume that Kenya, a market of possible interest, imposes a duty of 70 percent on bicycles, motor bikes, rickshaws, and similar products.

Smith estimates the total initial investment needed for the project is $450,000. To carry out the venture, Smith would establish a local company, the Ricko Company. The Smith Company would buy $200,000 of Ricko's shares. The remaining $250,000 could be sold to local African investors. Alternatively, Raj, Ltd. is willing to by $50,000 which would leave $200,000 in shares to be sold to local investors. Are there any problems with this proposal?

**No. 17**

Isco, a Florida company, is considering manufacturing refrigerators in Costa Rica. Assume that Guatemala has a refrigerator factory but Costa Rica does not. About 45 percent of the value of the final product would represent components imported from Isco's factory in Florida. What would be the maximum tax incentives available to Isco?

**No. 18**

Ito, a Japanese company, is contemplating an investment in Indonesia to produce widget Y. This widget has recently been approved for the AIJV lists. Since Malaysia already has a factory producing widget Y, that country decided not to participate in this particular AIJV program. Thailand, Indonesia, the Philippines, and Singapore are participants in this AIJV program.

Ito proposes to operate the plant through an Indonesian subsidiary, the PB Company. Ito would own 40 percent of PB's stock; Bang, an Indonesian firm, would own 30 percent; and Chula, a Thai company, would own the remaining 30 percent. The duty rates on widget Y are: Indonesia, 80 percent; Thailand, 30 percent; Philippines, 34 percent; Singapore, 50 percent; and Malaysia, 100 percent.

Can Ito's proposal qualify for AIJV treatment? What duties would be imposed on widget Y from the PB Company's plant in Indonesia if sent to:
    a.   Thailand?
    b.   Philippines?
    c.   Malaysia?
    d.   Singapore?
What duty will widget Ys from Malaysia pay on entering:
    e.   Indonesia?
    f.   Singapore?
    g.   Philippines?
    h.   Thailand?
After the expiration of four years, widget Ys entering the Philippines will pay what duty rate if from:
    i.   Indonesia?
    j.   Taiwan?
    k.   Singapore?
    l.   Malaysia?

**No. 19**

Assume the same facts as in question 18 and that the PB investment is actually made. By the end of the stipulated six-month period, no other investment in widget Y has been made in the ASEAN region (except the preexisting factory in Malaysia). Now two years later, Blue, a California company, wishes to begin producing widget Ys in the Philippines. Blue plans to sell only in the Philippine market. Meanwhile, Zud, a German firm, wants to set up a factory in Singapore to produce widget Y. Zud would sell almost all its widget Y production to Europe.

Are there any obstacles to Zud and Blue's proposed investments?

## SUGGESTED SOLUTIONS

### No. 1

a. Although Alpha is a foreign enterprise under Article 1 of Decision 24, the Andean Foreign Investment Code, Alpha will not have to divest because it was a preexisting enterprise. See Article 28 (Appendix H-4). If the company does not divest, however, it loses the right to send its goods to other ANCOM nations at the lower internal duty rates. Deprived of the larger market, Alpha will not enjoy the advantage of economies of scale and may become uncompetitive with other companies manufacturing for the larger market.

b. Beta may not sell the shares of Alpha to Salvage, another foreign enterprise, without permission of the Colombian government. Article 7.

c. Zed would also be a foreign enterprise under Article 1 of the code. This would be considered a new investment since Article 1 includes under "new" the expansion of an existing enterprise. As a new investment, Alpha would have to conclude a transformation agreement to reduce the percentage of foreign ownership to not more than 49 percent within 15 years. Article 30.

Moreover, since Colombia is one of the relatively more advanced nations, at least 15 percent of the shares must be locally owned when production begins. Article 30. The existing Colombian investment in Alpha ($250,000) will not amount to 15 percent of the total $3.7 million investment. But under Article 1, if Mr. Omega can obtain permission of the Venezuelan government, his investment may count toward the initial 15 percent as a subregional investor.

### No. 2

Under the Andean Foreign Investment Code, Delta might have to enter an agreement to transform itself into a mixed company. Since Bolivia is the site, the time period would be 20 years, and it would not be necessary to take in a local partner immediately. See Article 30 (appendix H-4).

If Delta will export 80 percent of its production outside the ANCOM region, it will not have to comply with the divestment provisions, but it will lose the advantage of selling to other ANCOM members at the reduced duty rates. See Article 34.

## No. 3

The right to buy into a national company is limited under Article 3 of the Andean Foreign Investment Code to cases where such is necessary to prevent imminent bankruptcy (Appendix H-4). Even then, the shares must first be offered to subregional investors. Moreover, if the foreign investment is approved, the foreign company has to satisy the divestment provisions reducing its participation to not more than 49 percent within 15 years.

## No. 4

Under Article 36 of the Andean Foreign Investment Code, they will not have to divest if the state has a determining capacity, even if the state's participation is less than 51 percent (Appendix H-4).

## No. 5

Se may not take back stock in Mu because Article 21, ¶ 1 of the Andean Foreign Investment Code prohibits capitalization of technology; that is, technology contributions may not be exchanged for shares of stock in the company (Appendix H-4). Article 21, ¶ 2 also forbids payment of royalties by a "foreign" enterprise to its parent or affiliated company. Although Mu is technically a "foreign" enterprise, some ANCOM nations will treat these companies as "mixed" enterprises if they have concluded a divestment agreement. If this is the case, Mu could pay royalties to Se.

The proposed licensing contract will contravene requirements of Article 20 of the code. Article 20(a) would forbid the tied purchase clause a, unless Se could show it was an exceptional case and the purchase price of the motors "corresponds to current levels in the international market."

Clause b, a grant back clause, is prohibited by Article 20(f), but sometimes such clauses are allowed if they are reciprocal so that both parties are bound to exchange information about improvements.

Clause c, the resale price provision, runs counter to Article 20(b) of the code.

Clause d, the export restrictions, may contravene the penultimate paragraph in Article 20 of the code. The prohibitions against sales to other Latin American nations will probably not be permitted. On the other hand, if a licensor has already given an exclusive license elsewhere, this may qualify as an "exceptional case." Thus, the prior legal obligation of Se to its French licensee may be recognized and the prohibitions of exports from Mu to Europe accepted.

Clause e will not be permitted because it violates Article 51.

The requirement that Mu pay a royalty for the trademark even if the mark is not used contravenes Article 25(d) of the code and will not be permitted.

## No. 6

Answers to the next four problems requires an analysis of ANCOM Decision 146 (Appendix H-8).

- a. 60 percent.
- b. 60 percent, zero after 1989, art. 11, ¶1.
- c. 60 percent, zero after 1992, art. 11, ¶2.
- d. 60 percent, zero after 1989, art. 12, ¶1.
- e. 60 percent, zero after 1992, art. 12, ¶2.
- f. 60 percent, the ANCOM common external tariff rate, art. 23, which applies to any non-ANCOM country.
- g. Zero, article 9.

## No. 7

- a. Zero, art. 9.
- b. 60 percent, zero after 1989 or 1992 depending upon when production started, art. 11.
- c. 29 percent, art. 17(a), gradually to be reduced to zero, art. 17(b).

## No. 8

- a. Zero, art. 9.
- b. 60 percent, zero after 1989 or 1992 depending upon when production started, art. 11.
- c. Zero, art. 16(a).
- d. 60 percent, gradually to be reduced to zero, art. 16(b) and (c).

## No. 9

- a. Zero, art. 14(a).
- b. 29 percent, to be gradually reduced to zero, art. 14(b).

## No. 10

Answers to the next four problems can be found in the LAIA convention (Appendix I-1).

- a. 49 percent, article 7ff., and the most-favored nation clause in the partial scope agreement.
- b. 49 percent, same reasons.
- c. 105 percent, Brazil is not a member of the partial scope agreement and there is no general most-favored nation clause in the LAIA accord.

    d.   105 percent, outside LAIA.
    e.   66 percent, not a member of the partial scope accord.
    f.   66 percent, outside LAIA.
    g.   40 percent, art. 7, and the terms of the partial scope agreement.
    h.   40 percent, the internal most-favored nation clause of the partial scope agreement means that Chile is also entitled to the lower rate conceded to Paraguay by Argentina.
    i.   66 percent, not a member of the partial scope agreement.
    j.   77 percent, not a member of the partial scope agreement.
    k.   77 percent, outside LAIA.
    l.   55 percent, partial scope agreement.
    m.   55 percent, most-favored nation clause of the partial scope agreement.

## No. 11

    a.   45 percent.
    b.   Zero, art. 18.
    c.   45 percent.
    d.   45 percent, not a LAIA member.
    e.   Zero, art. 18.
    f.   65 percent.
    g.   65 percent.
    h.   Zero, art. 18.
    i.   Zero, art. 18.

## No. 12

    a.   38 percent, not a member of the partial scope agreement.
    b.   38 percent, not a member of LAIA.
    c.   38 percent, the CACM extended no concession to Ecuador.
    d.   28 percent, under the agreement.
    e.   25 percent, under the agreement.
    f.   35 percent, not a member of CACM.
    g.   35 percent, not a member of the partial scope agreement.
    h.   35 percent, not a member of either group.
    i.   25 percent, art. 25(a), LAIA treaty.
    j.   25 percent, art. 25(a), LAIA treaty.

## No. 13

    a.   70 percent, ASEAN preference under accord, calculated as follows:

        100% Indonesian duty
    −   30% ASEAN preferential rate for Brazil
         70% Duty rate

b. 100 percent, not a member of the partial scope accord.
c. 100 percent, not a member of either group.
d. 100 percent, ASEAN made no concession to Bolivia.
e. 45 percent, Brazilian preferential rate under the accord, calculated as follows:

    50% Brazil's normal duty rate
    × 10% Brazil's preferential rate for ASEAN
    5% Amount of preference

    50% Brazil's normal duty rate
    − 5% Amount of preference
    45% Brazil's rate for this product from ASEAN

f. 50 percent, not a member of the accord.
g. 45 percent, entitled to concession made by Brazil, art. 27(a), LAIA Convention.
h. 50 percent, not a member of the partial scope accord.
i. 50 percent, not a member of either group.

## No. 14

Answers to these questions are in Article 5 of the LAIA Regional Preference Agreement (Appendix I-2).

a. 100 percent, not a LAIA member.
b. 95 percent, two "other" nations entitled to 5 percent preference.
c. 90 percent, good from least developed into "other nation" category entitled to 10 percent preference.
d. 93 percent, good from intermediate nation into "other" nation, entitled to 7 preference.
e. 50 percent.
f. 46.5 percent, calculated as follows:

    50% Colombia's normal duty rate
    × 7% LAIA regional preference for goods from least developed nation into intermediate nation
    3.5% Amount of preference

    50% Colombia's normal duty rate
    −3.5% Amount of preference
    46.5% Colombia's rate for this product from Paraguay

g. 48.5 percent, calculated as follows:

    50% Colombia's normal duty rate
×   3% LAIA regional preference for "other" nations from the
         intermediate nations
  1.5% Amount of preference

    50% Colombia's normal duty rate
−1.5% Amount of preference
48.5% Colombia's rate for this product from Brazil

h. 47.5 percent, calculated as follows:

    50% Colombia's normal duty rate
×   5% LAIA regional preference rate for goods from one intermediate
         nation to another intermediate country
  2.5%

    50% Colombia's normal duty rate
−2.5% Amount of preference
47.5% Colombia's rate for this product from Chile.

i. 200 percent
j. 196 percent
k. 194 percent
l. 190 percent

# No. 15

a. 60 percent; Colombia, Peru, and Venezuela were supposed to be at the final common external tariff by the end of 1983. Art. 61 of Cartagena Agreement (Appendix H-1) and art. 1 of the Lima Protocol (Appendix H-3).

b. 44 percent; CACM equalized duty rate or common external tariff; Panama is not a member of the CACM.

c. Should be somewhere between 40 and 60 percent because ANCOM members were supposed to have reached the minimum common external tariff level by the end of 1975 (Cartagena Agreement, art. 64) and Bolivia, as the less developed member, has until the end of 1988 to reach the final common external tariff (Lima Protocol, art. 2, Appendix H-3).

d. 25 percent, the LAIA partial accord rate.

e. 60 percent; Colombia should have been down to the ANCOM final common external tariff rate by the end of 1983. Since Brazil made a separate bilateral LAIA partial accord agreement with Colombia, Mexico is not entitled to the Brazilian rate because no most-favored nation rate is applicable to Mexico under the LAIA treaty.

f. Should have been zero by the end of 1983. Lima Protocol, art. 8.

g. Zero; the more developed nations of ANCOM were to have eliminated their duties against products from Bolivia and Ecuador by the end of 1973. Cartagena Agreement, art. 97(a).

## No. 16

Ghana is a member of ECOWAS, the Congo of ECCAS, and Zambia of the Eastern and Southern African PTA (See Appendixes D-1, B-1, and C-1). Thus, Smith will need to consider the rules of the various integration associations.

ECOWAS has already adopted a scheme for internal duty reductions; if this is implemented in practice, Ricko should be able to sell these vehicles all over West Africa duty free by 1989. Appendix D-4, art. 1, (Schedules I and II). ECCAS also envisions an eventual market free of tariff barriers, but when this will become effective is not yet clear.

The PTA scheme does not call for duty-free internal trade, but under article 4(2), Group IV(a) of the PTA Protocol on the Reduction and Elimination of Trade Barriers on Selected Commodities to be Traded Within the Preferential Trade Area, (Appendix C-2), these vehicles may be treated as a "consumer durable," entitled to a 40 percent preference. Thus, if Smith invests in Zambia, the product could enter Kenya at 42 percent, calculated as follows:

$$
\begin{array}{rl}
70\% & \text{Kenya's normal duty rate} \\
\times\ 40\% & \text{PTA preference} \\
\hline
28\% & \text{Amount of preference}
\end{array}
$$

$$
\begin{array}{rl}
70\% & \text{Kenya's normal duty rate} \\
-\ 28\% & \text{Amount of preference} \\
\hline
42\% & \text{PTA rate for this product}
\end{array}
$$

If Smith can convince the PTA authorities that these vehicles are of "particular importance to economic development," under Article 4(2), Group IV(d) the amount of the preference can increase to 70 percent, which should bring the Kenya duty down to 21 percent:

$$
\begin{array}{rl}
70\% & \text{Kenya's normal duty rate} \\
\times\ 70\% & \text{PTA preference} \\
\hline
49\% & \text{Amount of preference}
\end{array}
$$

70% Kenya's normal duty rate
– 49% Amount of preference
21% PTA rate for this product

If the Ricko investment is made in Ghana or the Congo (non-PTA members), the vehicles would be subject to the regular 70 percent duty on entering Kenya.

To obtain the benefit of these liberalized tariff structures, the project will have also to satisy the rules of origin requirements of the different integration units. Both the ownership structure and the local component requirements may pose difficulties.

An investment in Zambia would bring into play Rule 2(1)(a) of the PTA Protocol on Rules of Origin (Appendix C-4), which stipulate that a product may be treated as "local" only if the company is managed by nationals and is at least 51 percent owned by nationals. If Raj invests $50,000 and Smith $200,000, this gives a total of $250,000, which means that foreigners would own more than 51 percent of the company. Therefore, Ricko would lose the right to export to other PTA members at the preferential duty rates. To avoid this effect, Raj would probably have to be excluded from participation and the only foreign portion of the investment be limited to Smith's $200,000.

Moreover, to obtain the benefit of the lower duties, Rule 2(1)(b)(ii) and (iii) of that protocol requires a local component value of between 40 and 45 percent, whereas the investment proposal calls for only 35 percent locally added value. Thus, the arrangement has to be restructured to bring the local component up to the higher figures, for example, perhaps by manufacturing the pedals locally. Alternatively, if the PTA authorities can be persuaded that this product is of "particular importance" to economic development, the local component requirement can be as low as 25 percent. [Rule 2(1)(b)(iv)(aa).]

If the investment is in the Congo, the Protocol on the Rules of Origin for ECCAS (Appendix B-2) applies. For liberalized tariff treatment, Article 1(a) of Rule 2 requires, that the company be managed by a majority of local nationals and that at least 30 percent of the shares be held by nationals. In this case, both Smith and Raj could buy stock because their total share participation would be less than the 70 percent limit for foreign owners (i.e., $200,000 [Smith] + $50,000 [Raj] = $250,000 / $450,000 [total project] = 55.5 percent).

Rule 2, Article 1(b) also requires that local components account for 40 to 45 percent of the finished product; however, this standard can be reduced to 25 percent if vehicles are considered of particular importance to economic development. Rule 2, Article 1(b) (iv).

An investment in Ghana will trigger the norms of ECOWAS, whose rules of origin require local components amounting to 35 percent of the finished value [Appendix D-2, art. II(1)]. Moreover, to satisfy the origin standards, the percent of local equity ownership must reach 35 percent after 1983 and 51 percent after 1989, [Appendixes D-2, art. II(2) and D-3, art. I]. Otherwise, the vehicles will not be entitled to circulate within the market at the lower duty rates.

## No. 17

This proposed investment would be subject to the Central American Agreement on Fiscal Incentives (Appendix E-2). One will first have to determine under which category in Article 5 the proposal falls. Since this is a consumer good and since local components will account for more than 50 percent of the product, it will probably qualify as a Group A enterprise.

Next, one must determine whether this is a new or existing industry. Under Article 25, this would be classified as an "existing" industry because another member of the common market, Guatemala, already has a refrigerator plant (and more than seven years has expired).

As an existing Group A industry, the fiscal incentives available to this project are governed by Article 12. Thus, for example, the maximum exemption from income taxes would be two years, the maximum relief from customs duties would be six years, and so on.

## No. 18

To answer this question, see the Basic Agreements on ASEAN Industrial Joint Ventures (Appendix A-6). Since ASEAN nationals would own more than 51 percent of the stock, the proposal satisfies the article 1, ¶ 5 local ownership requirements. The duties of PB's widget Ys would be:

a. 15 percent. If PB receives AIJV status, widget Y is entitled to a 50 percent preference tariff from other participating countries under art. III (1).
b. 17 percent, same reason as in (a).
c. 100 percent, since Malaysia is not a participating member.
d. 25 percent, 50 percent preferential rate.
e. 80 percent, the full rate because Malaysia is not a participating AIJV country under art. III (2) and the Supplemental Agreement Amending the Basic Agreement (Appendix A-7).
f. 50 percent, for the same reason.
g. 34 percent, for the same reason.
h. 30 percent, for the same reason.
i. 17 percent, ASEAN Preferential Rate.
j. 34 percent, regular extraregional duty.
k. 17 percent, ASEAN Preferential Rate.
l. 17 percent, after four years all products on the AIJV lists circulate within ASEAN at the preferential rate, whether or not from participating countries. Art. III(8) and the Supplemental Agreement Amending the Basic Agreement.

## No. 19

Since no other project for this AIJV item was approved within six months, the PB Company is entitled to exclusivity under art. III(4). Thus, for the next three years, participating countries may not approve new plants to produce the same products. Therefore, the Blue investment would not be permitted. There is an exception to this rule, however, if 75 percent of the production is to be exported outside the ASEAN region. Therefore the Zud investment may be approved if the 75 percent requirement can be met [Appendix A-6, art. III(5)].

# 6

# COMECON: INTEGRATING
# PLANNED ECONOMIES

As explained in Chapter 1, integration among Communist nations has focused, not on tariff reduction, but on coordinated planning and resource allocation, as well as on improving scientific and technical cooperation. Likewise, achieving control over the technology transfer process is easier in command economies since all licensing is handled by governmental bodies, such as Licensintorg in the Soviet Union.[1]

The theoretical underpinnings of socialist integrations are rooted in the teachings of V. Lenin. The president of the USSR Commission for Collaboration of Planning, N. Baibakov, states that the basic principles of socialism

> include the great importance of central planning, the unity of politics and economics, the separations of the plan into its diverse links, the directive nature of the plan, the continuity in the planning process, as well as the calculation and strict control of the progress of performance of the economic plan. . . .[2]

Originally, the Council for Mutual Economic Assistance (COMECON) was designed to integrate economies within a body of contiguous states, that is, the Soviet Union and Eastern Europe. The addition of poor remote nations, like Mongolia, Vietnam, and Cuba, brought new challenges—not always welcomed. The Soviet Union had wanted COMECON to become a worldwide socialist organization, but the East European states complained about the economic burden of integrating with poor countries. For example, the per capital income of East Germany, the wealthiest COMECON member, is 40 times that of Vietnam. Reportedly, the East European countries prevented the Soviet Union from bringing Angola, Ethiopia, and Mozambique into COMECON.[3] (Apart from the integration context, the East Europeans have been generous and, as of 1982, had provided assistance to more than 6,400 industrial enterprises in the Third World.)[4]

In integrating command economies, the key questions concern how resources should be allocated and labor divided. In general, market forces are replaced by planning decisions. Consequently, a brief word about the authority structure of COMECON is necessary.[5]

## ORGANIZATIONAL STRUCTURE

Since COMECON operates on the theory of sovereign equality of its states, no measure may be adopted against the will of any member concerned. A project may nevertheless be undertaken by other states that wish to participate in it.[6] Amendment of the COMECON Charter also requires unanimous consent.[7] A Cuban authority contends that these rules are not intended to create a right of veto, but rather to promote negotiations aimed at achieving a consensus.[8]

The council makes "decisions" on organizational and procedural matters. On questions concerning economic, scientific, and technical cooperation, COMECON may only make recommendations.[9] COMECON also may conclude agreements both with member nations[10] and outside countries.[11] Some legal authorities believe that such pacts are binding international conventions; others argue that under the COMECON Charter such an accord would merely be a "gentleman['s] agreement."[12]

## INVESTMENT PLANNING AND ALLOCATION

In 1971 COMECON announced the adoption of the Comprehensive Program for Economic Integration, which set forth the goals and policies for the next 20 years. This program, however, did not contain specific measures for attaining these aims, and implementation has been less than satisfactory.[13] Even so, some 300 multilateral accords for economic and scientific coordination were concluded during the next nine years.[14] Among them were a 130,000-ton nickel-producing facility for Cuba and an ore concentration mill for Mongolia.[15]

For the foreseeable furture, Vietnam will probably be the site of raw material development projects, as Cuba and Mongolia are now. COMECON may, for instance, assist Vietnam in developing its petroleum resources. Since COMECON leaders have emphasized the need to equalize the standards of economic development of all its members, priority will probably be given to projects within these three developing nations.

To achieve a better division of labor and increase intraregional trade, a variety of specialized institutions have been created, such as the Common Center for Railway Freight Cars and the Organization for Collaboration in the

Ball Bearing Industry.[16] In 1973, the COMECON nations concluded the Agreement on Multilateral International Specialization in the Production of Elite [high-yield?] Seeds and Planting Materials. On the basis of tests conducted under this agreement, 750 high-yield varieties and hybrids have been introduced in different regions and planted in more than 12.5 million hectares (one hectare equals 2.5 acres).[17] The General Agreement on Co-operation in the Long-term Development of Interconnected Electric Power Systems was signed in 1977. This pact details ways to coordinate electrical power systems.[18]

Yuri V. Andropov, concerned about duplication, stressed the need for closer cooperation within COMECON. For instance, East Germany could increase its investments in robotics and microelectronics, fields in which it is well ahead of the other members. At the same time, that nation might yield other activities, perhaps auto manufacturing, to the remaining members. The Soviet Union has also urged that enterprises from different member nations merge their expertise and form one joint factory or groups of factories.[19] During the 1985 summit meeting of COMECON, accords were signed on production of industrial robots and on "a program of cooperation for saving and rational use of material resources through the year 2000."[20]

Opponents of rigid specialization argue that allocation decisions may be based on static assumptions. East Germany's comparative advantage in, say, engineering is to some extent a historical accident. To deny the less developed members the right to produce similar goods would be to deprive them of the right to develop such industrial capacity.

Also militating against specialization is the unwillingness of members to scrap certain lines of production. Moreover, there is fear the product quality may drop; Hungary allegedly abandoned production of radios in favor of clearly inferior Bulgarian sets. Conferees at COMECON meetings have suggested that assigning production to one country produces monopolistic tendencies and that, to avoid this result, allocations of a given item should be made to at least two nations.[21]

## TRADE POLICIES AND PRACTICES

COMECON countries conduct a major portion of their foreign trade with each other. During the 1970–75 period, reciprocal exports among member countries averaged 55 percent of all exports, while imports from partner nations amounted to 50 percent of the total imports.[22]

In the Soviet Union, some 70 foreign trade organizations (FTOs) conduct almost all international trade. In a recent revision of its regulations, the USSR has authorized Soviet manufacturers for the first time to sit on the boards of the foreign trade organizations of their respective industries, giving them a voice in policy decisions.[23] FTOs also do most of the importing and exporting in other COMECON countries; typically each nation has several dozen FTOs. In a few East European nations, certain large enterprises are permitted to sell directly to foreign buyers without going through the FTO middleman.[24]

## Procedures for Making Trade Agreements in COMECON

Foreign trade within COMECON is mostly bilateral and is arranged principally through three kinds of bilateral agreements. First, there is a long-term trade agreement that is negotiated and signed by the foreign trade ministries of the two governments. These pacts are operative for a period coinciding with the time frame set for the national plan of each nation, for instance, a five-year plan. These long-term agreements set forth which goods are to be supplied by each country to the other during which years.

Since COMECON lacks an effective multilateral payments system, generally the long-term agreement seeks to balance the trade, except where a credit is to be provided. Normally the agreement contains a formula or mechanism for setting the price in relation to the world market price over a preceding period.[25]

Next, each year a trade protocol is signed by the foreign trade ministries of the two governments. The chief purpose of the protocol is to adjust the provisions of the long-term agreement to current conditions.[26]

Finally come the FTO contracts, which provide for delivery of the specific goods. These agreements are usually signed by the appropriate FTO from each country. The contract specifies matters, such as quantity, assortment, technical description, price, and date and place of delivery. In nations where decentralization is fairly advanced, such as Hungary and Czechoslovakia, some FTO contracts are being negotiated before, rather than after, execution of the long-term intergovernmental agreement and the annual protocol. Then the foreign trade ministries, after consultation with their FTOs, try to negotiate inclusion of such goods within the intergovernmental agreements.[27]

## Economic Characteristics of Trade

Reciprocal foreign trade within the region increased about 4.2 times in comparable prices between 1960 and 1977. This reciprocal trade has also been characterized by a deep structural change. For example, in 1950 Bulgaria exported virtually no machinery and equipment, while in 1978 its exports of these items amounted to 2.1 billion roubles. Over the same period, Romania increased its deliveries of machinery and equipment 113 times.[28]

Traditionally, Westerners have believed that the Soviet Union was exploiting its COMECON partners in their trade relations. A new study, however, questions such an assumption. Rather, this examination concludes that in recent years the Soviet Union has granted Eartern Europe large trading subsidies, averaging $5.8 billion during 1974–78, rising to $10.4 billion in 1979 and a staggering $21.7 billion in 1980.

The subsidies result from the price formation theory used for intrabloc trade. For example, the Soviet export price for oil in 1980 was based on the average of world market prices in 1975–80. Poland provides an example of this distortion. Crude oil, natural gas, and cotton represent 31 percent of Polish imports from the Soviet Union. The foregoing study found that the Polish import price for Soviet oil was 52 percent below the average import price from the West, 26 percent below the Soviet export price to the West for natural gas, and 18 percent below the average import price from the West for cotton. Conversely, the Polish export price to the USSR for hard coal was 25 percent above the average export price to the West, for railroad cars 12 percent above, and 149 percent above for fishing trawlers. The assumption is that the Soviet Union bears these costs for a variety of reasons: increased economic stability in COMECON, access to an uninterrupted flow of technologically superior machinery, and reduced resistance to purchasing USSR goods.[29]

Some authorities have argued that the Soviet Union was willing to accept the burden of these subsidies to compel its COMECON partners to acquiesce in a comprehensive blueprint for integration along Soviet lines.[30] A United Nations technocrat questions this assumption. Pointing out that the Soviet Union has "simply not tried very hard to exploit its economic weight in the CMEA [COMECON] economic balance to enforce production specialization on any meaningful scale," he concludes, "It is therefore not likely to use the oil weapon in an extreme way, even if, as happened in the past, its partners were to display great reluctance to enact the type of production specialization it advocates."[31]

In any event, the Soviet Union has begun cutting back on these subsidies, reducing oil shipments, and raising prices.[32] In 1984 that country announced a proposal to build a natural gas pipeline to Eastern Europe, apparently to compensate those nations for any future declines in Soviet oil deliveries.[33]

### The COMECON Sales Convention

Without doubt, the outstanding juridical achievement of COMECON has been the unification of international sales law, with the adoption in 1958 of the General Conditions for the Delivery of Goods.[34] The West has tried hard to do the same thing, but with much less success. Not until 1980 was the United Nations Convention on Contracts for the International Sale of Goods[35] approved at a diplomatic conference. It is still too early to predict the response of the United States and other countries to this convention (although its content is similar to Article 2 of the American Uniform Commercial Code). True, it was easier for COMECON to achieve unification than for the disparate Western nations because the COMECON countries are more homogeneous in character, operate a similar system of trade, and have fairly similar domestic legal systems.

In promulgating "General Conditions," COMECON had a different purpose in mind from the Western drafters of sales legislation. The COMECON convention is intended to facilitate fulfillment of the intergovernmentally planned trade by the FTOs. The prime objectives are the actual completion of contracted deliveries, together with speed and simplicity in resolving disputes. Thus, the General Conditions sharply restrict the buyer's right to reject goods and provide for payment of a penalty as the basic monetary remedy, rather than compensation for damages. Throughout the convention, the "General Conditions" provide specific mechanical rules that are easy to apply quickly. Executing a national economic plan is absent as a motivation in the market economies of the West; thus, the right to obtain goods that conform precisely to contract specifications obtains more importance.[36]

The General Conditions govern all contracts to sell goods within the COMECON region; conversely the convention does not apply where one of the parties is not a member of COMECON.[37] Limited to the sale of tangible goods, the General Conditions cover such matters as formation of contracts, obligations of the seller for delivery and quality of the goods, breach of contract, remedies for breach, and force majeure.

Questions not resolved by the General Conditions are referred to the law of the nation of the seller. A number of the provisions are treated as mandatory; that is, the parties-FTOs cannot stipulate otherwise. An example is the requirement that disputes be submitted to arbitration by the national foreign trade arbitration tribunals.[38]

The earliest version of the General Conditions was adopted during the 1950s when the members were recovering from the war, industry was still disorganized, and goods were in short supply. Central economic planning had to do the best it could with limited resources. In this situation, delivery of some goods, even if they did not conform to all the contract specifications, contributed more to plan fulfillment than no delivery at all. Rejection of nonconforming goods would have incurred, in a time of scarcity, the additional costs of finding another buyer and reshipping the goods. Consequently, the General Conditions deny a buyer the remedy of rejection for nonconformity (except for contracts under time). Instead the buyer is compelled to accept the nonconforming goods and, after obtaining whatever repair or replacement is practical, to use them in the best possible way.[39]

Neverthless, the modern trend of arbitral tribunals has been to make rescission slightly more available. Some tribunals have reasoned that if the goods are extremely defective, in effect, no delivery has ever been made. This minority position appears to be a growing one. As the improved economic conditions within COMECON make goods more plentiful, the central planners are now aiming at better quality. And today, the FTO purchaser has a more realistic possibility of obtaining substitute goods elsewhere.[40]

To discipline sellers, the General Conditions used penalties as the primary monetary remedy. The drafters of the 1958 version chose penalties as being better calculated to attain the objective of completing scheduled physical deliveries. Even under the current version of this law, only a penalty is available for a delayed delivery or a delivery that cannot be used. The penalty is a mechanical one (for example, 0.05 percent of the value of the goods per day for the first 30 days, 0.08 percent per day for the next 30 days, and so on, up to a maximum penalty of 8 percent of the value of the goods). The amount of such penalty can obviously be substantially less than the actual losses incurred.[41]

The role of compensatory damages was substantially increased by the 1968, 1975, and 1979 revisions of the General Conditions. Under the 1979 revision, penalties remain the exclusive remedy for some breaches, damages for other, but for certain breaches both damages and penalties may be secured. Finally, damages alone may be recovered for certain breaches.[42]

Damages are now defined to include expenses incurred by the aggrieved party, loss or damage to the party's property, and also lost profits. Lost profits may be recovered, however, only when so provided in a bilateral agreement or the contract. Indirect damages are excluded.[43] One difficulty with applying the lost profits concept is that methods of calculating profitability as determined by domestic central planners may vary significantly among various industries and also among the COMECON countries.

All contract disputes in intra-COMECON trade must be submitted to the national foreign trade arbitration tribunal within the individual COMECON nation. Each member country has a permanent arbitration tribunal that specializes in foreign trade matters. Periodically, these national arbitrators meet at international conferences where they endeavor to reconcile differing interpretations of the General Conditions.[44] Although these tribunals arbitrate foreign trade disputes involving parties from any country in the world, 70 percent of their cases are between COMECON parties. Jurisdiction of the regular judicial courts over these disputes is excluded. COMECON has so far not succeeded in establishing a single multinational arbitral tribunal for these cases.

Accession by Cuba to the General Conditions, together with the possible future adherence of Vietnam, has added a new element. For example, prior to 1975, all the members were contiguous to each other; so ocean shipping was not a factor. Consequently, time periods were fairly short. In the 1975 revision, four time periods were lengthened solely for trade involving Cuba.[45]

### Extra-Regional Trade

Another recent development was the conclusion in 1978 of the Finland-COMECON General Conditions, which are now available for optional use in trade between any COMECON country and Finland. The COMECON-Finnish version has a special relevance for nations outside COMECON since it is designed for trade between a market economy and a centrally planned economy.[46]

Among Western nations the major trading partner of the COMECON countries is the EEC.[47] Nonetheless, the EEC has been described as unwilling to negotiate an overall trade agreement with COMECON on the grounds that the latter organization is merely an association of sovereign states, with no supranational institution analogous to the EEC Commission. COMECON, on the other hand, has wished to secure recognition by the EEC of the Council's authority to negotiate trade treaties on behalf of its member nations.[48]

As indicated below COMECON handled a similar problem concerning one of its financial institutions by amending its charter.[49] Now it is reported that during the 1985 COMECON summit meeting, the members concluded an agreement on the legal capabilities of COMECON itself.[50] Although the text of that pact is not yet available to this writer, one can speculate that it may have inserted similar clarifying language into the COMECON Charter, thereby allowing the organization to deal more effectively with outside groups, like the EEC.

## OTHER ASPECTS

### Financial Institutions

COMECON has created an International Investment Bank (IIB) to grant long- and medium-term credits for capital investments in member countries.[51] From 1971 to 1978, IIB approved loans for 61 projects involving 8,000 million transferable roubles.[52] In the late 1970s, IIB negotiated a $500 million loans from a consortium of western banks, led by a West German bank. In 1979, 12 Japanese banks lent IIB another $175 million.[53]

COMECON also established the International Bank for Economic Cooperation (IBEC).[54] Although COMECON has failed to establish a convertible currency or an effective multilateral payments system,[55] it has devised the "transferable rouble," which is used by IBEC to settle accounts of COMECON members.[56] Hungary has asked that steps be taken toward achieving a convertible rouble, but the Soviet Union believes such convertibility would disrupt its own domestic economy rather than help it.[57]

During the 1970s, IBEC's legal status was questioned in Great Britain. Article XI of the Agreement Concerning Multilateral Settlements in Transferable Roubles and the Organization of IBEC was thereupon amended to provide that IBEC is an international organization possessing the right to sign international agreements with states and international organizations.[58]

### Environmental Policy

Concerned about improving the environment, COMECON has concluded a multilateral agreement for cooperation in environmental protection.

Under this accord, a program for global monitoring of the environment has been created.[59]

## RESULTS

UNCTAD reports that the COMECON system has indeed contributed to production increases and stable high rates of overall economic growth. From 1950 to 1976, the national income of COMECON member countries increased by 690 percent and industrial output by 1,100 percent. Trade between the members increased 16 times between 1950 and 1975. "Mongolia and Cuba . . . accelerated significantly their economic development owing to cooperation with and assistance by their CMEA [COMECON] partners."[60]

One Soviet expert rejoices in the fact that from 1950 to 1970 the growth rate in real income averaged 8.2 percent for COMECON, but only 5 percent for the European Common Market.[61] Since COMECON started from a significantly lower base, its percentage increases surpassing those of the EEC is not that startling. Still, advocates of the socialist model would maintain that COMECON achieves a more equitable distribution of the benefits of increased production since this system focuses on the gradual leveling up of all its members and their citizens.[62]

## NOTES

1. Terence Roth and John J. Fialka, "Soviet Technology Yields Ideas That U.S. Firms Can Exploit, but Only a Few Make It to Market," *Wall Street Journal*, April 25, 1985, p. 37.

2. N. Baibakov, "Perfeccionamiento de la Planificación Socialista en los Países Miembros de CAME," *Cuestiones de la Economía Planificada* (Havana: Junta Central de Planificación de Cuba, July–August 1980), no. 4, p. 50; see also Margarita Maksimova (USSR), "Comments" in Bela Balassa, *Types of Economic Integration* (World Bank reprint series No. 69, 1976), p. 32.

3. Frederick Kempe, "Soviets to Press Allies for Economic Unity, Using Future Oil Deliveries as an Incentive," *Wall Street Journal*, June 11, 1984, p. 24.

4. "COMECON Connection," *SOUTH* (London), February 1985, pp. 63–72.

5. "Consejo de Ayuda Mutua Económica, Convención Sobre Capacidad Jurídica, Privilegios, e Inmunidades" (December 14, 1959, as amended through 1979), reprinted in *Cuestiones de la Economía Planificada* (Havana: Junta Central de Planificación de Cuba, January–February 1981), no. 7, p. 218. The 1960 English version of this convention appears in U.N.T.S. 368 (1960): 242. The original members were Albania, Bulgaria, Hungary, the German Democratic Republic, Poland, Rumania, the Union of Soviet Socialist Republics, and Czechoslovakia. Mongolia was admitted in 1962, Cuba in 1972, annd Vietnam in 1978. Albania has been inactive since 1961. Yugloslavia participates in some activities under a separate agreement. Thomas W. Hoya, *East West Trade: Comecon Law, American-Soviet Trade* (Dobbs Ferry, New York: Oceana, 1984), p. 7; see also Thomas L. Shillinglaw, "Recent Developments in the Council for Mutual Economic Assistance," *International Lawyer* 13 (1979): 523; *and* V. Kuznetosov, *La Integración Económica: Dos Modos de Abordar el Problema* (Moscow: Editorial Progreso, 1975).

6. "Estatutos [Charter], Consejo de Ayuda Mutua Económica," art. IV(3) (as amended through 1979), reprinted in *Cuestiones de la Economía Planificiada* (Havana: Junta Central de

Planificación de Cuba, January–February 1981, no. 7, p. 199 [hereinafter cited as "Estatutos"]. The 1960 version in English appears in U.N.T.S. 368 (1960): 264.

7. "Estatutos," supra, note 6, art. 17. It is reported that the Soviet Union at the thirty-second session in 1978 proposed that the charter be amended so that decisions now requiring unanimity would need only a majority vote. It is also understood that the Soviets wished to amend the charter to make participation in COMECON's integration projects mandatory rather than voluntary. Neither proposal was adopted. Shillinglaw, "Recent Developments," p. 524.

8. José Peraza Chapeau, "El CAME y Sus Estatutos," Cuestiones de la Economía Planificada (Havana: Junta Central de Planificación de Cuba, January–Febrary 1981), no. 7, p. 159.

9. "Estatutos," supra, note 6, art. IV(1) and (2).

10. Ibid., art. IV(4).

11. Ibid., art. III (2) (b).

12. Chapeau, "El CAME," p. 168.

13. Hoya, East West Trade, p. 5.

14. Mijail Kudriashov, "Finalidades, Principios, y Estructura del Consejo de Ayuda Mutua Económica," Cuestiones de la Economía Planificada (Havana: Junta Central de Planificación de Cuba, January–February 1981), no. 7, p. 130.

15. United Nations Conference on Trade and Development, Multilateral Schemes of the Countries Members of the Council for Mutual Economic Assistance and Opportunities for Developing Countries in Trade and Economic Co-operation Resulting from the Implementation of These Schemes, p. 6, TD/B/AC. 23/3/rev.1 (1978) [hereinafter cited as UNCTAD Report].

16. Lara Celaya, "Las Licencias y la Política Científico-Técnica," Revista Cubana de Derecho (Havana: La Unión Nacional de Juristas de Cuba, December–January 1980), no. 16, p. 210-11.

17. UNCTAD Report, supra, note 15, p. 8.

18. CMEA Secretariat, The Council for Mutual Economic Assistance—30 Years (Moscow, 1979), p. 52.

19. John F. Burns, "Slow Growth, High Prices Put Strains on Soviet Economic Alliance," International Herald Tribune (Paris ed.), May 13, 1983, p. 1.

20. Frederick Kempe, "To Dismay of Some COMECON Members, Soviets are Firm on Tighter Trade Ties," Wall Street Journal, July 1, 1985, p. 14; and David Ignatius, "Gorbachev Appoints 3 to Soviet Politburo, Stresses Need for Broad Economic Change," Wall Street Journal, April 24, 1985, p. 37.

21. Andrzej Korbonski, "Theory and Practice of Regional Integration: The Case of Comecon," in Regional Politics and World Order, eds. Richard A. Falk and Saul H. Mandlovitz (San Francisco: W. H. Freeman, 1973), pp. 159-62.

22. Raymundo Barros Charlin, "Derecho de la Integración: Estudios—Consideraciones Jurídico—económicas el Intercambio Comercial Con los Países Socialistas," Intergración Latinoamericana (Buenos Aires: INTAL, November 1982), no. 74, p. 24.

23. Roth and Filka, "Soviet Technology."

24. Hoya, East West Trade, p. 12.

25. Ibid., p. 13.

26. Ibid., p. 14.

27. Ibid., pp. 15-16.

28. CMEA Secretariat, supra note 18, pp. 74-75.

29. Jan Vanous and Micheal Marrese, "Soviet Subsidies to Eastern Economies," Wall Street Journal, January 15, 1982 (editorial page).

30. Kempe, "Soviets to Press Allies"; and Marie Lavigne, "The Soviet Union Inside Comecon," Soviet Studies 25, no. 2 (April 1983): 135-53.

31. Jozef M. van Brabant, "The USSR and Socialist Economic Integration—A Comment," Soviet Studies 26, no. 1 (January 1984): 134.

32. Henry S. Rowen and Vladimir G. Treml, "As Oil Prices Fall, Moscow's Woes Rise," Wall Street Journal, March 6, 1985 p. 30; and Frederick Kempe, "U.S.S.R. Pressures Hungarian Economy," Wall Street Journal, June 5, 1985, p. 38.

33. "Soviets Offer to Build Natural Gas Pipeline for East Bloc Allies," *Wall Street Journal*, July 3, 1984, p. 37.

34. The COMECON General Conditions were adopted in 1958, amended in 1964, significantly revised in 1968, revised again in 1975, and once again in 1979, effective in 1980. Hoya, *East West Trade*, p. 97. A translation of this document appears in Appendix I, p. 379 of Hoya's book.

35. U.N. Doc. A/CONF. 97/18(1980), reprinted in *International Legal Materials* 19 (1980): 671; and see J. Honnald, *Uniform Law For International Sales Under the 1980 United Nations Convention* (Deventer, Netherlands: Kluwer, 1982); Peter Winship, "Formation of International Sales Contracts under the 1980 Vienna Convention," *International Lawyer* 17 (1983): 1.

36. Hoya, *East West Trade*, pp. 99, 208.

37. Supra, note 34, art 1.

38. Hoya, *East West Trade*, pp. 99, 128.

39. Ibid., p. 205.

40. Ibid., pp. 209–10.

41. Ibid., pp. 212–13.

42. Ibid., pp. 214–15; and N. I. Tatischeva, "Perfeccionamiento de las Basis Jurídicas de la Colaboración de Países Miembros de CAME,"*Revista Cubana de Derecho*(Havana: Unión Nacional de Juristas de Cuba, December–January 1980), no. 16, pp. 146–47.

43. Supra, note 34, § 67-E.

44. Hoya, *East West Trade*, p. 146. The Cuban arbitration system is established by Decreto-Ley No. 10 of December 12, 1977; Decreto No. 23, July 3, 1978; Decreto No. 46 of September 18, 1979; Decreto No. 47 of September 1979; Decreto No. 60 of December 25, 1979, Reglamento Orgánico de los Organos del Sistema de Arbitraje Estatal; and Decreto No. 89 of May 21, 1981, Reglas de Procedimiento del Arbitraje Estatal, reprinted in *Revista Cubana de Derecho* (Havana: La Unión Nacional de Juristas de Cuba, September–December 1982), no. 20, pp. 3–72. See also Reyes Saliá, "El Sistema de Arbitraje Estatal en Cuba," ibid., p. 73; and Enrique Dahl, "Cuba's System of International Commercial Arbitration: A Convergence of Soviet and Latin American Trends," *Lawyer of the Americas* (University of Miami) 15 (1984): 441.

45. Hoya, *East West Trade*, p. 370.

46. Ibid., p. 296. An unofficial English translation of this convention appears in Professor Hoya's book, Appendix II, p. 443.

47. Peter Marsh, "The European Community and East-West Relations," *Journal of Common Market Law* 23 (September 1984): 1.

48. Thomas L. Shillinglaw, "Recent Developments in the Council for Mutual Economic Assistance," *International Lawyer* 13 (1979): 523, 527.

49. See Appendix J-4, art. XI.

50. Kempe, "To Dismay of Some COMECON Members."

51. Agreement on the Establishment of the International Investment Bank (January 1, 1971), reprinted in *International Legal Materials* 23 (1984): 641. See Appendixes J-2 and J-3.

52. CMEA Secretariat, supra, note 18, p. 78.

53. Shillinglaw, "Recent Developments," p. 529. See ibid., pp. 529–30, for a discussion of whether U.S. banks can participate in syndications for IIB loans without violating U.S. law.

54. Agreement Concerning Multilateral Settlements in Transferable Rubles and the Organization of the International Bank for Economic Cooperaton (May 19, 1964), as amended through November 23, 1977, reprinted in *International Legal Materials* 23 (1984): 650. See Appendixes J-4 and J-5.

55. Hoya, *East West Trade*, p. 5.

56. Ibid., and CMEA Secretariat, supra, note 18, p. 77.

57. Kempe, "Soviets to Press Allies."

58. Shillinglaw, "Recent Developments," p. 529.

59. CMEA Secretariat, supra, note 18, p. 69.

60. UNCTAD Report, supra, note 15.

61. Yuri Shishkov, *Two Systems of Economic Integration* (Moscow: Novosti Press Agency, 1974), p. 54.

62. For example, in West Germany for the 1950–57 period (before integration), the average annual growth rate of the net profits of the 50 largest companies outpaced the growth of their payroll by 14.3 percent. From 1957 to 1986, after integration, this lead went up to 37.9 percent. Ibid., pp. 58–59, 61.

# 7

# CONCLUSIONS AND RECOMMENDATIONS

As this study indicates, Third World integration associations have had their difficulties. Yet, considering the depth of their poverty and the extent to which their economies had been oriented toward the First World, the surprising fact is not that problems exist, but that the spirit of integration still lives. Despite periodic floundering, the developing countries do manage to regroup, to revise or rewrite treaties, and to stretch out deadlines—the overall movement toward integration continues to inch forward. From this quarter century of experimentation, some conclusions can be drawn, which form the basis for the following suggestions.

## TRADE INTEGRATION

### Procedures for Reducing Tariffs

Product by product negotiations do not seem to be the most fruitful way to achieve trade liberalization. The same is true for agreements to agree in the future. LAIA's new regional tariff preference shows promise, but the initial reductions are quite small. When later an effort to make deeper cuts threatens to have some real effect on trade, will affected interest groups be able to exert sufficient pressure to bring the process to halt as happened in LAFTA?

On the other hand, creating strict treaty requirements for across the board cuts according to rigid schedules may be unrealistic and therefore unenforceable. Yet two features here seem crucial: that the reductions be linear, not product by product; and that a schedule for phased reductions be established at once rather than left for later meetings.

Perhaps the best approach is to use linear cuts and fixed schedules, but to place those requirements, not in an international treaty, but in the legislation

102

of the integration unit. Legislation usually is not as difficult to change as a treaty. Thus, necessary modifications in deadlines and amounts of cuts could be more easily made. At the same time, this linear approach shifts the burden of proof by requiring that the nation or the industrialist that wishes relief from general across-the-board cuts will have to convince the decisionmakers of the special merits of its case. Obtaining an exception from an across the board reduction should be more difficult than merely persuading one's government not to place a product on the list of items to be proposed for a product by product session.

### Industries Not Yet in Existence

Integration units should develop lists of products that are not yet being produced in the region and immediately eliminate internal duties on those goods. Since no business depends on the tariff protection, such duties can be removed without injuring anyone. The same approach might be taken for economic sectors where the development is at a very low level and existing firms cannot meet the needs of the larger market.

As a comparative note, one might comment in passing that the United States formed its own common market in 1789 when the new Constitution prohibited the imposition of duties by the states[1] and delegated foreign commerce and the coinage of money to the federal government.[2] Since this occurred before the industrial revolution, the industry existing in the United States at the time was not powerful enough to prevent such internal trade liberalization. Developing countries should also press forward with internal duty abolition prior to the establishment of strong local industries that can subsequently pose an obstacle to trade liberalization.

### Nontariff Barriers

Lack of foreign exchange makes the use of nontariff barriers an attractive option. Because such restrictions can create severe distortions in trade patterns and disrupt integration, nations need to begin dismantling the most egregious barriers as soon as reasonably possible. Members of developing country integration units should consider first eliminating such limitations vis-à-vis partner states. This would have the effect of providing an additional preference for regional goods as against extrazonal products.

### Customs and Transportation Procedures

An integration unit would be well advised to concentrate upon simplifying customs regulations and reducing inspection for regional goods to a minimum. Establishment of special border units could be used to expedite regional trade.

## Interim Protection against Outside Competition

Although free trade may be a desirable long-term goal, most developing nations will need protective tariffs for their infant industries for some time. The same is true for the regional integration associations. Those that are common markets (or customs unions) are already required to build a common external tariff against products from outside.

Although free trade associations and trade preference organizations are not obligated to create common external tariffs, adopting such extraregional duties, at least for selected products, may be essential if the integration mechanisms are to operate effectively. For instance, preferences and concessions (e.g., the LAIA regional preference) will have little impact if the regional products have to compete against outside goods entitled to enter the market subject to little or no duty.

This, in fact, is frequently the situation today. A recent study revealed that 74 percent of the goods imported into Brazil are exempt from duty; while the duty-free imports into Mexico, Argentina, and Colombia amount to 60, 44, and 42 percent respectively.[3] With this magnitude of exemptions for nonarea imports, some experts believe it may be impossible to create an integrated Latin American economy. In appraising the ASEAN complementation schemes, Enrique Sabatté, a United Nations experts, concluded that they may fail because existing national duty rates in the region are often too low to protect the goods selected for complementation from outside competing goods.[4]

Consequently, Third World integration units seriously need to consider adopting minimum common external tariffs, for example, 15 percent, which would apply to goods from outside the region and which could not be eliminated by the individual member governments.[5] Use of a minimum and final common external tariff, as was done by ANCOM, might be appropriate to provide local business people with sufficient time to adjust. At some later date, reductions in such common external tariffs could be offered in exchange for concessions from extraregional nations or associations.

## Impact of Fiscal Incentives

Finally, under national investment incentive laws, companies within an integration region are often granted the right to import equipment and materials from outside the region duty free. Thus, regionally produced goods—even those selected for complementation programs—may be effectively denied market access to other local companies enjoying those fiscal incentives. Since these firms can buy extra-regional products duty free, there is little incentive for them to purchase the regional items.

Aggravating the situation is the fact that those same incentives probably had little influence on the initial investment decision. In general, scholars have been skeptical about the efficacy of tax incentives in producing investment.

The principal obstacles to investment in developing nations are the size of the market, the lack of natural resources, scarcity of local capital, and political instability. Tax incentives do little to reduce those risks. As Jack Heller and Kenneth M. Kauffman have written, "it is unlikely that. . . . [tax incentives] can induce substantially increased levels of new investments in most underdeveloped economies."[6] Thus, when a regional integration unit wishes to promote production of specific goods, such products need to be protected by duties against extraregional competitive goods. Member states therefore should be prohibited from using exemptions from customs duties on these particular products as an investment incentive.

Since the effectiveness of tax incentives is dubious and their cost to the limited treasuries of developing nations significant, it might be best to eliminate them altogether. Politically, however, such a course may be impossible. Even developing country leaders who question the value of fiscal incentives believe that they may perform the public relations function of showing a receptive attitude toward private investment.

If then tax incentives cannot be terminated, at least the amount of their drain on the national treasuries could be limited by capping them to eliminate competition among developing nations. By placing ceilings on the amount of the fiscal incentives available in the region, the CACM Agreement of Fiscal Incentives offers a useful model for other integration associations.

## A Regional "Similars" Law

Brazilian law for years has prohibited the import of machinery, parts, tools, or vehicles if a "national similar" exists. In determining whether a product will be treated as "similar," three basic criteria are considered: (1) whether the price of a locally made similar product is the same or less than the cost of the imported foreign item, calculated on the basis of "normal price" plus all taxes and fees incident to the importation; (2) whether the delivery time is similar; and (3) whether the quality and specifications are equivalent.[7] Once a Brazilian similar is found to exist, importation of the foreign good is forbidden.

Developing nation integration units might consider adopting a regional "similars" agreement. Under such a scheme, member states would prohibit importation of an item from outside the region if a similar product were available from a regional manufacturer.

## Dumping and Export Subsidies

In addition to entering the regional market at little or no duty, outside goods are often being dumped, that is, sold at a price below that charged in their home nation market. Or such goods may have received substantial exports subsidies from their home county. Either way, the extraregional good may as a result sell for less than the regionally produced item.

To offset such unfair advantages, the General Agreement of Tariffs and Trade (GATT) authorizes the imposition of compensatory duties by the importing nations. Within Third World integration units, a review should be made of each member's legislations on dumping and export subsidies. The integration associations should urge enactment of modern statutes on both subjects and could perhaps provide technical advice on enforcement mechanisms.

Again, it may be useful here to differentiate between products from regional partners and those from outside the association. For example, Nigeria might decide to impose countervailing duties on a subsidized product from Europe, but not from its ECOWAS partner, Senegal.

## INVESTMENT

### Encouraging Regional Investment by Local Firms

Integration associations need to find ways to encourage two different kinds of regional private investment. First, joint ventures among companies or individuals who are nationals of more than one country within the association should be promoted. For this purpose both the Andean Multinational Enterprise and the ASEAN Industrial Joint Ventures Program are worthy of study. Inducing local business people to enter such ventures could be an important step toward economic integration.

Secondly, domestic companies, wholly owned by nationals, must be persuaded to begin thinking in terms, not only of the larger market, but also of the bigger production and resource base.[8] National and intraregional laws should be reshaped to induce local entrepreneurs to move their various factors of production around the entire region, rather than plotting factor allocation merely on the basis of a single country. Such reworking of legal norms may call for revision of domestic laws on taxation, corporations, and capital markets, as well as the foreign exchange regulations and labor laws to ensure the same treatment for regional companies as for domestic firms. Integration associations could explore the possibility of treaties to avoid double taxations, using the CARICOM or ANCOM models as a starting point. To the extent that internal duties remain, they should be removed as against products from these indigenous multinational companies.

This ability to shift different production phases to various countries could prove to have another advantage. Suppose, for instance, the United States decides to remove a particular Brazilian product from the list of goods entitled to duty-free entry into the United States under the generalized system of preferences (GSP).[9] In this event, the item if made in Brazil would be charged the higher most-favored nation tariff rate. On the other hand, if the Brazilian firm were to transfer the final stages of its production process to Paraguay, then the finished product would be of Paraguayan origin and still entitled to GSP duty-free treatment by the United States.

## Preferential Treatment for Regional Investors

Article 48 of the LAIA treaty accords most-favored nation treatment for regional capital; that is, entrepreneurs from another LAIA nation will be treated no worse than investors from nonmember counties. That clause does recognize the possiblity of an exception to this norm if the members enter special agreements, providing more favorable treatment. Thus, the question arises: Why not create a system of preferences to favor regional investors over those from the outside?

In structuring such a system, the national laws on foreign and domestic investment would need to be analyzed. Then a system could be designed that would, to a significant extent, govern regional enterprises by the same rules as national companies. For instance, investments by nationals of LAIA countries outside ANCOM might be exempted from some of the provisions of the Andean Foreign Investment Code, for example, the fadeout requirements. Brazil, in applying its technology transfer regulations (similar to those of ANCOM), might interpret them more liberally on behalf of regional investors—or might waive them altogether.

Where such national treatment of regional companies proves politically unacceptable, a new category of "regional enterprises" could be created with such companies accorded treatment somewhat less favorable than for national firms and yet more favorable than for extraregional enterprises. Moreover, such laws might provide for a gradual merger of the concepts of "national" and "regional" enterprises so that both groups will eventually be considered "domestic" companies.

In additions, Third World integration units could develop regional treaties detailing the kinds of preferences to be provided to regional investors over nonregional companies. Of course, these suggestions run counter to the view that foreign investors should be treated the same as domestic companies (national treatment), a position reflected in the recent Argentine law[10] and strongly advocated by President Reagan in his U.S. bilateral investment treaty program.[11]

Basically, this question is a matter of economic philosophy. If one believes free markets and unfettered capitalism are the best road to development, then the "equal treatment" approach follows logically. If, on the other hand, the leaders feel, as seems true in many developing nations, that capitalism needs to be channeled into certain courses to achieve desirable political and social ends, then a good deal of directive behavior is to be expected. Lessening the "dependencia" or dependence on the industrialized world probably will call for some preferential treatment of regional business over outside enterprises, rather than equal treatment for all.

## Coping with Monopolistic Tendencies

Both the integration units in the socialist and the nonsocialist world have to deal with the problem of how to induce efficiency in enterprises that have been assigned exclusive or semi-exclusive production rights. In the absence of effective competition, either internally or externally, how can such companies be motivated to attain high quality standards?

Although antitrust norms can be found in the laws of Latin American countries, their implementation is at best sketchy.[12] The regional agreements on competition discussed above are virtually without teeth. The fact is that in the typical developing nation a small group of enterprises controls the bulk of production. This permits such companies to affect the conduct of other small firms and provides a wide field for maneuvering through the use of tied purchases and sales agreements, resale price fixing, and exclusivity agreements. The capital that does exist tends to be highly concentrated.

In light of these realities, most developing nations may pay homage to the principle of free competition but really show little concern with problems of dominance and monopolistic structure. Emphasis has been more on government control of the companies and regulation of consumer prices than on striving for the elusive goal of free competition. Moreover, the desire to encourage priority investments often awards the investors monopolistic privileges.

The rigorous enforcement of antitrust norms, which contributed so much to growth in the EEC and in the United States, is unlikely to prove a viable course for the Third World, at least in the near future. Hence, other alternatives should be sought.

In creating complementation or sectorial programs, the favored industries often gain monopolistic advantages as they are protected by tariff barriers against outside competition. Although perhaps necessary for infant industries, such protection should cease after a period of years and the mature industry be subjected to the invigorating winds of competition. Placing a time limit on the duration of the tariff in advance could help prepare these companies for the coming change. For example, a protective common tariff could be structured to automatically decline by, say, 50 percent after ten years and phase out completely perhaps in the fifteenth year.

For political or security reasons, all nations insist on insulating certain industries from outside competition. Developing countries and their regional organizations can be expected to do the same. To the extent feasible, this protection should be confined to those products where there is more than one healthy internal producer.

Finally, when integration associations are allocating production rights to specific countries or enterprises, they should endeavor, whenever possible, to make such an assignment to at least two different countries or to two different companies. Such a scheme might further be structured to open allocations of the same products to additional firms or nations at some future date.

**Agricultural Projects**

Shortage of food crops has become a significant problem in many developing regions. Latin America can no longer produce enough food to meet the basic needs of its population. Consequently, it is essential that a better balance be struck between developing the manufacturing sector and the agricultural sector. Regional projects in agroindustry and fertilizer production should be given special attention.

**Integrating the Private Sector into
the Decision-Making Process**

During my visits to the headquarters of ANCOM and LAIA in the spring of 1983, officials of both groups told me that these associations had failed to involve the private sector adequately in their original planning. Both LAIA and ANCOM have now formed consultative groups of private business people to advise on future directions. Since the success of many of these units ultimately depends on decisions by private investors, this is a prudent course. The experience of ASEAN with formalizing the role of the ASEAN Chambers of Commerce and Industry seems worthy of consideration by other integration organizations.

## PUBLIC INFORMATION

As this book shows, these integration associations are complex. At the same time, most integration efforts are doomed to failure unless their schemes are understood and implemented by the business community and the government agencies. The integration associations need to embark on intensive campaigns to educate journalists, industrialists, and other individuals who can affect the functioning of the regional market. For instance, easily understood manuals and lectures should be prepared and delivered to customs officers at all levels.

The secretariats of the various integration units need to coordinate closely with local chambers of commerce. Short, practically oriented seminars should be held for business people and imaginative information brochures widely distributed. Civil servants of geographically enormous integration associations, like LAIA, should not stay rooted at the headquarters, but must go out into the field and talk with entrepreneurs in Cali (Colombia), Concepción (Chile), and Maracaibo (Venezuela); obviously, the dialogue should be two way.

## INTEGRATION AND THE LAW

### Unification of Law in Integrated Regions

Recently, Dr. Sunaryati Hartono of Indonesia issued a call for the nations of ASEAN to create uniform laws in the fields of corporations, foreign investment, and trade.[13] Pointing out that the legal systems of the different ASEAN members represent a melange of Dutch civil law, Adat laws (ethnic group norms), Islamic law, Spanish civil law, German civil law (Thailand), and British common law, as well as recent legal influence from the United States, she concluded that these five nations have ended up with confusing and often conflicting rules. For instance, the term *public corporation* means one thing in some countries and something else in other ASEAN members. The same is true of the term *foreign enterprise*. Rather than continuing their separate legal development, these nations need to design a special legal regime for ASEAN trade and commerce.

This appeal is one that should not be limited to ASEAN; other integration units may also find it prudent gradually to begin a process of legal harmonization. Probably the greatest difficulty would be encountered in the African organizations where the heritage of French civil law would confront that of British common law. So complex will be this task that it may have to be approached quite gradually. On the other hand, the members of LAIA and ANCOM started off with a similar Ibero-French legal system. As various Latin American nations have modernized specific laws, divergence has occurred. Nonetheless, with basically the same legal foundation, these nations should be able to achieve some harmony in fields crucial for regional trade.

COMECON's success in unifying much of intraregional sales law is a major accomplishment. For those who reject that model, the United Nations International Sales Convention offers another alternative.

### Legal Education

Enforcement of the elaborate network of rules flowing from integration structures requires involvement of the legal profession. Practising lawyers should become familiar with the detailed workings of the complicated tariff regulations, the investment laws, and the industrial policies. Both judges and lawyers will have to be able to determine when an incorrect duty has been levied. Attorneys and courts must ensure that importers, exporters, and other business people can depend on litigation for appropriate enforcement of their rights under these associations. Law students should be taught about the practical impact of these new systems on their commercial law.

Lawyers' associations and law schools might organize one-day conferences to provide attorneys with the knowledge they need to apply these new rules. Scholars familiar with the intricacies of a particular association could greatly assist in this implementation process by writing short articles that explain the workings of the system to practitioners and judges. The legal profession, in drafting these various treaties and laws, has proved itself innovative and imaginative. That same profession is now called upon to make these laws effective by training the practitioners, officials, and the judiciary.

### Exchange of Legal Information Among Associations

Although these Third World associations have devised sophisticated, multifaceted schemes to achieve integration, the mechanisms created in one part of the world may be unknown in other sections of the globe.

To some extent language is the culprit. For instance, COMECON's work is conducted in Russian, a language not accessible to experts in many nations. The Institute for Integration of Latin America, under assistance from the Inter-American Development Bank, has prepared a wealth of studies and materials. Most of this information, however, is in Spanish, a language understood by few in Africa or Asia.

Thus, there is a genuine need to create channels whereby the knowledge and experience gained by one integration organization can be shared by others. Lawyers, professors, and jurists from one region should be given an opportunity to make on-site studies at these associations in other areas. Key reports and papers should be translated into a world language, comprehensible to a larger public.

## INCREASING SOUTH-SOUTH LINKAGES

It is not clear how much collective bargaining power has been gained by these integration units. ASEAN has used its joint authority in negotiating with the EEC, Japan, and the United States. It would appear useful for Third World nations to combine their efforts. In seeking concessions from the industrialized world, LAIA certainly presents a stronger negotiating party than Bolivia. Should LAIA, CARICOM, and CACM all join forces someday, they might constitute a formidable bloc.

Perhaps some good will come out of the present world crisis. It could be the force that compels the Third World to reduce its dependence on the industrialized North and to multiply South-South trade and investment links. In looking at the Latin American situation, the Chilean economist Ricardo Ffrench Davis concludes that the present crisis "instead of being a negative factor, should encourage implementation through LAIA of the regional system of margins of preference as a device designed to enhance intra-regional export opportunities."[14] This same reasoning applies equally to poor regions in Asia and Africa.

An encouraging development in the new LAIA treaty is that it permits member nations to conclude integration agreements with outside nations and integration organizations. This new flexibility creates the possiblity of, for example, an agreement between ANCOM and ASEAN or between Venezuela and the CACM.

The division of the Third World into these various trading blocs may create problems for those countries that have been left out, such as the

Dominican Republic. Taiwan and South Korea are in the anomalous position of being newly industrialized nations whose prosperity is threatened by the increasing protectionism of the developed world. It may therefore be appropriate for Third World integration units to form some special trade and investment linkages with these left out countries. CARICOM, for instance, might create a free trade association with Panama in which case a common market (CARICOM) would be located inside a free trade association. Taiwan and ASEAN might work out preferential tariff arrangements for selected products.

Another issue today is whether some type of integration—perhaps limited—can be accomplished among selected socialist nations and capitalist countries. An observer might conclude that the profound differences in their forms of integration constitute an insurmountable obstacle to integration. So, it is argued, Tanzania with its socialist-oriented economy could never have successfully integrated with Kenya, a basically market economy. Does this mean that Nicaragua, whose leaders expect to reserve a significant portion of their economy for the planned sector, cannot effectively participate as a member of the Central American Common Market?

M. Maksimova of the Soviet Union would answer such questions, "no." She writes:

> In the modern world there are tasks demanding collective effort—those of developing to the utmost international economic ties, of promoting genuinely equal and mutually advantageous co-operation among all countries, irrespective of socio-economic system. This task applies equally to the socialist, the capitalist and the developing countries, whether within integration groupings or outside them. It presupposes joint action both on a bilateral and multilateral basis, and many diverse forms of ties and cooperation between countries and integration groups of countries in the common interests of all peoples. I am referring, above all, to the interests of ensuring peaceful life all over the world, of raising the material and cultural standards of the broad masses of people in all countries, the successful solution of problems facing mankind in the fields of energy, natural resources, environmental protection, the wiping out of famine and disease, the exploration of outer space and the oceans, the full development of the forces of production.[15]

COMECON members are already involved in 12 joint projects in Iraq, 13 in India, and 30 in Egypt. Usually, such multilateral cooperation has consisted of equipment and technical know-how flowing from Eastern Europe with the resources and labor furnished by the developing nation.[16]

Moreover, in recent years several members of COMECON have changed their attitudes toward foreign investment. Vietnam,[17] Cuba,[18] Hungary,[19] Rumania,[20] and Yugoslavia[21] have all enacted legislation authorizing joint ventures with private foreign companies. Likewise, it will be recalled that Argentina has now concluded a LAIA "partial scope" agreement with Cuba. Thus, an entrepreneur investing in Cuba may secure access to the larger COMECON market and, at least, one LAIA member. Perhaps the time may soon come when access to the entire Latin American market will be added.

New forms of integration will have to be developed for the future. The United Kingdom and the People's Republic of China have concluded their agreement on Hong Kong.[22] Without doubt, some innovative arrangements will result as that market economy adjusts to living inside the command system of China. Will some as yet unimagined integration scheme permit renewed ties between Taiwan and the People's Republic of China under circumstances that save face and preserve important values on both sides? Finally, can the EEC develop some new techniques for working with COMECON in ways that would enrich both groups? One may certainly hope so. In such a case the integration models will have evolved to offer the world renewed prospects for reducing international tension by providing greater access to material well-being for all.

## NOTES

1. U. S. Const., art. I, § 10.

2. Ibid., art. I, § 8.

3. "Editorial: La Integración Regional Como Respuesta Latinoamericana a la Crisis Económica," *Integración Latinoamericana* (Buenos Aires: INTAL, March 1984), no. 88, p. 2 [hereinafter cited as "Editorial"]; and Julio Berlinski and Heber Camelo y María Pazmiño, "Importaciones Exentas de Araceles en Algunos Países de la ALADI," *Integración Latinoamericana* (Buenos Aires: INTAL, April 1984), no. 89, p. 3.

4. Enrique Sabatté, *Selection of Technological Families for Complementary Industrial Cooperation in ASEAN Countries: Project Findings and Recommendations* (Unpublished report for United Nations Industrial Development Organization, February 8, 1979), pp. 44, 55.

5. "Editorial," supra, note 3, p. 3; and see César Peñaranda C., "Estrategia para La Integración Económica en América Latina," ibid. p. 27.

6. *Tax Incentives For Industry in Less Developed Countries* (Cambridge, Mass.: Harvard International Program in Taxation, 1963), p. 65; and George E. Lent, "Tax Incentives in Developing Countries," in *Readings on Taxation in Developing Countries*, 3rd ed., eds. R. Bird and O. Oldman, (Baltimore, Johns Hopkins University Press, 1975), p. 363.

7. Brazil Decree Law 37 of November 18, 1966, art. 18, (1966) 7 Coleção (legis.) 56, D. O. November 21, 1966.

8. See Eduardo White, "Cooperación Empresarial entre Países Semi Industrializados: El Caso de Argentina-Brasil," *Integración Latinoamericana* (Buenos Aires: INTAL, May 1984), no. 90, p. 19.

9. 19 U.S.C. §§ 2461, 2462, and 2464 (1974, as amended 1979).

10. Argentine Foreign Investments Law of August 19, 1976, No. 21, 382 (1976); C Anales 2071, as amended by Law of April 25, 1980, No. 22, 208 (1980) B Anales 1024; see also Enrique Dahl, "Argentina's System of Foreign Investments," *Fordham International Law Journal* 6 (1982): 49.

11. The U. S. prototype provides that each nation "shall permit such investments to be established and acquired on terms and conditions that accord treatment no less favorable than the treatment it accords in like situations to investments of its own nationals or companies or to nationals and companies of any third country, whichever is most favorable." Treaty Between the United States and _____ Concerning the Reciprocal Encouragement and Protection of Investments, January 21, 1983, art. II, ¶1, Office of United States Trade Representative, Press Release

(January 13, 1982); see also "Note, Developing a Model Bilateral Investment Treaty," *Law & Policy in International Business* 15 (Washington, D.C.: Georgetown University Law School, 1983): 15.

12. See Beverly May Carl, "Latin American Antitrust Laws and Their Equivalents: Impact on Reorganization and Licensing by Transnational Enterprises," in *Reorganization of Multinational Enterprises, Legal and Tax Aspects*, Alain A. Levasseur and Enrique Dahl, eds., (University Press of America, Baltimore, in press).

13. "Editorial: El Problema de la Deuda Externa en América Latina: Tendencias y Perspectivas en 1983," *Integración Latinoamericana* (September 1983), no. 83, p. 16.

14. "Legal Development and the Promotion of Intra ASEAN Trade and Investment," speech by Dr. Sunaryati Hartono, as reported in "Asean Commercial Law Urged for Region," *The Bulletin* (Manila), April 17, 1985.

15. As quoted in Bela Balassa, *Types of Economic Integration* (Washington, D.C.: World Bank reprint series No. 69, 1976), p. 36. Throughout the 1970s, various representatives of ANCOM met with COMECON officials to explore possible linkages between the two organizations. See Carlos Muñis Ortega, *La Integración Economica de los Países Socialistas: el CAME en la Economía Mundial* (Bogota, Colombia, Ediciones Librería del Profesional, published after 1982), pp. 147–49.

16. United Nations Conference on Trade and Development, *Multilateral Schemes of the Countries Members of the Council for Mutual Economic Assistance and Opportunities for Developing Countries in Trade and Economic Co-operation Resulting from the Implementaton of These Schemes*, TD/B/AC.23/3/rev. 1 (1978), p. 11.

17. "Vietnam, Regulation of Foreign Investments, Decree 115/CP," (April 18, 1977); see also Tang Thi Thanh Trai Le, "The Foreign Investment Code of the Socialist Republic of Vietnam," *International Lawyer* 13 (1979); 329.

18. "Cuba, Legislative Decree No. 50 on Economic Association between Cuban and Foreign Entities," (February 15, 1982), reprinted in *International Legal Materials* 21 (Washington, D.C.: American Society of International Law, 1982): 1106.

19. "Hungary, Decree on Economic Association with Foreign Participation" (October 3, 1972), reprinted in *International Legal Materials* 12 (1973): 989.

20. "Rumania, Decree on Joint Enterprises," (1973), reprinted in *International Legal Materials* 12 (1973): 65.

21. Yugoslavia, Law on Investment of Resources of Foreign Persons in Domestic Organizations of Associated Labor," (1978 as amended through 1984), reprinted in *International Legal Materials* 24 (1985): 318.

22. "Joint Declaration of the Government of the United Kingdom of Great Britain and Northern Ireland and the Government of the People's Republic of China on the Questions of Hong Kong," (Beijing: Foreign Language Press, 1984).

# APPENDIXES:

SELECTED PROVISIONS FROM
INTEGRATION AGREEMENTS

## APPENDIX A-1
## ASEAN: Joint Communiqué, 1st Ministerial Meeting 1967
## (The ASEAN Declaration)

. . .

The Presidium Minister for Political Affairs/Minister for Foreign Affairs of Indonesia, the Deputy Prime Minister of Malaysia, the Secretary for Foreign Affairs of the Philippines, the Minister for Foreign Affairs of Singapore and the Minister of Foreign Affairs of Thailand:

. . .

## DO HEREBY DECLARE:
*FIRST*, the establishment of an Association for Regional Co-operation among the countries of South-East Asia to be known as the Association of South-East Asian Nations (ASEAN).

. . .

5. To collaborate more effectively for the greater utilization of their agriculture and industries, the expansion of their trade, including the study of the problems of international commodity trade, the improvement of their transportation and communication facilities and the raising of the living standards of their peoples;

. . .

Reprinted from Michael Haas, ed., *Basic Documents of Asian Regional Organizations*, vol. 6 (Dobbs Ferry, New York: Oceana, 1979).

## ASEAN: Treaty of Amity and Cooperation in Southeast Asia, 1976

### 2. Industrial Cooperation
    (i) Member states shall cooperate to establish large-scale ASEAN industrial plants, particularly to meet regional requirements of essential commodities.

    (ii) Priority shall be given to projects which utilize the available materials in the member states, contribute to the increase of food production, increase foreign exchange earnings or save foreign exchange and create employment.

### 3. Cooperation in Trade
    (1) Member states shall cooperate in the fields of trade in order to promote development and growth of new production and trade and to improve the trade structures of individual states and among countries of ASEAN conducive to further development and to safeguard and increase their foreign exchange earnings and reserves.

    (ii) Member states shall progress towards the establishment of preferential trading arrangements as a long term objective on a basis deemed to be at any particular time appropriate through rounds of negotiations subject to the unanimous agreement of member states.

    (iii) The expansion of trade among member states shall be facilitated through cooperation in ASEAN industrial projects.

    (iv) Member states shall accelerate joint efforts to improve access to markets outside ASEAN for their raw materials and finished products by seeking the elimination of all trade barriers in those markets, developing new usage for these products and in adopting common approaches and actions in dealing with regional groupings and individual economic powers.

    (v) Such efforts shall also lead to cooperation in the field of technology and production methods in order to increase the production and to improve the quality of export products, as well as to develop new export products with a view to diversifying exports.

### 4. Joint Approach to International Commodity Problems and other World Economic Problems
    (i) The principle of ASEAN cooperation on trade shall also be reflected on a priority basis in joint approaches to international commodity problems and other world economic problems such as the reform of international

Reprinted from Michael Haas, ed., *Basic Documents of Asian Regional Organizations*, vol. 6 (Dobbs Ferry, New York: Oceana, 1979).

monetary system and transfer of real resources. in the United Nations and other relevant multilateral fora, with a view to contributing to the establishment of the New International Economic Order.

(ii) Member states shall give priority to the stabilization and increase of export earning of these commodities produced and exported by them through commodity agreements including bufferstock scheme and other means.

. . .

# APPENDIX A-3
## ASEAN: Agreement on ASEAN Preferential Trading Arragements (February 24, 1977)

### ARTICLE 3

The Contracting States agree to adopt the following instruments for Preferential Trading Arrangements: long-term quantity contracts; purchase finance support at preferential interest rates; preference in procurement by Government entities; extension of tariff preferences; liberalization of non-tariff measures on a preferential basis; and other measures.

### ARTICLE 4

The Preferential Trading Arrangements shall be applied to Basic Commodities particularly rice and crude oil; products of the ASEAN industrial projects; products for the expansion of intra-ASEAN trade; and other products of interest to Contracting States.

. . .

### ARTICLE 7

1. Pre-tender notices for international tenders in respect of procurement by Government entities should be sent to the Missions of the Contracting States in the relevant ASEAN capital.

2. Subject to such provisions as may be embodied in supplementary agreements on Government procurement and to the rules of origin to be subsequently decided, Contracting States shall accord each other a preferential margin of 2½% which should not exceed US$40,000 worth of preferences per tender in respect of international tenders for Government procurement of goods and auxilliary services from untied loans submitted by ASEAN countries vis-a-vis non-ASEAN countries.

3. The preferential margin should be applied on the basis of the lowest evaluated and acceptable tender.

### ARTICLE 8

1. An effective ASEAN margin of tariff preference should be accorded on a product-by-product basis.

---

Reprinted from *Malaya Law Review* (Kuala Lumpur) 20 (1978): 415.

2. Where tariff preferences have been negotiated on multilateral or bilateral basis, the concessions so agreed should be extended to all Contracting States on an ASEAN most-favoured-nation basis, except where special treatment is accorded to products of ASEAN industrial projects.

3. In the negotiations on tariff preferences, considerations for the balancing of preferences should take into account the possibility of using other instruments of preferential trading arrangements.

4. The effective ASEAN margin of tariff preferences to be accorded to the selected products should take into account existing levels of tariffs in the respective Contracting States.

• • •

## ARTICLE 10

1. Nothwithstanding the provisions of Articles 5, 6, 7, 8, 9 and 15 of this Agreement, the Contracting States shall establish special preferential trading arrangements in respect of products of ASEAN industrial projects which shall be embodied in supplementary agreements. Such supplementary agreements shall include the provision that trade preferences shall be extended exclusively to the products of the ASEAN industrial projects within agreed time frames and subject to such other conditions as may be set forth in the supplementary agreements.

2. The products of the ASEAN Industrial Complementation Projects shall qualify for preferential trading arrangements, provided that these individual industrial complementation schemes or projects fall within the guidelines approved by competent Committees of ASEAN Economic Ministers and that the specific schemes or projects are approved by the Committee on Industry, Minerals and Energy.

## CHAPTER IV
## MAINTENANCE OF CONCESSIONS

## ARTICLE 11

Contracting States shall not diminish or nullify any of the concessions as agreed upon through the application of any new charge or measure restricting trade, except in cases provided for in this Agreement.

## CHAPTER V
## EMERGENCY MEASURES

### ARTICLE 12

1. If, as a result of the implementation of this Agreement, imports of a particular product eligible for Preferential Trading Arrangements are increasing in such a manner as to cause or threaten to cause serious injury to sectors producing like or similar products in the importing Contracting States, the importing Contracting State may suspend provisionally and without discrimination, the preferences included in this Agreement.

2. Without prejudice to existing international obligations, a Contracting State, which finds it necessary to institute or intensify quantitative restrictions or other measures limiting imports with a view to forestalling the threat of or stopping a serious decline in its monetary reserves or limiting exports due to serious decline in supplies shall endeavour to do so in a manner which safeguards the value of the concessions agreed upon.

3. Where, however, emergency measures are taken in pursuance to this Article, immediate notice of such action must be given to the Committee referred to in Article 13 and such action may be the subject of consultations as provided for in Article 14.

. . .

# APPENDIX A-4
## ASEAN: Rules of Origin for the Asean Preferential Trading Arrangements
### (1977)

For determining the origin of products eligible for preferential concessions under the Agreement on ASEAN Preferential Trading Arrangements, the following Rules shall be applied:

RULES 1. ORIGINATING PRODUCTS—Product covered by preferential trading arrangements within the framework of this Agreement, imported into the territory of a Contracting State from another Contracting State which are consigned directly within the meaning of Rule 5 hereof, shall be eligible for preferential concessions if they conform to the origin requirement under any one of the following conditions:

(a) Products wholly produced or obtained in the exporting Contracting State as defined in Rule 2; or
(b) Products not wholly produced or obtained in the exporting Contracting State, provided that the said products are eligible under Rule 3 or Rule 4.

RULE 2. WHOLLY PRODUCED OR OBTAINED—Within the meaning of Rule 1(a), the following shall be considered as wholly produced or obtained in the exporting Contracting State:

(a) mineral products extracted from its soil, its water or its seabeds;
(b) agricultural products harvested there;
(c) animals born and raised there;
(d) products obtained from animals referred to in paragraph (c) above;
(e) products obtained by hunting or fishing conducted there;
(f) products of sea fishing and other marine products taken from the sea by its vessels;
(g) products processed and/or made on board its factory ships exclusively from products referred to in paragraph (f) above;
(h) used articles collected here, fit only for the recovery of raw materials;
(i) waste and scrap resulting from manufacturing operations conducted there;
(j) goods produced there exclusively from the products referred to in paragraph (a) to (i) above.

---

Reprinted from *Malaya Law Review* (Kuala Lumpur) 20 (1978): 415.

### RULE 3. NOT WHOLLY PRODUCED OR OBTAINED

(a) (i) Subject to sub-paragraph (ii) below, for the purpose of implementing the provisions of Rule 1(b) and subject to the provisions of Rule 4, products worked on and processed as a result of which the total value of the materials, parts or produce originating from non-ASEAN countries or of undetermined origin used does not exceed 50% of the FOB value of the products produced or obtained and the final process of manufacture is performed within the territory of the exporting Contracting State.

    (ii) In respect of Indonesia, the percentage referred to in sub-paragraph (i) above is 40%. On certain categories of manufactured products to be agreed upon from time to time, the requirement of 50% of non-ASEAN content may apply.

(b) In respect of the ASEAN industrial projects, the per cent criterion of Rule 3(a) may be waived.

(c) The value of the non-originating materials parts or produce shall be:—

    (1) The CIF value at the time of importation of the products or importation can be proven; or

    (2) The earliest ascertainable price paid for the products of undetermined origin in the territory of the Contracting State where the working or processing takes place.

### RULE 4. CUMULATIVE RULE OF ORIGIN—

Products which comply with origin requirements provided for in Rule 1 and which are used in a Contracting State as inputs for a finished product eligible for preferential treatment in another Contracting State/States shall be considered as a product originating in the Contracting State where working or processing of the finished product has taken place provided that the aggregate ASEAN content of the final product is not less than 60%.

### RULE 5. DIRECT CONSIGNMENT—

The following shall be considered as directly consigned from the exporting Contracting State to the importing Contracting State:

(a) if the products are transported without passing through the territory of any other non-ASEAN country;

(b) the products whose transport involves transit through one or more intermediate non-ASEAN countries with or without transhipment or temporary storage in such countries, provided that:

    (1) The transit entry is justified for geographical reason or by considerations related exclusively to transport requirement;

(2) the products have not entered into trade or consumption there; and

(3) the products have not undergone any operation there other than unloading and reloading or any operation required to keep them in good condition.

## RULE 6. TREATMENT OF PACKING

(a) Where for purposes of assessing customs duties a Contracting State treats products separately from their packing, it may also, in respect of its imports consigned from another Contracting State, determine separately the origin of such packing.

(b) Where paragraph (a) above is not applied, packing shall be considered as forming a whole with the products and no part of any packing required for their transport or storage shall be considered as having been imported from outside the ASEAN region when determining the origin of the products as a whole.

RULE 7. CERTIFICATE OF ORIGIN—A claim that products shall be accepted as eligible for preferential concession shall be supported by a Certificate of Origin issued by a government authority designated by the exporting Contracting State and notified to the other Contracting States in accordance with the Certification Procedures to be developed and approved by the Committee on Trade and Tourism.

· · ·

# APPENDIX A-5
## ASEAN: Basic Agreement on Asean Industrial Complementation
### (June 18, 1981)

## ARTICLE I: GENERAL PROVISIONS

. . .

3. A participating country in an AIC package is an ASEAN country allocated a specific product or products in such an AIC package. There should be at least four participating ASEAN countries in an AIC package, unless otherwise recommended by COIME and approved by the AEM.

. . .

## ARTICLE IV:
### PRIVILEGES AND OBLIGATIONS UNDER THE ASEAN INDUSTRIAL COMPLEMENTATION PROGRAMME

1. An existing product in an AIC package shall, from the date of AEM final approval of such AIC package, enjoy exclusivity privileges for a period of two (2) years.

2. A product is deemed to be an Existing product in an AIC package if it is already being manufactured in ASEAN at the time COIME considers that product for possible allocation. Any product not covered by the above mentioned definition of Existing product shall be deemed New.

3. A new AIC product in an AIC Package shall enjoy exclusivity privileges for a period of 3 years from the actual date of start-up or from the target date of start-up agreed at the time of AEM approval of such AIC package, which ever date comes first. In exceptional cases where a New AIC product in an AIC package requires a longer period of exclusivity, the AEM may consider extending the period of exclusivity by another year.

4. Exclusivity shall mean:

   i. For the country allocated a particular product, it would be entirely at its discretion as to how it would organize its production facilities to meet the ASEAN requirements for that product.

---

Reprinted from *International Legal Materials* 22 (Washington, D.C.: American Society of International Law, 1983): 1229.

ii. For the other participating countries, such countries cannot set-up new production facilities or expand existing ones to make the same product as that of the country for which such product was allocated unless 75% of its production is for export outside the ASEAN region.

iii. Notwithstanding paragraph 4 (ii) above, the other participating countries' firmly planned projects to produce Existing products in ASEAN and which products have been allocated to another country as part of the AIC package, shall be allowed to proceed. For this purpose a firmly planned project refers to that which has already obtained written government approval or has already opened letters of credit for the importation of machinery and equipment or has already commissioned the fabrication of such machinery and equipment.

iv. For purposes of paragraph 4 (ii), a production facility is deemed to have been set up when it is in commercial operation.

5. The products in an AIC package shall qualify for preferences, in accordance with the Agreement on ASEAN-PTA.

6. During the period of exclusivity, special preferences outside the Agreement on ASEAN Preferential Trading Arrangements (PTA) can be granted such as mandatory sourcing and recognition of local content, applicable only to specific countries.

7. Privileges and obligations shall only apply to participating countries.

. . .

# APPENDIX A-6
## ASEAN: Basic Agreement on Asean Industrial Joint Ventures (1983)

## ARTICLE I

. . .

1. An ASEAN INDUSTRIAL JOINT VENTURE (AIJV) product is any processed or manufactured product which is included in the final list of AIJV products approved by the ASEAN Economic Ministers (AEM) and referred to in Article II, paragraph 3.

2. An AIJV product may be an existing product or a new product;
   a) An existing product is one which is being processed or manufactured in any of the participating countries at the time of its inclusion in the final list.
   b) Any product not covered by the definition of an existing product is a new product.

3. An AIJV is any entity which:

   a) produces an AIJV product in any of the participating countries;
   b) has equity participation from nationals of at least two participating countries;
   c) satisfies the equity ownership provisions specified in paragraph 5 of this Article.

4. With respect to a particular AIJV product, a participating country is an ASEAN member country which has indicated its intention to participate by way of providing tariff preference as provided for Article III for that AIJV product in the final list approved by the AEM. An ASEAN member country which has not indicated its intention to so participate is a non-participating country with respect to that particular AIJV product.

5. A minimum ASEAN equity ownership of 51 per cent shall be required for any proposed AIJV except that this requirement shall not apply to an entity in any of the following cases:

   a) where the participating countries in a proposed AIJV product agree to a higher equity participation by non-ASEAN investors;

Reprinted from *International Legal Materials* 22 (Washington, D.C.: American Society of International Law, 1983): 1235.

b) where more than 50 per cent of the product produced by such entity will be exported to non-ASEAN markets;

c) where the product is already being produced by an entity in a participating country prior to its inclusion in the final list; or

d) where an entity has already been approved by a participating country to produce that product prior to the inclusion of the product in the final list.

6. The investors in an AIJV shall be free to locate their projects in any of the participating countries.

7. The approval by the AEM of the final list carries with it the pre-commitment to extend a minimum 50 per cent margin of tariff preference to AIJV products by participating countries as provided for in Article III paragraphs 1 and 6.

8. Non-participating countries in an AIJV product shall waive tariff preferences extended under Article III subject to the conditions therein stated.

. . .

## ARTICLE II

1. The Committee on Industry, Minerals and Energy (COIME) shall invite nominations for AIJV products from the ASEAN-CCI [ASEAN Chamber of Commerce and Industry] and ASEAN member countries. All nominations for existing AIJV products shall be accompanied by details of existing production facilities, such as ownership, location and production capacities. These shall be compiled at a COIME meeting into a tentative list of AIJV products.

. . .

3. The final list shall be submitted to the AEM for approval and thereafter be made available to the ASEAN-CCI and national Chambers of Commerce and Industry in ASEAN member countries.

4. For new AIJV products, interested parties shall be given six months from the date the final list is approved by the AEM to obtain approval from the appropriate government agencies to produce such products.

5. At the end of the stipulated six month period, all participating countries shall inform COIME of those applications for the production of new AIJV products, for which approval has been granted. Any product for which approval

has not been granted within the stipulated six month period shall be automatically deleted from the list.

6. COIME shall inform all member countries of those new AIJV products for which approval has been granted.

7. For existing AIJV products, interested parties shall seek their respective governments' confirmation that their entities qualify as AIJVs under this Agreement, after the inclusion of their AIJV products in the final list approved by the AEM.

. . .

## ARTICLE III
### PRIVILEGES AND OBLIGATIONS UNDER THE
### ASEAN INDUSTRIAL JOINT VENTURE PROGRAMME

*New AIJV Products*

1. Where an application for the production of an AIJV product has been approved by any participating country, and due notification thereof has been given to COIME, all participating countries shall extend a minimum margin of tariff preference of 50 per cent for that AIJV product within 90 days of its commercial production.

2. The tariff preference described in Article III paragraph 1 shall apply, during the initial three year period, only to AIJVs in participating countries. The three year period shall commence from the actual date of commercial production of the AIJV product, or upon expiry of 30 months from the date the AEM approved the inclusion of that product in the final list, whichever is earlier.

3. Non-participating countries shall waive their rights under Chapter II, Article 8, paragraph 2 of the ASEAN PTA for the three year period. Participating countries shall also similarly waive their rights, during the three year period, in respect of entities which are not AIJVs within their countries but produce the same AIJV products. At the end of the initial three year period for a given AIJV product, non-participating countries shall be deemed to be participating countries and shall extend the same margin of tariff preference for that AIJV product. Furthermore, after the initial three year period, any entity in any ASEAN member country which produced the same AIJV product, irrespective of whether or not it qualifies as an AIJV, shall enjoy the same margin of tariff preference.

4. In the event that there is only one approved project for a new AIJV product by the end of the stipulated six month period, the participating countries shall grant to that AIJV exclusivity privileges. Exclusivity privileges shall continue for a period of three years commencing from the actual data of commercial production of the AIJV product or upon the expiry of 30 months from the date the AEM approved the inclusion of that product in the final list, whichever is earlier. In the event that there is more than one approved project for a new AIJV product, exclusivity privileges shall not be granted.

5. Exclusivity privileges in this Agreement shall mean that during the exclusivity period of three years, the participating countries cannot set up new production facilities for the same product, other than the approved project, unless 75 per cent of its production is for export to non-ASEAN countries. A production facility is deemed to have been set up when it is in commercial production.

*Existing AIJV Products*

6. The participating countries shall extend to an existing AIJV product the same tariff preferences as provided for in Article III paragraph 1 within 90 days from the date the AEM approves the inclusion of that product in the final list.

7. The tariff preferences described in Article III paragraph 6 shall apply, during the initial three year period, only to AIJVs in participating countries. The three year period shall commence from the actual date of implementation of tariff preferences.

8. Non-participating countries shall waive their rights under Chapter II, Article 8, paragraph 2 of the ASEAN PTA for the three year period. Participating countries shall also similarly waive their rights, during the three period, in respect of entities which are not AIJVs within their country but produce the same AIJV products. At the end of the initial three year period for a given AIJV product, non-participating countries shall be deemed to be participating countries and shall extend the same margin of tariff preference for that AIJV product. Furthermore, after the initial three year period, any entity in any ASEAN member country which produces the same AIJV product, irrespective of whether or not it qualifies as an AIJV, shall enjoy the same margin of tariff preference.

9. Existing AIJV products shall not be granted exclusivity privileges.

· · ·

# APPENDIX A-7
## ASEAN: Supplementary Agreement to Amend the Basic Agreement on Asean Industrial Joint Ventures (November 7, 1983)

. . .

NOW THE PARTIES HAVE AGREED AS FOLLOWS:

(1) That the term "three year period" referred to in paragraphs 2 and 7 of Article III of the Agreement be amended to read as "four year period". The amended version of paragraphs 2 and 7 of Article III of the Agreement is to read as follows:

"The tariff preference described in Article III paragraph 1 shall apply, during the initial four year period, only to AIJVs in participating countries. The four year period shall commence from the actual date of commercial production of the AIJV product, or upon expiry of 30 months from the date the AEM approved the inclusion of that product in the final list, whichever is earlier.

The tariff preferences described in Article III paragraph 6 shall apply, during the initial four year period, only to AIJVs in participating countries. The four year period shall commence from the actual date of implementation of tariff preferences."

(2) That paragraphs 3 and 8 of Article III of the Agreement be amended to read as follows:

"Non-participating countries shall waive their rights under Chapter II, Article 8 paragraph 2 of the ASEAN PTA for the four year period. Non-participating countries need not extend a margin of preference to participating countries on AIJV products. Non-participating countries, which so desire and upon notification and concurrence of COIME, may become participating countries at any time and shall extend the same margin of tariff preference for that AIJV product.

Participating countries shall waive their right under Chapter II, Article 8 paragraph 2 of the ASEAN PTA for the four year period in respect of entities which are not AIJVs but produce the same products within their countries. After the four year waiver period for an AIJV product, any entity in any member country which produces that AIJV product, irrespective of whether it qualifies as an AIJV or not, shall enjoy the margin of tariff preference in the participating countries for that particular AIJV product."

. . .

Reprinted from *International Legal Materials* 22 (Washington, D.C.: American Society of International Law, 1983): 1243.

# ECCAS: Treaty for the Establishment of the Economic Community of Central African States (October 19, 1983)

## ARTICLE 6
### Procedures for establishing the Community

1. The Economic Community of Central African States shall be established progressively over a twelve year-period subdivided into three four year-stages.

2. Each stage shall have allotted to it a schedule of actions to be undertaken and pursued concurrently, as follows:

> (a) first stage: stability of the fiscal and customs regime existing at the date of entry into force of the Treaty, and the carrying out of studies to determine the timetable for the gradual removal of tariff and non-tariff obstacles to intra-Community trade; setting a timetable for increases or decreases in the custom tariffs of Member States in adaptation to a common external tariff;
>
> (b) second stage: setting up a free trade zone (application of the timetable for the gradual elimination of tariff and non-tariff obstacles to intra-Community trade);
>
> (c) third stage: establishment of the customs union (adoption of the common external tariff).

. . .

## COURT OF JUSTICE

## ARTICLE 16
### Establishment and powers

1. There is established a Court of Justice of the Community.

2. The Court of Justice shall be responsible for observance of the law in the interpretation and application of this Treaty and shall decide disputes submitted to it under this Treaty.

3. The Court of Justice shall accordingly:

> (a) oversee the legality of the decisions, directives and regulations of Community institutions;

Reprinted from *International Legal Materials* 23 (Washington, D.C.: American Society of International Law, 1984): 947.

(b) decide on appeals lodged by Member States of the Conference on the grounds of lack of jurisdiction, exceeding jurisdiction and infringement of the substance of the provisions of this Treaty;

(c) make interlocutory decisions on:

- the interpretation of this Treaty;
- the effectiveness of the decisions, directives and regulations formulated by Community institutions;

(d) give advisory opinions on any legal matter at the request of the Conference or Council.

4.  Powers to deal with other disputes may be granted to the Court by decisions taken by the Conference by virtue of this Treaty.

## ARTICLE 17
### Decisions of the Court

The decisions of the Court of Justice shall be binding on Member States and institutions of the Community.

## ARTICLE 18
### Organization

The composition, procedure and constitution of the Court and other matters concerning it shall be determined by the Conference.

.   .   .

## ARTICLE 22
### Relationships between the personnel of the General
### Secretariat and the Member States

1.  In the performance of their duties the Secretary-General, the Deputy Secretary-General, the Financial controller, the Accountant and the personnel of the General Secretariat shall be responsible only to the Community.

Accordingly they may neither seek nor accept instructions from any Government or any national or international authority outside the Community.

.   .   .

## LIBERALIZATION OF TRADE

### ARTICLE 27
Customs Union

The Member States agree gradually to establish between them during a transition period, as specified in Article 5 of the pre-Treaty, a Customs Union involving:

(a) the elimination between Member States of customs duties, quotas, trade restrictions and bans and administrative obstacles to trade;

(b) the adoption by Member States of a common external customs tariff.

### ARTICLE 28
Elimination of customs duties between Member States

1. In the first stage Member States shall refrain from the establishment of any new customs duties between them and from increasing those they apply in their mutual trade relations. They shall make regular submissions to the Secretary-General of any information concerning customs duties, for study.

2. At the end of the first stage Member States shall progressively reduce and eventually eliminate customs duties between them in accordance with a programme to be determined by the Conference on a Council proposal.

3. The Conference may at any time on the Council's recommendation decide that any customs duty may be reduced more rapidly or eliminated sooner. However, the Council shall study the question at least twelve months before the date on which such reduction or elimination is to apply to some or all of the goods and to some or all of the Member States and shall submit the result of this study to the Conference for a decision.

### ARTICLE 29
Establishment of a common external customs tariff

1. The Member States agree to the gradual establishment of a common external customs tariff applicable to goods imported into Member States from third countries.

2. At the end of the first stage and during the second stage Member States shall, in accordance with a programme to be proposed by the Council, eliminate differences between customs duties in their respective customs tariffs.

3. At the end of the second stage and during the third stage the Council shall propose to the Conference the adoption of a common customs and statistical nomenclature for all Member States.

## ARTICLE 30
### Treatment of intra-Community trade

1. At the end of the second stage no Member State shall levy customs duties on goods originating from one Member State and transferred to another Member State. Similar considerations shall apply to goods from third countries which are traded in freely in the Member States and transferred from one Member State to another.

2. The definition of this concept of products originating from Member States and the rules governing the application of this Article shall be given in the protocol annexed hereto as Annex I.

3. Goods originating from third-party countries in respect of which import formalities have been completed and customs duties paid in a Member State and which have not benefited from a partial or total rebate of such duties shall be considered as being traded in freely in such a Member State.

4. Member States shall not adopt legislation implying direct or indirect discrimination directed against identical or similar products of any other Member State.

## ARTICLE 31
### Deflection of trade

1. For the purposes of the Article, trade is said to be deflected if:

(a) imports of any particular product by a Member State from another Member State increase significantly; and
(b) this increase in imports causes or would cause serious injury to production which is carried on in the territory of the importing Member State.

2. In case of deflection of trade to the detriment of a Member State resulting from the abusive reduction or elimination of duties and charges levied by another Member State as a result of unregistered trade or for any other reason, the Member State concerned shall submit a report to the Secretary-General who shall submit the matter to the Council.

The Council shall propose the necessary measures to the Conference.

## ARTICLE 32
### Internal taxation

1. Member States shall not apply directly or indirectly to goods originating from Member States and imported into every Member State internal taxation in excess of that applied to like domestic goods and otherwise impose such taxation for the effective protection of such goods.

2. Member States shall progressively eliminate all internal taxation made for the protection of like domestic goods in the same conditions as specified in Article 28 hereof. Where by virtue of obligations under an existing contract entered into by a Member State the latter is unable to comply with the provisions of this Article, the Member State shall duly notify the Council of Ministers of this fact and shall not, subject to Article 31, extend or renew such contract at its expiry.

## ARTICLE 33
### Non-tariff restrictions on intra-Community trade

1. Except as is provided in this Article, each of the Member States undertakes that upon the definitive entry into force of this Treaty it shall gradually relax and eventually remove, at the latest by the end of the second stage and in accordance with paragraph 2 of this Article, prohibitions which apply to the transfer to that State of goods orginating in the other Member States and that, except as may be provided or permitted by this Treaty, it will thereafter refrain from imposing any further restrictions or prohibitions on such goods.

2. Except as is provided in this Article, the Commission shall, after considering proposals submitted to it by the Secretary-General, recommend to the Council for its approval a programme for the gradual relaxation and eventual elimination, at the latest by the end of the second stage, of all the existing quotas, restrictions or prohibitions which apply in a Member State to the import of goods originating in the other Member States, provided that the Council may subsequently decide that all the quotas, restrictions or prohibitions shall be relaxed more rapidly or removed earlier than is approved under the provisions of this paragraph.

3. The special provisions on restrictions, prohibitions, quotas, dumpings, grants and discriminatory practices shall be the subject of a protocol on non-tariff hindrances to trade annexed hereto as Annex II.

## ARTICLE 34
### Exceptions

1.  Notwithstanding the provisions of Article 33, a Member State may, after having given notice to the other Member States of its intention to do so, introduce or continue to impose restriction or prohibitions affecting:

(a) the application of security laws and regulations;

(b) the control of arms, ammunition and other war equipment and military items;

(c) the protection of human, animal or plant health or life or the protection of public morality;

(d) the transfer of gold, silver, platinum and precious stones;

(e) the protection of national treasures of artistic or archaeological value or the protection of industrial and commercial property;

(f) the control of nuclear materials, radio-active products or any other equipment used in the development or exploitation of nuclear energy;

(g) the control of strategic products.

2.  However, such prohibitions or restrictions shall in no case be a means of arbitrary discrimination or a disguised restriction on trade between Member States.

3.  If a Member State encounters balance-of-payments difficulties arising from the application of the provisions of this Chapter, the Member State may, provided that it has taken all reasonable steps to overcome the difficulties, impose for the purpose only of overcoming such difficulties for a specified period to be determined by the Council, quantitative or the like restrictions or prohibitions on goods originating from the other Member States.

4.  For the purpose of protecting an infant or strategic industry a Member State may, provided that it has taken all reasonable steps to protect such industry, impose for the purpose only of protecting such industry for a specified period to be determined by the Council, impose quantitative or the like restrictions or prohibitions, on similar goods originating from the other Member States.

5.  A Member State imposing quantitative or the like restrictions or prohibitions under paragraphs 3, 5 and 6 of this Article shall send a report to the Secretary-General who shall submit the matter to the Council in order to determine for how long such measures may continue.

6.  The Council shall keep under review the operation of any quantitative or

the like restrictions or prohibitions imposed under the provisions of Article 1, 3 and 4 of this Article and take appropriate action.

## ARTICLE 35
### Most-favoured-nation treatment

1. The Member States shall accord to one another in relation to intra-Community trade the most-favoured-nation treatment. In no case shall trade concessions granted to a third country under an agreement with a Member State be more favourable than those applicable under the Treaty.

2. The text of agreements coming under paragraph 1 of this Article shall be sent to the Secretary-General by the States parties to it.

3. Any agreement between a Member State and a third country under which tariff concessions are granted shall not be incompatible with the obligations of that Member State hereunder.

4. No Member State may conclude with any third country an agreement whereby the latter would grant such Member State tariff concessions not granted to the other Member States.

## ARTICLE 36
### Re-export of goods and intra-Community transit

Under this Article the Member States undertake:

(a) to facilitate the re-export of goods among them in accordance with the Protocol on the Re-Export of Goods annexed hereunto as Annex III while awaiting the stage of establishment of the customs union;

(b) to grant freedom of transit through their territories to goods proceeding to or from another Member State in accordance with the provision of the Protocol on Intra-Community Transit annexed hereto as Annex IV.

## ARTICLE 37
### Customs administration

The Member States shall in accordance with the provisions of the Protocol on Customs Co-operation annexed hereto as Annex V take measures to harmonize and standardize their customs regulations and procedures to ensure the effective application of the provisions of this Chapter and to facilitate the movement of goods and services across their frontiers.

## ARTICLE 38
### Deflection of trade arising from barter agreements

1. If a barter agreement in a specific category of articles between a Member State or a physical or legal person thereof and a third country or a physical or legal person thereof leads to a substantial deflection of trade in such category to the detriment of articles imported from and manufactured in any other Member State in favour of articles imported under the barter agreement, the Member State importing such articles shall take effective steps to obviate such deflection.

2. To determine whether a deflection of trade has occurred in a specific category of articles within the meaning of this Article, consideration shall be given to all the relevant trade statistics and other data on the category of articles available for the six months prior to a complaint from a Member State affected concerning deflection of trade and to the average of two comparable six-month periods during the 24 months prior to the first importation of goods under the barter agreement.

3. The Secretary-General shall submit the matter to the Council which shall consider it and submit it to the Conference for a decision.

## ARTICLE 39
### Establishment of the Fund for Compensation for
### Loss of Revenue

1. There is established a Fund for Compensation for Loss of Revenue.

2. A Protocol concerning the resources and use of the Fund is attached hereto as Annex VI.

## CHAPTER V

## FREEDOM OF MOVEMENT, RESIDENCE AND
## RIGHT OF ESTABLISHMENT

## ARTICLE 40

1. Citizens of Member States shall be deemed to be citizens of the Community. Accordingly, Member States agree, in accordance with the Protocol on Freedom of Movement and Right of Establishment annexed hereto as Annex VII, gradually to facilitate procedures for the freedom of movement and right of establishment within the Community.

2. For the purposes of Protocol VII legal persons complying with existing legislation in a Member State shall be deemed to be natural persons.

## CHAPTER VI

## CO-OPERATION IN THE CURRENCY, FINANCIAL AND PAYMENTS FIELD

### ARTICLE 41
### Currency, finance and payments

1. Member States agree to harmonize their currency, financial and payments policies in order to create confidence in their respective currencies, to ensure satisfactory operation of the Community and to further the achievement of its aims and to improve currency and financial co-operation between them and the other African countries.

2. For the purpose of paragraph 1 of this Article the General Secretariat acting in liaison with the particular subregional committees concerned with the Association of Central African Banks shall:

(a) prepare for the Council's attention recommendations on harmonization and the economic and financial policies of Member States:
(b) give continuous attention to the balance-of-payments problems of Member States and undertake any studies relating thereto;
(c) study the development of the economies of Member States;
(d) make recommendations to the Council about the short-term creation of bilateral clearing systems among Member States and the long-term establishment of a multilateral clearing system and monetary union.

3. Under the Protocol on the Clearing House annexed hereto as Annex VIII, Member States undertake to boost intra-Community trading in goods and services through the channel of a compensation chamber.

### ARTICLE 42
### Movement of capital

Upon the entry into force hereof the Conference shall, at the proposal of the Council and subject to the approval of the Consultative Commission, take steps for the progressive co-ordination of national exchange policies with regard to movements of capital between Member States and third States.

. . .

## ECCAS: Protocol on the Rules of Origin

### ANNEX I

## PROTOCOL ON THE RULES OF ORIGIN FOR PRODUCTS TO BE TREATED [TRADED] BETWEEN THE MEMBER STATES OF THE ECONOMIC COMMUNITY OF CENTRAL AFRICAN STATES

. . .

### RULE 2
Rules of Origin of Community goods

1. Goods shall be regarded as originating in a Member State if they are consigned directly from a Member State to a consignee in another Member State and:

(a) they have been produced in the Member States by enterprises which are subject to management by a majority of nationals and to at least 30 per cent equity holding by nationals of the Member States or a Government or Governments of the Member States or institutions, agencies, enterprises or corporations of such Government or Governments; and

(b) where the goods satisfy one of the criteria set out in items (i) to (v) of this subparagraph:

    (i) they have been wholly produced as defined in Rule 3 of this Protocol;

    (ii) they have been produced in the Member States and the c.i.f. value of materials imported from outside the Member States or of undetermined origin which have been used at any stage in the production of the goods does not exceed 60 per cent of the total cost of materials used in the production of the goods;

    (iii) they have been produced in the Member States essentially from materials imported from outside the Member States or of undetermined origin and the value added resulting from the process of production, including the value of the materials, originating from Member States, accounts for at least 45 per cent of the ex-factory cost, provided that the Council may, upon the recommendations of the Commission, raise the percentage of the value added required;

Reprinted from *International Legal Materials* 23 (Washington, D.C.: American Society of International Law, 1984): 966.

(iv) subject to the provisions of subitem (iii) of this subparagraph:

- they have been produced in the Member States and designated in a list by the Council upon the recommendation of the Commission to be goods of particular importance to the economic development of the Member States, and containing not less than 25 per cent of value added; or
- they have been produced in the Member States and are consumed in large quantities throughout the Member States and have been designated in a list by the Council upon the recommendation of the Commission to be goods currently in short supply within the Member States and containing value added of not less than 30 per cent; or
- they have been produced in the Member States and are designated in a list by the Council upon the recommendation of the Commission to be goods whose production is based on local raw materials and which include a local value added of at least 60 per cent;

(v) subject to such exemptions as may be determined by the Council:

- they have been imported into the Member States and have undergone a process of substantial transformation, that is to say, a process of production as a result of which such goods are classified or become classifiable under a CCCN [the applicable system of tariff nomenclature] tariff heading other than the CCCN tariff heading under which they were imported, and are contained in a list to be known as "List A"; or
- they have been imported into the Member States and have not undergone a process of substantial transformation as defined in item (a) of this subparagraph but which in the opinion of the Council shall nevertheless be deemed to have undergone a process of substantial transformation as prescribed in item (a) of this subparagraph, and are contained in a list to be known as "List B".

2. The Council may determine how long the goods contained in the lists referred to in items (iv) and (v) of subparagraph (b) of paragraph 1 of this Rule shall remain on such lists and may from time to time amend them as may be necessary.

3. Raw materials or semi-finished goods originating in accordance with the provisions of this Protocol in any of the Member States and undergoing working or processing either in one or two or in more States shall for the purpose of determining the origin of a finished product be deemed to have originated in the Member States where the final processing or manufacturing takes place.

## RULE 3
### Goods wholly produced in the Member States

For the purposes of item (i) of subparagraph (b) of paragraph 1 of Rule 2 of this Protocol, the following are among the products which shall be regarded as wholly produced in the Member States:

(a) mineral products extracted from the ground or sea-bed or oceans of the Member States;

(b) vegetable products harvested within the Member States;

(c) live animals born or raised within the Member States;

(d) products and by-products obtained within the Member States from live animals referred to in paragraph (c) of this Rule;

(e) products obtained by hunting or fishing conducted within the Member States;

(f) products obtained from sea fishing and other products obtained from the sea and from rivers and lakes within the Member States by vessels registered in a Member State or flying its flag;

(g) local craft articles made exclusively from the products referred to in subparagraphs (a), (b) and (c) of this Rule;

(h) products manufactured in an enterprise where management is by a majority of nationals of one or more Member States exclusively from the products referred to in paragraph (f) of this Rule;

(i) scrap and waste resulting from processing or working operations in Member States and disused articles, provided that such articles have been collected from users within the Member States and are fit only for the recovery of raw materials;

(j) goods produced within the Member States exclusively or mainly from one or both of the following:

    (i)   products referred to in paragraph (a) to (i) of this Rule;

    (ii)  materials containing no element imported from outside the Member States or of undetermined origin.

## RULE 4
### Application of percentage of imported materials and value-added criteria

For the purpose of subparagraph (a) of paragraph 1 and items (ii), (iii) and (iv) of subparagraph (b) of paragraph 1 of Rule 2 of this Protocol:

(a) any material which meets the condition specified in item (i) of subparagraph (b) of paragraph 1 of Rule 2 of this Protocol shall be regarded as containing no elements imported from third States;

(b) the value of any materials imported from third States shall be their c.i.f. value at the place of entry into the customs territory of the Community on clearance for consumption, or on temporary admission at the time of importation into a Member State where they were used in a process of production, less the amount of any transport costs incurred in transit through the Member States;

(c) if the value of any materials imported from third States cannot be determined in accordance with paragraph (b) of this Rule their value shall be the earliest ascertainable price for them in the Member State where they were used in a process of production;

(d) if the origin of any materials cannot be determined, such materials shall be deemed to have been imported from third States and their value shall be the earliest ascertainable price paid for them in the Member State where they were used in a process of production.

## RULE 5
### Processes not conferring origin

Notwithstanding the provisions of items (ii), (iii), (iv) and (v) of sub-paragraph (b) of paragraph 1 of Rule 2 of this Protocol, the following operations and processes shall be considered as insufficient to support a claim that goods originate from a Member State:

(a) packing, bottling, placing in flasks, bags, cases and boxes, fixing on cards or boards and all other simple packing operations;

(b) (i)   simple mixing of ingredients imported from third States;

   (ii)  simple assembly of components and parts imported from third States to consititute a complete product;

   (iii) simple mixing and assembly where the costs of the ingredients, parts and components imported from third States and used in any of such processes exceed 60 per cent of the total costs of the ingredients, parts and components used;

(c) operations to ensure the preservation of merchandise in good condition during transportation and storage such as ventilation, spreading out, drying, freezing, placing in brine, sulphur dioxide or other aqueous solutions, removal of damaged parts and similar operations;

(d) operations for improving the presentation or merchantable quality of merchandise or for packing them for transportation, such as the breaking up or assembly of packages, the sorting and grading of goods and changes of packing;

(e) marking, labelling or affixing other similar distinguishing signs on products or their packages;

(f) simple operations consisting of removal of dust, sifting or screening, sorting, classifying and matching, including the making up of sets of goods, washing, painting and cutting up;

(g) a combination of two or more operations specified in paragraphs (a) to (f) of this Rule;

(h) slaughter of animals.

. . .

# APPENDIX B-3
## ECCAS: Protocol on Non-tariff Hindrances to Trade

## ANNEX II
## PROTOCOL ON NON-TARIFF HINDRANCES TO TRADE

### ARTICLE 2
Quota-fixing, restrictions and prohibitions

Notwithstanding the provisions of Article 33 of the Treaty, a Member State having balance-of-trade difficulties due to imports from another Member State may, provided that it has done everything to overcome such difficulties and given written notification thereof to the Council, the country concerned and the Secretary-General, introduce temporary quota-fixing measures, restrictions or prohibitions or any other equivalent measures on goods originating from such other Member State for a temporary period to be determined by the Council.

### ARTICLE 3
Dumping and grants

1.  The Member States shall prohibit the practice of dumping and exporting subsidized goods within the Community.

2.  Where a Member State is injured by dumping and subsidy practices it may ban the import of the goods benefiting from such practices and originating from one or more Member States. It shall send a report to the Secretary-General of the Community who shall refer the matter to the Council to decide on the action to be taken.

. . .

Reprinted from *International Legal Materials* 23 (Washington, D.C.: American Society of International Law, 1984): 971.

# APPENDIX B-4
## ECCAS: Protocol on the Re-export of Goods

### ANNEX III
## PROTOCOL ON THE RE-EXPORT OF GOODS WITHIN THE ECONOMIC COMMUNITY OF CENTRAL AFRICAN STATES

### ARTICLE 2
### General provisions

1. The Member States agree that re-exports bound for any Member State shall be exempted from the payment of import or export duties in the importing State, provided that this paragraph shall not preclude the levying of normal administrative and service charges applicable to the import or export of similar goods in accordance with their customs laws and regulations.

. . .

### ARTICLE 3
### Refund and remission of duties and taxes

1. Where import duties on goods have been charged and collected by the Importing State, that State shall refund all such duties less import subsidies, if any, to the re-exporter of those goods in its territory when the goods are re-exported to another Member State in an unused condition provided that the re-export is made within twelve months from the date on which the goods are received in the importing State.

2. Where imported goods have been admitted for warehousing, transit or trans-shipment under customs bond without payment of customs duties, no import or export duties shall be charged in respect of such goods when they are subsequently re-exported by the importing State.

3. Notwithstanding the provisions of paragraph 1 and 2 of this Article, the importing States shall, in accordance with their customs laws and regulations, be free to withhold or charge part of the duties collected or collectable where the goods have been re-packed, assembled, preserved, blended or otherwise processed in the importing State, provided that no duties shall be refunded where the processed goods qualify as originating in the importing State under the provisions of Annex I to the Treaty.

. . .

Reprinted from *International Legal Materials* 23 (Washington, D.C.: American Society of International Law, 1984): 972.

# APPENDIX B-5
## ECCAS: Protocol Relating to the Freedom of Movement and Rights of Establishment

### ANNEX VII

### ARTICLE 3
#### Movement of people

1. Nationals of Member States shall have freedom of movement within the Community provided that they hold a national identity card, a valid passport or a laissez-passer and an international health carnet.

2. Citizens of Member States travelling as tourists must prove that they can support themselves and will not take up a job during their stay. They must also furnish proof of right of abode. Subject to existing regulations in each Member State, tourists may move around and stay in the territory of a host Member State for a period not exceeding three months.

3. Notwithstanding the provisions of paragraph 1 of this Article, the free movement of business men shall be subject to the holding of a special certificate issued by the National Chamber of Commerce of each Member State or the particular nationals authorities concerned.

4. The free movement of workers, subject to limitations on the grounds of public order, public safety and public health, shall include the right:
    (a) to accept a job offered in a Member State and for this purpose to have freedom of movement in the territories of Member States;
    (b) to stay in the territory of a Member State in order to work there in accordance with the laws, regulations and administrative arrangements governing the employment of workers who are nationals of such Member States;
    (c) after having had a job, to remain in the territory of the Member State, in conditions to be determined by the Conference, with a view to finding further work or becoming established in such State.

### ARTICLE 4
#### Right of establishment

1. The right of establishment shall include the right of access to unsalaried liberal or craft work and to practice them and the establishment and management of enterprises under the conditions defined by the various legislations and investment codes of the Member States of the Community.

Reprinted from *International Legal Materials* 23 (Washington, D.C.: American Society of International Law, 1984): 989.

2. Subject to the provisions of paragraph 3 of Article 2 of this Protocol, nationals of Member States of the Community who are established in another Member State shall have the same rights and freedoms as the nationals of the latter State except for political rights.

3. However, the rights and freedoms referred to in this Article shall not be a bar to the sovereign right of the Governments of Member States to expel nationals of another Member State. The latter State shall be immediately informed of the action taken against its national by the Government concerned, which shall do everything appropriate to safeguard the property and interest of the expelled person.

4. The nationals of Member States may practice liberal professions in the territory of another Member State subject to the conditions laid down by the national legislation of the latter State.

5. Salaried workers who are nationals of one Member State and employed in the territory of another Member State may, when they have ceased any kind of salaried activity establish themselves in such territory or practice a non-salaried activity if they comply with the conditions they had to comply with at the time of their entry into such State.

6. In order to facilitate the application of the provisions of this Article the Secretary-General shall make particular efforts *inter alia* to:

(a) study as a priority matter the activities where freedom of establishment is or will be a particularly useful contribution to the expansion of production and trade;

(b) collect in close collaboration with the national administrations concerned any useful particulars on activities or special situations within the Community.

. . .

# APPENDIX B-6
## ECCAS: Protocol on the Clearing House

ANNEX VIII
PROTOCOL ON THE CLEARING HOUSE FOR THE
ECONOMIC COMMUNITY OF CENTRAL AFRICAN STATES

ARTICLE 2
Establishment and objectives

1. There is established a Clearing House for bilateral and multilateral settlements between the banks of Member States.

. . .

ARTICLE 5
Legal status

1. The Clearing House is an international financial institution having legal capacity and the authority to purchase and alienate chattels movable and immovable, conclude contracts and go to law.

2. The Clearing House shall enjoy the immunities and privileges normally granted to international financial institutions. The Executive Secretary of the Clearing House shall conclude a corresponding Headquarters agreement with the Government of the host country.

. . .

ARTICLE 8
Unit of account

1. All the transactions of the Clearing House shall be expressed in Community units of account whose value, and the rate of exchange of national currencies, shall be determined by the Committee. Accordingly, each Bank shall be liable for giving regular information to the Clearing House about the value of its currency.

2. When the Committee considers that the economic situation makes it impossible to use fixed exchange rates for defining the unit of account, the effective exchange rates on the currency markets concerned shall be used.

Reprinted from *International Legal Materials* 23 (Washington, D.C.: American Society of International Law, 1984): 990.

3. Every Bank shall send a daily cable or telex giving the rate of exchange at market closure between its national currency and one or more of the convertible currencies specified by the Committee in accordance with subparagraph (h) of paragraph 3 of Article 6 of this Protocol.

4. Any alteration in the exchange rate of a currency declared by a Bank in accordance with paragraph 1 of this Article shall be immediately notified by such Bank to the Clearing House and to the other Banks in order that the exchange rate for such currency may be adjusted consequentially.

5. Every Bank guarantees to every other Bank the conversion of its currency into Community units of account at the declared exchange rate or at the rates of exchange determined in accordance with paragraph 1 of this Article.

6. In respect of eligible transactions, Member States guarantee the settlement of the amount due by their Bank in any agreed currency or currencies in accordance with the exchange rate on the date of settlement, as notified by the Clearing House.

## ARTICLE 9
### Credits, transactions and exceptions

1. Member States agree that the Committee shall from time to time determine the maximum limits of net debt and net credit positions for each Bank.

2. Notwithstanding paragraph 1 of this Article, each Bank may on its own initiative and advising the Clearing House accordingly, increase the amount of net credit position referred to in the previous paragraph.

3. Net debit balances at the end of the transaction period shall be settled in convertible currencies by the debtor Banks within a settlement period to be determined by the Committee.

4. The Clearing House shall be immediately notified of inter-Bank transactions under this Protocol in accordance with the rules or regulations determined by the Council.

5. The provisions of this Protocol shall apply to all eligible transactions between Member States.

6. Gifts and loans among Governments of the Member States may, after consultation with the banks concerned, be implemented through the channels of the Clearing House.

7. Payments for transactions between Member States of the same monetary zone shall not be subject to this Protocol for as long as such States have a common currency.

## ARTICLE 10

1. Any debtor Bank failing to comply with paragraph 3 of Article 9 of this Protocol at the end of a settlement period shall immediately forfeit the right to any further credit and the right to vote and shall levy its export income and other incomes of the subregion only through the channels of the Clearing House. The debtor Bank shall then be liable to negotiate with the Committee on the date and arrangements for paying its debit balance.

2. The Member States agree that in cases in which balances still exist after the settlement date has been notified to a debtor Bank, the delay shall be deemed to be a breach of this Article and shall incur the payment of daily interest at an increasing rate to be determined by the Committee.

3. Any Bank wishing to withdraw from the Clearing House shall give the Chairman in Office of the Council written notification of its intention one year in advance and at the expiry of the notification period shall cease to be a Member of the Clearing House unless it revokes its decision in the meantime.

4. During the one-year period referred to in paragraph 3 of this Article, any Member Bank wishing to withdraw from the Clearing House shall nevertheless comply with this Protocol and shall remain liable to discharge its obligations thereunder, *inter alia* to discharge its debit balance in respect of the Clearing House.

# APPENDIX C-1
## PTA: Treaty for the Establishment of the Preferential Trade Area for Eastern and Southern African States (December 21, 1981)

### ARTICLE 10
### Tribunal of the Preferential Trade Area

1. There is hereby established a judicial organ to be known as the Tribunal of Preferential Trade Area which shall ensure the proper application or interpretation of the provisions of this Treaty and adjudicate upon such disputes as may be referred to it in accordance with Article 40 of this Treaty.

2. The Statute and other matters relating to the Tribunal shall be prescribed by the Authority.

. . .

### ARTICLE 12
### Liberalization of trade

The Member States agree in accordance with the provisions of this Treaty to:

(a) the gradual reduction and eventual elimination of customs duties and nontariff barriers to trade conducted among themselves; and

(b) the gradual evolution of a common external tariff in respect of all goods imported from third countries with a view to the eventual establishment of a common market among themselves.

### ARTICLE 13
### Customs duties

1. The Member States shall reduce and eventually eliminate in accordance with the provisions of the Protocols on the gradual reduction and elimination of customs duties and co-operation in customs matters annexed to this Treaty respectively, as Annexes I and II, customs duties imposed on or in connexion with the importation or exportation of the commodities which are set out in the Common List.

2. During a period of ten years from the definitive entry into force of this Treaty, a Member State may not be required to reduce or eliminate customs

Reprinted from *International Legal Materials* 21 (Washington, D.C.: American Society of International Law, 1982): 479.

duties except in accordance with the provisions of paragraph 1 of this Article. During this period of ten years the Member States shall not impose any new customs duties or increase existing ones on goods appearing on the Common List and shall transmit to the Secretary-General all information on customs duties for study by the Customs and Trade Committee.

3. The Commission shall, after considering proposals from the Customs and Trade Committee submitted to it by the Secretary-General, recommend to the Council for its approval, a programme for the progressive reduction of customs duties among the Member States with a view to eliminating such duties not later than ten years after the definitive entry into force of this Treaty. Such a programme shall take into account the effects of the reduction and elimination of customs duties on the revenues of the Member States: Provided that the Council may subsequently decide that any customs duties shall be reduced more rapidly or eliminated earlier than is approved under the provisions of this paragraph.

## ARTICLE 14
### Common external tariff

For the purposes of this Treaty, the Commission shall, on the recommendation of the Customs and Trade Committee, submit from time to time to the Council for its approval, a programme for the gradual establishment of a common external tariff.

## ARTICLE 15
### Preferential treatment

1. For the purpose of this Treaty, goods shall be accepted as eligible for preferential treatment if such goods:
(a) originate in the Member States; and
(b) are during the period of ten years specified in paragraph 2 of Article 13 of this Treaty contained in the Common List.

2. Goods shall be accepted as originating in the Member States where they satisfy the conditions prescribed in the Protocol on Rules of Origin annexed to this Treaty as Annex III.

## ARTICLE 16
### Non-tariff restrictions on goods

1. Except as is provided in this Article and in accordance with Annex I to this Treaty, each of the Member States undertakes that upon the definitive entry

into force of this Treaty, it shall relax and remove the then existing quota, quantitative or the like restrictions or prohibitions on goods which apply to the transfer to that State, of goods originating in the other Member States and which are contained in the Common List. Except as may be provided or permitted by this Treaty, the Member States will thereafter refrain from imposing any further restrictions or prohibitions on such goods.

2. Except as is provided in this Article, the Commission shall, after considering proposals from the Customs and Trade Committee submitted to it by the Secretary-General, recommend to the Council for its approval a programme for the gradual relaxation and eventual elimination, not later than ten years from the definitive entry into force of this Treaty, of all the existing quota, quantitative or the like restrictions or prohibitions which apply in a Member State to the import of goods originating in the other Member States. Except as may be provided for or permitted by this Treaty, the Member States will thereafter refrain from imposing any further restrictions or prohibitions on such goods;

Provided that the Council may subsequently decide that any quota, quantitative or the like restrictions or prohibitions shall be relaxed more rapidly or removed earlier than is approved under the provisions of this paragraph.

3. The provisions of paragraphs 1 and 2 of this Article shall not extend to the following:

(a) export prohibitions or restrictions temporarily applied to prevent or relieve critical shortages of foodstuffs or other products essential to the exporting Member State;

(b) import and export prohibitions or restrictions necessary to the application of standards or regulations for the classification, grading or marketing of commodities in international trade;

(c) import restrictions on any agricultural or fisheries product, imported in any form, necessary to the enforcement of governmental measures which operate;

(i) to restrict the quantities of the like domestic product permitted to be marketed or produced, or if there is no substantial domestic production of the like product, of a domestic product for which the imported product can be directly substituted; or

(ii) to remove a temporary surplus of the like domestic product, or, if there is no substantial domestic production of the like product, of a domestic product for which the imported product can be directly substituted, by making the surplus available to certain groups of domestic consumers free of charge or at prices below the current market level; or

(iii) to restrict the quantities permitted to be produced of any animal product the production of which is directly dependent, wholly or mainly, on the imported commodity, if the domestic production of that commodity is relatively negligible.

4. Notwithstanding the provisions of the Article, a Member State may, after having given notice to the other Member State of its intention to do so, introduce or continue to impose restrictions or prohibitions affecting:

(a) the application of security laws and regulations;

(b) the control of arms, ammunition and other war equipment and military items;

(c) the protection of human, animal or plant health or life or the protection of public morality;

(d) the transfer of gold, silver and precious stones;

(e) the protection of national treasures; or

(f) the control of nuclear materials, radio-active products or any other material used in the development or exploitation of nuclear energy.

5. If a Member State encounters balance-of-payments difficulties arising from the application of the provisions of this Chapter, that Member State may, provided that it has taken all reasonable steps to overcome the difficulties, impose for the purpose only of overcoming such difficulties for a specified period to be determined by the Council, quantitative or the like restrictions or prohibitions, on goods originating from the other Member States.

6. For the purpose of protecting an infant or strategic industry the products of which are contained in the Common List, a Member State may, provided that it has taken all reasonable steps to protect such infant or strategic industry, impose for the purpose only of protecting such industry for a specified period to be determined by the Council, quantitative or the like restrictions or prohibitions on similar goods originating from the other Member States.

7. A Member State imposing quantitative or the like restrictions or prohibitions under praragraphs 3, 5 and 6 of this Article shall inform the other Member States and the Secretary-General as soon as possible of such restrictions.

8. The Council shall keep under review the operation of any quantitative or the like restrictions or prohibitions imposed under the provisions of paragraphs 3, 5 and 6 of this Article and take appropriate decisions thereon.

## ARTICLE 17
### Dumping

1. The Member States undertake to prohibit the practice of dumping goods within the Preferential Trade Area.

2. For the purposes of this Article, "dumping" means the transfer of goods originating in a Member State to another Member State for sale:

(a) at a price lower than the comparable price charged for similar goods in the Member State where such goods originate (due allowance being made for the differences in the conditions of sale, in taxation, in transport costs or for any other factors affecting the comparability of price); and

(b) under circumstances likely to prejudice the production of similar goods in that Member State.

### ARTICLE 18
#### Most favoured nation treatment

1. The Member States shall accord to one another in relation to trade between them the most favoured nation treatment.

2. In no case shall trade concessions granted to a third country under an agreement with a Member State be more favourable than those applicable under this Treaty.

3. Any agreement between a Member State and a third country under which tariff concessions are granted shall not derogate from the obligations of that Member State under this Treaty.

4. The provisions of this Article shall apply only with respect to commodities contained in the Common List.

### ARTICLE 19
#### Re-exportation of goods and transit facilities

1. The Member States shall undertake to facilitate trade in re-exports among themselves. However, in certain cases to be jointly agreed upon, a Member State from which the goods to be re-exported originate, may object to the re-export of such goods.

2. Each Member State shall grant freedom of transit through its territory of goods proceeding to or from another Member State indirectly through that territory in accordance with the provisions of the Protocol on transit trade and transit facilities annexed to this Treaty as Annex V.

3. The Member States agree that the goods imported into their territories from the Republic of South Africa shall not be re-exported into the territories of another Member State and that goods imported into the Member States from a Member State shall not be re-exported to the Republic of South Africa.

4. The Member States further agree that goods being imported or re-exported in contravention of the provisions of paragraphs 1 and 3 of this Article shall not benefit from the transit facilities and privileges provided for in this Treaty.

• • •

## ARTICLE 30
### Protocol in respect of Botswana, Lesotho and Swaziland

The Member States agree that a Protocol on the unique situation of Botswana, Lesotho and Swaziland within the context of the Preferential Trade Area to be annexed to this Treaty as Annex XII shall, taking into account their membership of the Southern African Customs Union, regulate such unique situation and the granting to Botswana, Lesotho and Swaziland of temporary exemptions from the full application of certain provisions of this Treaty.

## ARTICLE 31
### Special provisions in respect of The Comoros and Djibouti

The Member States, recognizing the special economic conditions of The Comoros and Djibouti, agree to grant them temporary exemptions from the full application of certain provisions of the Treaty as provided for in this Treaty.

• • •

## ARTICLE 40
### Procedure for the settlement of disputes

Any dispute that may arise among the Member States regarding the interpretation and application of the provisions of this Treaty shall be amicably settled by direct agreement between the parties concerned. In the event of failure to settle such disputes, the matter may be referred to the Tribunal by a party to such dispute and the decision of the Tribunal shall be final.

• • •

## ARTICLE 46
### Membership or association of other countries

The Member States may together negotiate with any African State not included among those referred to in paragraph 2 of Article 2 of this Treaty but which is an immediate neighbour of a Member State and which has transmitted to the Secretary-General its intention of becoming a Member State of or entering into other co-operative arrangements with the Preferential Trade Area.

• • •

# APPENDIX C-2
## PTA: Protocol on the Reduction and Elimination of Trade Barriers on Selected Commodities to be Traded within the Preferential Trade Area

### ARTICLE 3
#### The Common List-establishment and effect

1. The Member States agree to the establishment of a Common List of selected commodities which shall have originated in the Member States, referred to in this Protocol as "the Common List", which shall be annexed to this Protocol and the accordance of preferential treatment to such selected commodities when traded among the Member States.

2. The Common List shall include selected commodities which are of both export and import interest to the Member States and shall be amended from time to time by the Council on the recommendation of the Committee.

3. The Member States agree to reduce and eliminate among themselves in accordance with the provisions of this Protocol, customs duties and non-tariff barriers with respect to the commodities appearing in the Common List.

### ARTICLE 4
#### Classification of goods and determination of tariff concessions

1. The Member States agree to adopt a common percentage for the reduction of customs duties to be applied to each commodity or group of commodities appearing in the Common List.

2. For the purposes of paragraph 1 of this Article, the Member States agree that the commodities appearing in the Common List shall be classified under various groups in respect of which the basic rates shall be progressively reduced and eventually eliminated commencing with reductions by percentages on various groups of commodities as follows:

- Group I:       Food (excluding luxury items)     • 30 per cent
- Group II:      Raw materials:
                 (a) Agricultural                  • 50 per cent
                 (b) Non-agricultural              • 60 per cent
- Group III:     Intermediate goods                • 65 per cent

Reprinted from *International Legal Materials* 21 (Washington, D.C.: American Society of International Law, 1982): 498.

- Group IV:     Manufactured consumer goods
(excluding luxury items)
  - (a) Durable consumer goods
(excluding (c) and (d) below     • 40 per cent
  - (b) Non-durable consumer goods
(excluding (c) and (d) below)     • 35 per cent
  - (c) Highly competing consumer
goods     • 30 per cent
  - (d) Consumer goods for particular
importance to economic
development     • 70 per cent
- Group V:     Capital goods (including transport
equipment)     • 70 per cent
- Group VI:     Luxury goods     • 10 per cent

3. Notwithstanding the provisions of paragraphs 1 and 2 of this Article, The Comoros and Djibouti shall, during the period of two years after the definitive entry into force of the Treaty, be at liberty to reduce their customs duties by 25 per cent only of the rates of tariff reductions applicable to the Member States in accordance with the provisions of paragraphs 1 and 2 of this Article. Thereafter, the rate of tariff reductions that shall be applicable to The Comoros and Djibouti shall be determined at every round of negotiations in accordance with the provisions of paragraph 1 of Article 7 of this Protocol.

4. The Member States agree that where there are no customs duties in respect of any commodity contained in the Common List, no customs duty shall be introduced on such commodities when traded within the Preferential Trade Area.

5. Commodities, which are contained in the Common List shall be accorded the most favoured nation treatment by the Member States.

## ARTICLE 5
### Non-tariff barriers and concessions

1. Subject to the Treaty and unless otherwise specified, non-tariff barriers in respect of commodities appearing in the Common List shall be relaxed or eliminated as follows:

| Non-tariff barriers | Concessions |
|---|---|
| (a) Quantitative restrictions | • Preferential treatment in allocation of quotas. |
| (b) Export and import licencing | • Preferential treatment in issuing licences. |
| (c) Foreign exchange licencing | • Preferential treatment in issuing licences. |
| (d) Stipulation of import sources | • Preferential treatment |
| (e) Prohibition or temporary prohibition of imports | • Exempted where possible |
| (f) Advance import deposits | • Preferential treatment |
| (g) Conditional permission for imports | • Exempted |
| (h) Special charges for acquiring foreign exchange licences | • Preferential treatment |

2. The Member States undertake to keep under constant review the non-tariff barriers to trade among themselves with a view to progressively relaxing and eventually abolishing them.

## ARTICLE 6
### Basic rates and standstill provisions

1. The Member States undertake not to increase customs duties and non-tariff barriers in respect of commodities appearing in the Common List with effect from the date on which agreement is reached to include such commodities in the Common List.

2. For the purposes of paragraph 3 of Article 3 of this Protocol the Member States agree that:

(a) the customs duties applied by them on the date of the definitive entry into force of the Treaty shall be the basic rates on which tariff reductions in respect of commodities appearing in the Common List shall be based, and that for other commodities which may subsequently be added to the Common List their basic rates shall be as specified in subparagraph (b) of paragraph 6 of Article 7 of this Protocol; and

(b) the non-tariff barriers applied by them on the date of the definitive entry into force of this Protocol shall be those on which concessions in respect of commodities appearing in the Common List shall be based.

3. The Member States, shall not later than one hundred and eighty days after agreement is reached in pursuance of the provisions of this Protocol for the reduction or elimination of a tariff or non-tariff barrier in respect of a commodity appearing in the Common List, give effect to such reduction or elimination.

. . .

# APPENDIX C-3
## PTA: Protocol Relating to Customs Co-operation within the Preferential Trade Area for Eastern and Southern African States

### ARTICLE 4
Simplification and harmonization of customs procedures

1. The Member States undertake to promote the simplification and harmonization of customs laws, regulations and procedures to facilitate the movement of goods and services across their common frontiers.

2. For the purpose of paragraph 1 of this Article the Member States undertake to:
   (a) adopt uniform, comprehensive and systematic tariff classification of goods with a common and specific basis of description and interpretation in accordance with internationally accepted standards;
   (b) adopt a standard system of valuation of goods based on principles of equity, uniformity and simplicity of application in accordance with internationally accepted standards and guidelines;
   (c) agree on common terms and conditions governing temporary admission procedure including the list or range of goods to be covered and the nature of manufacturing or processing to be authorized;
   (d) implement the customs requirement for the re-exportation of goods affected by Annex IV of the Treaty;
   (e) implement the customs requirements for the transit of goods as prescribed in Annex V of the Treaty;
   (f) harmonize and simplify customs formalities and documents in accordance with the provisions of Annex X of the Treaty; and
   (g) adopt common procedures for the establishment and operation of free zones, free ports, customs supervised factories and export drawbacks.

3. The Member States undertake to use the Customs Co-operation Council Nomenclature as a basis for the classification of goods in their customs tariffs and may accordingly set up sub-headings covering those products or categories of products to which they apply preferential treatment among themselves.

4. The Member States undertake to harmonize their customs and statistical nomenclature and standardize their foreign trade statistics to ensure comparability and reliability of the relevant information.

· · ·

Reprinted from *International Legal Materials* 21 (Washington, D.C.: American Society of International Law, 1982): 501.

## APPENDIX C-4
## PTA: Protocol on the Rules of Origin for Products to be Traded between the Member States of the Preferential Trade Area

### RULE 2
### Rules of Origin of Preferential Trade Area goods

1. Goods shall be accepted as originating in a Member State if they are consigned directly from a Member State to a consignee in another Member State and:

(a) they have been produced in the Member States by enterprises which are subject to management by a majority of nationals and to at least 51 per cent equity holding by nationals of the Member States or a Government or Governments of the Member States or institutions, agencies enterprises or corporations of such Government or Governments; and

(b) where the goods satisfy one of the criteria set out in items (i) to (v) of this subparagraph:

(i) they have been wholly produced as defined in Rule 3 of this Protocol;

(ii) they have been produced in the Member States and the c.i.f. value of materials imported from outside the Member States or of undetermined origin which have been used at any stage in the production of the goods does not exceed 60 per cent of the total cost of materials used in the production of the goods;

(iii) they have been produced in the Member States essentially from materials imported from outside the Member States or of undetermined origin and the value added, resulting from the process of production, accounts for at least 45 per cent of the ex-factory cost:

> Provided that the Council may,
> upon the recommendations of
> the Committee, raise the percentage
> of the value added required;

(iv) notwithstanding the provisions of the items (iii) of this subparagraph:

(aa) they have been produced in the Member States and designated in a list by the Council upon the recommendation of the Committee to be goods of particular importance to the economic development of the Member States, and containing not less than 25 per cent of value added; or

Reprinted from *International Legal Materials* 21 (Washington, D.C.: American Society of International Law, 1982): 505.

(bb) they have been produced in the Member States and are consumed in large quantities throughout the Member States and have been designated in a list by the Council upon the recommendation of the Committee to be goods currently in short supply within the Member States and containing value added of not less than 30 per cent.

(v) subject to such exemptions as may be determined by the Council:

(aa) they have been imported into the Member States and have undergone a process of substantial transformation, that is to say, a process of production as a result of which such goods are classified or become classifiable under a CCCN [the applicable tariff nomenclature] tariff heading other than the CCCN tariff heading under which they were imported, and are contained in a list to be known as "List A"; or

(bb) they have been imported into the Member States and have not undergone a process of substantial transformation as defined in item (aa) of this subparagraph but which in the opinion of the Council shall nevertheless be deemed to have undergone a process of substantial transformation as prescribed in item (aa) of this subparagraph, and are contained in a list to be known as "List B".

2. Notwithstanding the provisions of subparagraph (a) of paragraph 1 of this Rule:

(a) the amount of equity holding that shall apply to enterprises referred to in that subparagraph with respect to The Comoros and Djibouti shall during the period of five years from the definitive entry into force of the Treaty, be not less than 25 per cent and thereafter the Council shall upon the recommendations of the Commission determine the amount of equity holding that shall apply to such enterprises;

(b) the amount of equity holding that shall apply to enterprises referred to in that subparagraph with respect to Mauritius shall during the period of two years from the definitive entry into force of the Treaty, be not less than 30 per cent and during the next successive period of two years not be less than 40 per cent and shall at the end of the sixth year from the definitive entry into force of the Treaty, be not less than 51 per cent;

(c) the amount of equity holding that shall apply to enterprises referred to in that subparagraph with respect to Botswana, Lesotho and Swaziland shall during the period of five years from the definitive entry into force of the Treaty be not less than 30 per cent and thereafter the Council shall upon the recommendations of the Commission determine the amount of equity holding that shall apply to such enterprises;

(d) the amount of equity holding that shall apply to enterprises referred to in that subparagraph with respect to Zimbabwe shall during the period of two years from the definitive entry into force of the Treaty, be not less than 30 per cent and during the next successive period of two years be not less than 40 per cent and shall at the end of the fifth year from the definitive entry into force of the Treaty, be not less than 51 per cent.

3. The Council may determine how long the goods contained in the lists referred to in items (iv) and (v) of subparagraph (b) of paragraph 1 of this Rule shall remain on such lists and may from time to time amend them as may be necessary.

4. Raw materials or semi-finished goods originating in accordance with the provisions of this Protocol in any of the Member States and undergoing working or processing either in one or two or in more States shall for the purpose of determining the origin of a finished product be deemed to have originated in the Member States where the final processing or manufacturing takes place.

## RULE 3
### Goods wholly produced in the Member States

For the purposes of item (i) of subparagraph (b) of paragraph 1 of Rule 2 of this Protocol, the following are among the products which shall be regarded as wholly produced in the Member States:

(a) mineral products extracted from the ground or sea-bed of the Member States;

(b) vegetable products harvested within the Member States;

(c) live animals born or raised within the Member States;

(d) products and by-products from animals born or raised within the Member States;

(e) products obtained by hunting or fishing conducted within the Member States;

(f) products obtained from the sea and from rivers and lakes within the Member States by a vessel of a Member State;

(g) products manufactured in a factory of a Member State exclusively from the products referred to in paragraph (f) of this Rule;

(h) used articles fit only for the recovery of materials, provided that such articles have been collected from users within the Member States;

(i) scrap and waste resulting from manufacturing operations within the Member States;

(j) goods produced within the Member States exclusively or mainly from one or both of the following;

    (i)    products referred to in paragraphs (a) to (i) of this Rule;

    (ii)   materials containing no element imported from outside the Member States or of undetermined origin.

## RULE 4
### Application of percentage of imported materials and value added criteria

For the purpose of subparagraph (a) of paragraph 1 and items (ii), (iii) and (iv) of subparagraph (b) of paragraph 1 of Rule 2 of this Protocol:

    (a)  any material which meets the condition specified in item (i) of paragraph (b) of paragraph 1 of Rule 2 of this Protocol shall be regarded as containing no elements imported from outside the Member States;

    (b)  the value of any materials which can be identified as having been imported from outside the Member States shall be their c.i.f. value accepted by the customs authorities on clearance for home consumption, or on temporary admission at the time of last importation into the Member State where they were used in a process of production, less the amount of any transport costs incurred in transit through other Member States;

    (c)  if the value of any materials imported from outside the Member States cannot be determined in accordance with paragraph (b) of this Rule their value shall be the earliest ascertainable price for them in the Member State where they were used in a process of production;

    (d)  if the origin of any materials cannot be determined, such materials shall be deemed to have been imported from outside the Member States and their value shall be the earliest ascertainable price paid for them in the Member State where they were used in a process of production.

## RULE 5
### Processes not conferring origin

Notwithstanding the provisions of items (ii), (iii), (iv) and (v) of subparagraph (b) of paragraph 1 of Rule 2 of this Protocol, the following operations and processes shall be considered as insufficient to support a claim that goods originate from a Member State:

    (a)  packing, bottling, placing in flasks, bags, cases and boxes, fixing on cards or boards and all other simple packing operations;

    (b)  (i)   simple mixing of ingredients imported from outside the Member States;

         (ii)  simple assembly of components and parts imported from outside the Member States to constitute a complete product;

         (iii) simple mixing and assembly where the costs of the ingredients, parts and components imported from outside the Member States and used in any of such processes exceed 60 per cent of the total costs of the ingredients, parts and components used;

(c) operations to ensure the preservation of merchandise in good condition during transportation and storage such as ventilation, spreading out, drying, freezing, placing in brine, sulphur dioxiode or other aqueous solutions, removal of damaged parts and similar operations;

(d) changes of packing and breaking up of or assembly of consignments;

(e) marking, labelling or affixing other like distinguishing signs on products or their packages;

(f) simple operations consisting of removal of dust, sifting or screening, sorting, classifying and matching, including the making up of sets of goods, washing, painting and cutting up;

(g) a combination of two or more operations specified in paragraphs (a) to (f) of this Rule;

(h) slaughter of animals.

# APPENDIX C-5
## PTA: Protocol on Clearing and Payments Arrangements

### ARTICLE 4
### Establishment in the Clearing House

1. There shall be established a Clearing House for the multilateral clearing and settlement of payments in respect of eligible transaction among the Member States at such time as the Committee may determine:

> Provide that the Committee may, as an interim
> measure, designate a monetary authority of a
> Member State on such terms and conditions as the
> Committee and such monetary authority may agree,
> to perform the duties of the Clearing House.

2. The functions of the Clearing House shall be:
   (a) to undertake clearing operations in respect of eligible transactions among the Member States;
   (b) to regulate and oversee transfers of payments expressed in UAPTA and made in pursuance of eligible transactions;
   (c) to facilitate the efficient and speedy transfers of payment between the Member States, the efficient use of credit facilities available through the Clearing House and the use of national currencies expressed in UAPTA for transactions made within the framework of the Preferential Trade Area; and
   (d) to undertake such other activities as the Council may on the recommendation of the Committee, determine.

3. The Clearing House shall, subject to the Treaty, have such staff who shall be subject to such administrative regulations as the Committee may determine.

4. The Head Office of the Clearing House shall be established at a place to be determined by the Council.

### ARTICLE 5
### Unit of account and exchange rate guarantee

1. The Committee, after consultation with the Council, shall establish a unit of account for the Preferential Trade Area referred to in this Protocol as "UAPTA" and determine its value.

Reprinted from *International Legal Materials* 21 (Washington, D.C.: American Society of International Law, 1982): 525.

2. The Clearing House shall compute and determine, from time to time, the value of each national currency in terms of the UAPTA [the unit of account for the PTA] and inform the monetary authority of each Member State accordingly. For this purpose, each monetary authority shall communicate to the Clearing House, as may be requested, the official exchange rate of its currency against its intervention currency or reference currency, as the case may be.

3. Any change in the official exchange rate of the currency of a Member State shall be notified immediately by its monetary authority to the Clearing House.

4. The Member States shall guarantee the free convertibility of the amounts due from their monetary authorities in respect of eligible transactions into any agreed currency or currencies at the rate of exchange prevailing on the date of transaction as notified by the Clearing House.

ARTICLE 6
Clearing and settlement of transactions

1. The Member States agree that the clearing of payments with respect to eligible transactions among themselves shall be undertaken on a multilateral basis as provided for in this Protocol:

> Provided that during a transitional period to be determined by the Council on the recommendation of the Committee which shall not exceed a period of five years from the definitive entry into force of the Treaty, such Member States which are unable upon the definitive entry into force of the Treaty to enter into multilateral clearing and payments arrangements with other Member States as provided for in this paragraph, shall, subject to Article 14 of this Protocol, be at liberty to maintain bilateral clearing and payments arrangements with other Member States in respect of eligible transactions.

2. The Member States agree that the Committee shall determine the maximum limits of net debit and net credit positions for each monetary authority on the basis of the volume of trade of each Member State within the Preferential Trade Area.

3. Notwithstanding the provisions of paragraph 2 of this Article, a monetary authority may on its own initiative and advising the Clearing House accordingly, increase the amount of net credit position referred to in paragraph 2 of this Article.

4. The net debit balance outstanding against a debtor monetary authority at the end of the transactions period shall be settled in convertible currency by the debtor monetary authority within a settlement period to be determined by the Committee.

5. The Member States agree that where, contrary to the provisions of paragraph 4 of this Article, debit balances remain outstanding after the due date for settlement has been notified to a debtor monetary authority, such delay in settling the debts shall be deemed to be a breach of the provisions of this Article and shall as such attract a daily interest charge at progressive rates to be determined by the Committee.

6. A monetary authority which, contrary to the provisions of paragraph 5 of this Article, fails to settle the outstanding debit balances due either at the end of the payment period or settlement period in accordance with the rules and regulations prescribed by the Committee, shall be deemed to be in violation of the provisions of this Article and the Committee may recommend to the Council that such a monetary authority be suspended by the Council from the Clearing House for such period as it may determine, and shall also be subject to such additional sanctions as may be contained in the rules and regulations prescribed by the Committee.

### ARTICLE 7
#### Payments restrictions

1. The Member States undertake not to impose any restrictions on the making of bona-fide payments and transfers relating to concluded eligible transactions among themselves.

2. The Member States agree to communicate to each other through the Clearing House the exchange control regulations applied by them, and to include in such regulations provisions to facilitate the smooth functioning of the Clearing House.

3. The Member States agree to co-operate in measures designed to make the exchange control regulations of each other effective:

> Provided that such measures and regulations are
> consistent with the provisions of the Treaty.

## APPENDIX D-1
## ECOWAS: Treaty of the Economic Community of West African States (Lagos, 1975).

## CHAPTER III
## CUSTOMS AND TRADE MATTERS

### ARTICLE 12
### Liberalization of Trade

There shall be progressively established in the course of a transitional period of fifteen (15) years from the definitive entry into force of this Treaty, and as prescribed in this Chapter, a Customs Union among the Member States. Within this Union, customs duties or other charges with equivalent effect on imports shall be eliminated. Quota, quantitative or like restrictions or prohibitions and administrative obstacles to trade among the Member States shall also be removed. Furthermore, a common customs tariff in respect of all goods imported into the Member States from third countries shall be established and maintained.

### ARTICLE 13
### Customs Duties

1. Member States shall reduce and ultimately eliminate customs duties and any other charges with equivalent effect except duties notified in accordance with Article 17 and other charges which fall within that Article, imposed on or in connection with the importation of goods which are eligible for Community tariff treatment in accordance with Article 15 of this Treaty. Any such duties or other charges are hereinafter referred to as "import duties."

2. Within a period of two (2) years from the definitive entry into force of this Treaty, a Member State may not be required to reduce or eliminate import duties. During this two-year period, Member States shall not impose any new duties and taxes or increase existing ones and shall transmit to the Executive Secretariat all information on import duties for study by the relevant institutions of the Community.

3. Upon the expiry of the period of two (2) years referred to in paragraph 2 of this Article and during the next succeeding eight (8) years, Member States shall progressively reduce and ultimately eliminate import duties in accordance with

Reprinted from *International Legal Materials* 14 (Washington, D.C.: American Society of International Law, 1975): 1200.

a schedule to be recommended to the Council of Ministers by the Trade, Customs, Immigration, Monetary and Payments Commission. Such a schedule shall take into account, inter alia, the effects of the reduction and elimination of import duties on the revenue of Member States and the need to avoid the disruption of the income they derive from import duties.

4. The Authority may at any time, on the recommendation of the Council of Ministers, decide that any import duties shall be reduced more rapidly or eliminated earlier than is recommended by the Trade, Customs, Immigration, Monetary and Payments Commission. However, the Council of Ministers shall, not later than one calendar year preceding the date in which such reductions or eliminations come into effect, examine whether such reductions or eliminations shall apply to some or all goods and in respect of some or all the Member States and shall report the result of such examination for the decision of the Authority.

## ARTICLE 14
### Common Customs Tariff

1. The Member States agree to the gradual establishment of a common customs tariff in respect of all goods imported into the Member States from third countries.

2. At the end of the period of eight (8) years referred to in paragraph 3 of Article 13 of this Treaty and during the next succeeding five (5) years, Member States shall gradually, in accordance with a schedule to be recommended by the Trade, Customs, Immigration, Monetary and Payments Commission, abolish existing differences in their external customs tariffs.

3. In the course of the same period, the above-mentioned Commission shall ensure the establishment of a common customs nomenclature and customs statistical nomenclature for all the Member States.

## ARTICLE 15
### Community Tariff Treatment

1. For the purposes of this Treaty, goods shall be accepted as eligible for Community tariff treatment if they have been consigned to the territory of the importing Member State from the territory of another Member State and originate in the Member States.

2. The definition of products originating from Member States shall be the subject of a protocol to be annexed to this Treaty.

3. The Trade, Customs, Immigration, Monetary and Payments Commission shall from time to time examine whether the rates referred to in paragraph 2 of this Article can be amended to make them simpler and more liberal. In order to ensure their smooth and equitable operation, the Council of Ministers may from time to time amend them.

## ARTICLE 18
### Quantitative Restrictions on Community Goods

1. Except as may be provided for or permitted by this Treaty, each of the Member States undertakes to relax gradually and to remove ultimately in accordance with a schedule to be recommended by the Trade, Customs, Immigration, Monetary and Payments Commission and not later than ten (10) years from the definitive entry into force of this Treaty, all of the then existing quota, quantitative or like restrictions or prohibitions which apply to the import into that State of goods originating in the other Member States and thereafter refrain from imposing any further restrictions or prohibitions.

2. The Authority may at any time, on the recommendation of the Council of Ministers, decide that any quota, quantitative or like restrictions or prohibitions shall be relaxed more rapidly or removed earlier than is recommended by the Trade, Customs, Immigration, Monetary and Payments Commission.

3. A Member State may, after having given notice to the other Member States of its intention to do so, introduce or continue or execute restrictions or prohibitions affecting:
   (a) the application of security laws and regulations;
   (b) the control of arms, ammunition and other war equipment and military items;
   (c) the protection of human, animal or plant health or life, or the protection of public morality;
   (d) the transfer of gold, silver and precious and semiprecious stones; or
   (e) the protection of national treasures; provided that a Member State shall not so exercise the right to introduce or continue to execute the restrictions or prohibitions conferred by this paragraph as to stultify the free movement of goods envisaged in this Article.

## ARTICLE 19
### Dumping

1. Member States undertake to prohibit the practice of dumping goods within the Community.

2. For the purposes of this Article, "dumping" means the transfer of goods originating in a Member State to another Member State for sale:

(a) at a price lower than the comparable price charged for similar goods in the Member States where such goods originate (due allowance being made for the differences in the conditions of sale or in taxation or for any other factors affecting the comparability of prices); and

(b) under circumstances likely to prejudice the production of similar goods in that Member State.

### ARTICLE 20
#### Most Favoured Nation Treatment

1. Member States shall accord to one another in relation to trade between them the most favoured nation treatment and in no case shall tariff concessions granted to a third country under an agreement with a Member State be more favourable than those applicable under the Treaty.

2. Copies of such agreements referred to in paragraph 1 of this Article shall be transmitted by the Member States which are parties to them, to the Executive Secretariat of the Community.

3. Any agreement between a Member State and a third country under which tariff concessions are granted, shall not derogate from the obligations of that Member State under this Treaty.

### ARTICLE 21
#### Internal Legislation

Member States shall refrain from enacting legislation which directly or indirectly discriminates against the same or like products of another Member State.

### ARTICLE 22
#### Re-exportation of Goods and Transit Facilities

1. Where customs duty has been charged and collected on any goods imported from a third country into a Member State such goods shall not be re-exported into another Member State except as may be permitted under a Protocol to this Treaty entered into by the Member States.

2. Where goods are re-exported under such a Protocol, the Member States from whose territory such goods are re-exported shall refund to the Member State into whose territory such goods are imported the customs duties charged

and collected on such goods. The duties so refunded shall not exceed those applicable on such goods in the territory of the Member State into which such goods are imported.

3. Each Member State, in accordance with international regulations, shall grant full and unrestriced freedom of transit through its territory of goods proceeding to or from a third country indirectly through that territory to or from other Member States; and such transit shall not be subject to any discrimination, quantitative restrictions, duties or other charges levied on transit.

4. Notwithstanding paragraph 3 of this Article;
   (a) goods in transit shall be subject to the customs law; and
   (b) goods in transit shall be liable to the charges usually made for carriage and for any services which may be rendered, provided such charges are not discriminatory.

5. Where goods are imported from a third country into one Member State, each of the other Member States shall be free to restrict the transfer to it of such goods whether by a system of licensing and controlling importers or by other means.

6. The provisions of paragraph 5 of this Article shall apply to goods which, under the provisions of Article 15 of this Treaty, fail to be accepted as originating in a Member State.

. . .

## ARTICLE 25
### Compensation for Loss of Revenue

1. The Council of Ministers shall, on the report of the Executive Secretary and recommendation by the appropriate Commission or Commissions, determine the compensation to be paid to a Member State which has suffered loss of import duties as a result of the application of this Chapter.

2. A protocol to be annexed to this Treaty shall state precisely the methods of assessment of the loss of revenue suffered by Member States as a result of the application of this chapter.

. . .

## ARTICLE 27
### Visa and Residence

1. Citizens of Member States shall be regarded as Community citizens and

accordingly Member States undertake to abolish all obstacles to their freedom of movement and residence within the Community.

2. Member States shall by agreements with each other exempt Community citizens from holding visitors' visas and residence permits and allow them to work and undertake commercial and industrial activities within their territories.

. . .

## ARTICLE 50
### Establishment

There is hereby established a Fund to be known as the Fund for Co-operation, Compensation and Development hereinafter referred to as the "the Fund".

. . .

## ARTICLE 52
### Uses of the Fund

The Fund shall be used to:
(a) finance projects in Member States;
(b) provide compensation to Member States which have suffered losses as a result of the location of Community enterprises;
(c) provide compensation and other forms of assistance to Member States which have suffered losses arising out of the application of the provisions of this Treaty on the liberalisation of Trade within the Community;
(d) guarantee foreign investments made in Member States in respect of enterprises established in pursuance of the provisions of this Treaty on the harmonisation of industrial policies;
(e) provide appropriate means to facilitate the sustained mobilisation of internal and external financial resources for the Member States and the Community; and
(f) promote development projects in the less developed Member States of the Community.

. . .

## ARTICLE 56
### Procedure for the Settlement of Disputes

Any dispute that may arise among the Member States regarding the interpretation or application of this Treaty shall be amicably settled by direct agreement. In the event of failure to settle such disputes, the matter may be referred to the Tribunal of the Community by a party to such disputes and decisions of the Tribunal shall be final.

. . .

# ECOWAS: Protocol Relating to the Definition of the Concept of Products Originating from Member States (November 5, 1976, as amended by Supplementary Protocol of May 29, 1979).

## ARTICLE II
### Rules of Origin of Community Goods

1. The promotion of trade in goods originating in Member States as well as the collective economic development of the Community requires indigenous ownership and participation. Goods shall be accepted as originating in Member States for purposes of trade liberalisation if:

(a) they have been wholly produced as defined in Article V of this Protocol; or

(b) they have been produced in a Member State other than by any of the operations and processes listed in Article IV of this Protocol or with the material from a foreign or undetermined origin used in the process of production of goods whose C.I.F. value does not exceed 60% of the total cost of the material employed in the production or with the material of Community origin whose value must not in any case be less than 40% of the total cost of the material used in the process of production or with the raw material of Community origin representing in quantity at least 60% of the whole raw material used in the production; or

(c) if the goods have been produced from material of a foreign or undetermined origin and having received in the process of production a value added of at least 35% of the ex factory price of the finished product; and

2. If the Enterprises producing these goods attain a desirable level of indigenous ownership and participation. The Commission shall, on the basis of appropriate statistics, make proposals to the Council of Ministers to determine orientations and levels relating to ownership and participation.

. . .

## ARTICLE IV
### Processes not conferring origin

For the purpose of sub-paragraphs (b) and (c) of paragraph 1 of Article II of of this Protocol, the following operations and processes shall be considered as insufficient to support a claim that goods originate from a Member State:

---

Reprinted from ECOWAS *Official Journal* 1 (June 15, 1979): 12.

(a) packing, bottling, placing in flasks, bags, cases, boxes, fixing on cards or boards and all other simple packing operations;

(b) mixing of products except as provided for in Article VIII of this Protocol;

(c) operations to ensure the preservation of merchandise in good condition during transportation and storage such as ventilation, spreading out, drying, freezing, placing in brine, sulphur dioxide or other aqueous solutions, removal of damaged parts and similar operations;

(d) changes of packing and breaking up or assembly of consignments;

(e) simple assembly of parts of a product to constitute a complete product;

(f) marking or labelling for distinguishing products or their packages;

(g) simple operations consisting of removal of dust, sifting or screening, sorting, classifying, matching including the making up of sets of goods, washing, painting and cutting up;

(h) a combination of two or more operations specified in sub-paragraphs (a) to (g) of this Article;

(i) slaughter of animals.

## ARTICLE V

For the purpose of sub-paragraph (a) of paragraph 1 of Article II of this Protocol, the following are among the products which shall be regarded as wholly produced in the Member States:

(a) mineral products extracted from the ground or sub-soil or sea bed of the Member States;

(b) vegetable products harvested within the Member States;

(c) live animals born and/or raised within the Member States;

(d) products obtained within the Member States from live animals in (c) above;

(e) products obtained by hunting or fishing conducted within the Member States;

(f) products obtained from the sea and from rivers and lakes within the Member States by a vessel of a Member State;

(g) products manufactured in a factory of a Member State exclusively from the products referred to in sub-paragraph (f) of this Article;

(h) used articles fit only for the recovery of materials, provided that such articles have been collected from users within the Member States;

(i) scrap and waste resulting from manufacturing operations within the Member States;

(j) goods produced within the Member States exclusively or mainly from one or both of the following:
  (i) products within sub-paragraphs (a) to (i);
  (ii) materials containing no element imported from outside the Member States or of undetermined origin.

# ECOWAS: Decision Relating to the Fixing of the Desirable Level of National Participation in the Equity Capital of Industrial Enterprises Whose Products Benefit from Preferential Duty (May 15, 1980)

. . .

## ARTICLE 1

i. The level of participation by nationals of Member States in the equity capital of industrial enterprises as well as the corresponding periods of implementation are hereby fixed as indicated below:

— 28 May 1981   20%
— 28 May 1983   35%
— 28 May 1989   51%

ii. The list of enterprises fulfilling the conditions fixed . . . shall be drawn up and sent to the Executive Secretariat by the competent authority responsible for industrial affairs in each Member State on the basis of a dossier presented by the enterprises concerned and containing the following information:
   a. Identity of the Industrial enterprise, legal status, headquarters
   b. Nature of activity
   c. Equity capital and its ownership structure

   — percentage held by the Member State
   — percentage held by nationals of the Member State
   — percentage held by nationals of other Member States
   — percentage held by foreigners

The Executive Secretariat shall give to each enterprise concerned an Authorisation Number that shall necessarily be quoted on the ECOWAS Certificate of Origin, and shall inform Member States accordingly.

## ARTICLE 2

Paragraph 2 of Article 11 of the Protocol relating to the definition of originating products shall be consequently modified.

. . .

Reprined from ECOWAS Official Journal 2 (June 1980): 5.

# APPENDIX D-4
## ECOWAS: Decision Relating to Trade Liberalization in Industrial Products

### ARTICLE 1

TRADE LIBERALIZATION IN INDUSTRIAL PRODUCTS AND ELIMINATION OF TARIFF BARRIERS SHALL BE GOVERNED BY THE FOLLOWING SCHEDULES:

### SCHEDULE I

a. Products of Community Enterprises
   Such products shall be liberalized immediately they are produced and they shall have free access to the Community market duty free.

b. Priority Industrial Products to enjoy Accelerated Liberalization
   Such products shall be liberalized over a period of four (4) years at the following rate: 25, 50, 75 and 100 per cent which shall be implemented on the 28th of May of the years 1981, 1982, 1983 and 1984 respectively.

c. Other Products
   Such products shall be liberalized over a period of six (6) years at the following rate: 15, 30, 50, 70, 90 and 100 per cent which shall be implemented on the 28th of May of the years 1981, 1982, 1983, 1984, 1985 and 1986 respectively.

2. THE TARIFF ELIMINATION SCHEME STIPULATED IN SCHEDULE I ABOVE SHALL APPLY TO IVORY COAST, GHANA, NIGERIA AND SENEGAL.

### SCHEDULE II

a. Products of Community Enterprises
   Such products shall be liberalized immediately they are produced and they shall have free access to the Community market duty free.

b. Priority Industrial Products to enjoy Accelerated Liberalization
   Such products shall be liberalized over a period of six (6) years at the rate of 15, 30, 50, 70, 90 and 100 per cent which shall be implemented on the 28th of May of the years 1981, 1982, 1983, 1984, 1985 and 1986 respectively.

Reprined from *ECOWAS Official Journal* 2 (June 1980): 6.

c. Other Products

Such products shall be liberalized over a period of eight (8) years at the rate of 10, 20, 30, 45, 60, 75, 90 and 100 per cent which shall be implemented on the 28th of May of the years 1981, 1982, 1983, 1984, 1985, 1986, 1987 and 1988 respectively.

3. THE TARIFF ELIMINATION SCHEME STIPULATED IN SCHEDULE II ABOVE SHALL APPLY TO BENIN, CAPE VERDE, GAMBIA, GUINEA, GUINEA BISSAU, UPPER VOLTA [BURKINA FASO], LIBERIA, MALI, MAURITANIA, NIGER, SIERRA LEONE AND TOGO.

## ARTICLE II
## ELIMINATION OF NON-TARIFF BARRIERS

For the purposes of eliminating non-tariff barriers the following scheme shall apply:

1. All Member States shall be treated on the same level.
2. The method of liberalization shall be left to the discretion of Member States.
3. Liberalization shall be undertaken at a faster rate than tariff barriers and shall be eliminated over a period of four (4) years commencing from the 28th May, 1981.

. . .

# APPENDIX D-5
## ECOWAS: Decision Relating to Application of the Compensation Procedures for the Loss of Revenue Suffered by Member States as a Result of the Liberalization Programme

. . .

## ARTICLE 1

### CHAPTER I: DEFINITIONS AND PROCEDURES

The loss of revenue suffered by a Member State due to the implementation of the Treaty constitutes the total shortfall in receipts recorded by that Member State as a result of Trade Liberalization within the Community.

This is equal to the difference between the revenue that would have accrued if the most favoured nation rate or the general rate, whichever, was applicable and consolidated on 28 May, 1979, and the actual revenue collected by using the preferential rate of duty derived from the liberalization programme as decided by the Council of Ministers.

## ARTICLE 2

The preferential rate of duty shall be the difference between the rate applicable to the third country benefitting from the most favoured Nation clause and the product of this rate by applying the liberalization rate resulting from the liberalization programme, decided by the Authority of Heads of State and Government.

In the event of the favoured Nation rate not granted to third country, the preferential rate of taxation shall be the difference between the rate of common duties consolidated in May, 1979 and the product of this rate derived by applying the liberalization rate resulting from the Liberalization programme decided by the Authority of Heads of State and Government.

. . .

## ARTICLE 11
### CHAPTER III: PAYMENT OF COMPENSATION

The payment of compensation to a Member State shall be calculated subject to deductions of any shortfalls in revenue recorded in respect of originating products imported by this Member State which may be identified as re-exported goods.

---

Reprinted from ECOWAS *Official Journal* 2 (June 1980): 7–8.

## ARTICLE 12

Losses in revenue resulting from the preferential duties shall be fully compensated for. However, for reasons of solidarity the Council of Ministers decided that one fifth (1/5) of the losses suffered by the four more developed countries, i.e. Ivory Coast, Ghana, Nigeria and Senegal shall be subjected to redistribution in the following manner:

i. During the first five (5) years of the trade liberalization, this one fifth (1/5) shall be made fully available to the least developed States and shall be inversely proportional to the coefficient of the contribution of Member States to the budget of the Community.

ii. After this period of five (5) years, this one fifth (1/5) shall be given to all the sixteen Member States on the above-mentioned basis.

. . .

## ECOWAS: Protocol Relating to Free Movement of Persons, Residence and Establishment
### (May 1, 1979)

. . .

## GENERAL PRINCIPLES ON MOVEMENT OF PERSONS, RESIDENCE AND ESTABLISHMENT

### ARTICLE 2

1. The Community citizens have the right to enter, reside and establish in the territory of Member States.

2. The right of entry, residence and establishment referred to in paragraph 1 above shall be progressively established in the course of a maximum transitional period of fifteen (15) years from the definitive entry into force of this protocol by abolishing all other obstacles to free movement of persons and the right of residence and establishment.

3. The right of entry, residence and establishment which shall be established in the course of a transitional period shall be accomplished in three phases, namely:

  **Phase I —Right of Entry and Abolition of Visa**
  **Phase II —Right of Residence**
  **Phase III—Right of Establishment**

4. Upon the expiration of a maximum period of five (5) years from the definitive entry into force of this Protocol the Commission, based upon the experience gained from the implementation of the first phase as set out in Article 3 below, shall make proposals to the Council of Ministers for further liberalization towards the subsequent phases of freedom of residence and establishment of persons within the Community and these phases shall be dealt with in subsequent Annexes to this Protocol.

## PART III

## IMPLEMENTATION OF THE FIRST PHASE: ABOLITION OF VISAS AND ENTRY PERMIT

### ARTICLE 3

1. Any citizen of the Community who wishes to enter the territory of any

---

Reprinted from *ECOWAS Official Journal* 1 (June 1979): 3.

other Member States shall be required to possess valid travel document and international health certificate.

2. A citizen of the Community visiting any Member State for a period not exceeding ninety (90) days shall enter the territory of that Member State through the official entry point free of visa requirements. Such citizen shall however, be required to obtain permission for an extension of stay from the appropriate authority if after such entry that citizen has cause to stay for more than ninety (90) days.

## ARTICLE 4

Notwithstanding the provisions of Article 3 above, Member States shall reserve the right to refuse admission into their territory Community any citizen who comes within the category of inadmissible immigrants under its laws.

## PART IV

## MOVEMENT OF VEHICLES FOR THE
## TRANSPORTATION OF PERSONS

## ARTICLE 5

In order to facilitate the movement of persons transported in private or commercial vehicles the following provisions shall apply:

### 1. Private Vehicles

A private vehicle registered in the territory of a Member State may enter the territory of another Member State and remain there for a period not exceeding ninety (90) days upon presentation of the documents listed hereunder to the competent authority of that Member State:

(i) **Valid driving license**
(ii) **Matriculation Certificate (Ownership Card) or Log Book**
(iii) **Insurance Policy recognised by Member States**
(iv) **International customs carnet recognised within the Community.**

### 2. Commercial Vehicles

A commercial vehicle registered in the territory of a Member State and carrying passengers may enter the territory of another Member State and remain there for a period not exceeding fifteen (15) days upon presentation of the documents listed hereunder to the competent authority of that Member State:

  (i) **Valid driving license**
  (ii) **Matriculation Certificate (Ownership Card) or Log Book**
  (iii) **Insurance Policy recognised by Member States**
  (iv) **International customs carnet recognised within the Community.**

During the period of fifteen (15) days the commercial motor vehicle shall however not engage in any commercial activities within the territory of the Member State entered.

. . .

## APPENDIX D-7
### ECOWAS: Protocol Relating to the Re-Exportation Within ECOWAS of Goods Imported from Third Countries
### (November 5, 1976)

### ARTICLE II
### Customs Duty Collected to be Refunded in the Collecting State

1. Where any goods, which are imported into a Member State of the Community from a third country and in respect of which customs duty has been charged and collected in that State (in this paragraph referred to as "the Collecting State") are transferred to one of the other Member States of the Community (in this paragraph referred to as "the Consuming State") the following provisions shall apply:

    (a) An administrative fee representing 0.5% of the c.i.f. value of every consignment being re-exported is to be charged by the Collecting State.

    (b) The Collecting State shall refund to the importer within its territory, the full amount of duty paid on the goods while other costs such as c.i.f., port charges, etc. involved in the importation are to be included in the invoiced price to be paid by the importer in the Consuming State.

    (c) The Consuming State shall charge and collect the duty payable on such goods.

2. Where goods which are imported into a Member State of the Community from a third country and in respect of which customs duty is charged and collected in that State (in this paragraph referred to as "the Collecting State") are wholly or in part used in Collecting State in the manufacture of other goods (in this Article referred to as "the manufactured goods"), and the manufactured goods are subsequently transferred to another Member State of the Community (in this Article referred to as "the Consuming State"), the Collecting State shall refund to the importer within its territory the full amount of the duty collected in respect of the goods imported and used in the production of the manufactured goods subsequently transferred in the Consuming State.

## APPENDIX E-1
## CACM: General Treaty of Central American Economic
## Integration (Managua, Nicaragua, 1960)

· · ·

**Article I**  The contracting States agree to set up among themselves a common market which should be fully established in not more than five years from the date of the entry into force of this Treaty. They also undertake to set up a customs union among their territories.

**Article II**  For the purposes of the previous Article, the contracting Parties shall undertake to complete the establishment of a Central American free trade area within a period of five years and to adopt a uniform Central American tariff in accordance with the terms of the Central American Agreement on the Equalization of Import Charges.

### Chapter II

### TRADE REGIME

**Article III**  The signatory States shall grant free trade rights for all products originating in their respective territories, with the sole limitations included in the special regimes referred to in Annex A of this Treaty.

Accordingly, the natural products of the contracting countries and products manufactured in them shall be exempt from import and export duties, including consular fees, and all other taxes, surcharges and imposts levied on such imports and exports or on the occasion of their importation and exportation, whether such duties, fees, taxes, surcharges, and imposts are national, municipal, or of any other nature.

The exemptions provided for in this article shall not include taxes or charges for lighterage, docking, warehousing, and handling of goods or any other charges which may be legitimately levied by port, warehouse, and transport services; nor shall they include exchange differentials resulting from the existence of two or more rates of exchange or from any other exchange measures adopted in any of the contracting countries.

Goods originating in the territory of the contracting States shall be accorded national treatment in all of them and shall be exempt from any restrictions or measures of a quantitative nature, apart from control measures which are legally applicable in the territories of the contracting States for reasons of a public health, security or police character.

Reprinted from Inter-American Institute of International Legal Studies, *Instruments Relating to the Economic Integration of Latin America*, vol. 2 (Dobbs Ferry, New York: Oceana, 1975), p. 385.

**Article XI** No contracting State shall grant, directly or indirectly, any subsidy in favor of the export of goods intended for the territories of the other States, or establish or maintain any system resulting in the sale of a given commodity for export to another contracting State at a price lower than the established price for the sale of the said commodity on the domestic market, making due allowance for differences in the conditions of sale and taxation, as well as for other factors affecting price comparability.

. . .

**Article XII** Since it would be a practice contrary to the aims of this Treaty, each contracting State shall, through the legal means at its disposal, prevent the exportation of goods from its territory to that of the other States at a price lower than their normal value, if this would jeopardize or threaten to jeopardize production in the other countries or retard the establishment of a domestic or Central American industry.

A commodity shall be considered to be exported at a lower price than its normal value if the price of the said commodity is less than:

a) the comparable price, under normal trade conditions, for a similar commodity when intended for consumption in the domestic market of the exporting country; or

b) the highest comparable price for a similar commodity exported to a third country under normal trade conditions; or

c) the cost of production of the commodity in the country of origin plus a reasonable addition in respect of the sales cost and profit.

. . .

## CENTRAL AMERICAN BANK FOR ECONOMIC INTEGRATION

**Article XVIII** The signatory States agree to establish the Central American Bank for Economic Integration which shall have the legal status of a corporate body. The Bank shall act as an instrument for the financing and promotion of integrated economic growth, on the basis of balanced regional development. To this end, the contracting States shall sign the Agreement setting up the said institution, which Agreement shall remain open for the signature or adhesion of any other Central American State which may wish to become a member of the Bank.

It shall be laid down, however, that members of the Bank may not obtain guarantees or loans from the said institution if they have not previously deposited the instruments of ratification of the following international agreements:

. . .

# APPENDIX E-2
## CACM: Central American Agreement on Fiscal Incentives to Industrial Development
### (July 31, 1962)

**Article 3** The contracting States will not grant to manufacturing industries fiscal privileges of a kind, amount, or duration different from those provided in this Agreement. Excepted from this provision are exemptions granted with respect to municipal or local taxes.

The contracting States will not grant fiscal exemptions to productive activities not included in Article 2 above, except to the following, which may be regulated by laws or provisions of a national character:

a) Mineral-extracting industries;
b) Industries extracting petroleum and natural gas;
c) Forestry and the extraction of lumber;
d) Pisciculture and fishing;
e) Service industries and activities;
f) Agricultural activities; and
g) The construction of low-cost housing. In this case it will be possible to grant exemptions from customs on imports of construction materials only when Central American substitutes adequate in quality, quantity, and price are not available.

The exceptions referred to in the foregoing subheadings shall not include typically manufacturing processing of the products obtained, which will be controlled by the provisions of this Agreement.

. . .

**Article 5** Enterprises which fulfill the conditions enumerated in Chapter III will be classified as belonging to one of the following groups: A, B, and C.

Classified in Group A will be those enterprises which:

a) Produce industrial raw materials or capital goods; or
b) Produce articles of consumption, containers, or semimanufactured products, provided that at least fifty percent of the total value of the raw materials, containers, or semimanufactured products used are of Central American origin.

Reprinted from Inter-American Institute of International Legal Studies, *Instruments Relating to the Economic Integration of Latin America*, vol. 2 (Dobbs Ferry, New York: Oceana, 1975), p. 479.

Classified in Group B will be those enterprises which combine the three following requirements:

a) Produce articles of consumption, containers, or semimanufactured products;
b) Give rise to important net benefits in the balance of payments and to a high value added in the industrial process;
c) Utilize entirely, or in a high proportion, in terms of value, non-Central American raw materials, containers, and semimanufactured products.

Classified in Group C will be those enterprises which:

a) Do not satisfy the requirements indicated for Groups A and B;
b) Simply assemble, pack, cut up, or dilute products; or
c) Belong to the industries expressly enumerated in Annex 1 to this Agreement.

For the purpose of applying this article, use shall be made of the definitions established in Annex 2 of this Agreement. For the purpose of classifying the enterprises in Group A, subheading (a), use shall be made of the list of capital goods and of raw materials of industrial origin which will be adopted, for this purpose, by the Executive Council of the General Treaty of Central American Economic Integration, within a period of thirty days from the date the present Agreement enters into force.

· · ·

**Article 7**  The industrial enterprises in Group A and B shall be classified as belonging to new or existing industries.

Classified as new industries will be those manufacturing articles which:

a) Are not produced in the country; or
b) Are produced in the country by rudimentary methods of manufacture, provided that the new plant satisfies the two following conditions:
    i) It fills an important part of the unsatisfied demand in the market of the country; and
    ii) It introduces radically different technical processes of manufacture which change the existing structure of the industry and lead to an improvement in productivity and a reduction in costs.

In order to determine whether an enterprise fulfills the requirements enumerated in section (b), it will be necessary for the authorities charged with the application of this Agreement in each country, before classifying one of these enterprises as belonging to the group of new industries, to request and receive a favorable technical opinion of the Permanent Secretariat of the General Treaty.

All other industries not included under the headings (a) and (b) above shall be classified as belonging to the group of existing industries.

## Chapter V
## FISCAL BENEFITS

**Article 8** The fiscal benefits which will be granted in accordance with this Agreement are the following:

I. Total or partial exemption from customs duties and other related charges (including the consular fees but not charges for specific services) which are levied on the importation of the articles mentioned below when the latter are indispensable for the establishment or operation of the enterprises and cannot be taken care of by adequate Central American substitutes:
a) Machinery and equipment;
b) Raw materials, semimanufactured products, and containers;
c) Fuels strictly for the industrial process, except gasoline. This exemption will not be granted to industrial enterprises for their transport operations, nor for the generation of their own power when there already exists an adequate supply from public service plants.

II. Exemption, for the enterprise and its owners, from the tax on income and on profits with respect to revenues derived from qualified activities. The exemption will not be granted when these enterprises or their owners are subject in other countries to taxes which would make this exemption ineffective.

III. Exemption from taxes on assets and on net worth payable by the enterprise or its owners or stockholders by reason of qualified activities.

• • •

**Article 11** Enterprises classified in Group A as belonging to new industries will receive the following benefits:
a) Total exemption from customs duties and other related charges, including consular fees, for ten years, on the importation of machinery and equipment;
b) Exemption from customs duties and other related charges, on the importation of raw materials, semimanufactured products and containers, as follows: one hundred percent during the first five years; sixty percent during the three following years; and forty percent during the two years then following;
c) Total exemption from customs duties and other related charges, including consular fees, for five years, on the importation of fuels strictly for the industrial process, except gasoline;

d) Total exemption from taxes on income and profits for eight years; and

e) Total exemption from taxes on assets and on net worth for ten years.

**Article 12**   Enterprises classified in Group A as belonging to existing industries will receive the following benefits:

a) Total exemption from customs duties and other related charges, including consular fees, for six years on the importation of machinery and equipment;

b) Total exemption from taxes on income and profits for two years; and,

c) Total exemption from taxes on assets and on net worth for four years.

**Article 13**   Enterprises classified in Group B as belonging to new industries will receive the following benefits:

a) Total exemption from customs duties and other related charges, including consular fees, for eight years, on the importation of machinery and equipment;

b) Exemption from customs duties and other related charges, including consular fees, on the importation of raw materials, semimanufactured products, and containers, as follows: one hundred percent during the first three years and fifty percent during the two following years;

c) Exemptions from customs duties and other related charges, including consular fees, on the importation of fuels strictly for the industrial process, except gasoline, as follows: one hundred percent during the first three years and fifty percent during the two following years;

d) Total exemption from taxes on income and profits during six years; and

e) Total exemption from taxes on assets and on net worth for six years.

**Article 14**   Enterprises classified in Group B as belonging to existing industries will receive total exemption from customs duties and other related charges, including consular fees, on machinery and equipment for a period of five years.

**Article 15**   Enterprises classified in Group C will receive total exemption from customs fees and other related charges, including consular fees, on the importation of machinery and equipment for a period of three years.

**Article 16**   Classified enterprises which produce raw materials or capital goods and which during the period of their concession utilize or come to utilize Central American raw materials which represent at least fifty percent of the total value of the raw materials will enjoy the benefit of total exemption from the taxes referred to by letters (d) and (e) of Article 11, and (b) and (c) of Article 12, above, of the present Agreement, for an additional period of two years.

**Article 17**   Qualified enterprises, which propose to install plants in an industry in which other enterprises of the same country are enjoying fiscal benefits corresponding to new industries in accordance with this Agreement, will have a right to the same benefits in return for fulfilling equivalent commitments and obligations, but only for the time elapsing before the expiration of the benefits corresponding to the first concession granted.

Once the period referred to in the preceding paragraph is over, and if this period is shorter than that corresponding to existing industry, the enterprises shall receive the benefits of existing industries, but only for the time that must elapse to complete the time period of the latter, in accordance with the terms of their executive order or decrees of classification.

**Article 18**   The period of exemption for the tax on income or profits will begin to be counted from the tax period in which the classified industry begins its production, or, if it had already been in production, from the tax period in which the order or decree of classification enters into effect.

The first year of the period of exemption for taxes on assets or net worth will be that in which the order or decree of classification was published.

**Article 19**   The period of exemptions on customs duties and other related charges, in the case of machinery and equipment, will begin on the date on which the first importation is made of any of these goods.

The period of custom exemption for raw materials, semimanufactured products, containers, and fuels will begin to be counted from the date on which the first importation of any of these articles is effected.

. . .

**Article 25**   During the first seven years the present Agreement is in force, the enterprises which propose to dedicate themselves to industries which already exist in one or more of the countries, but not in others, may be classed in the latter as new industries, being granted the benefits corresponding to this condition and to the classification assigned to them within the three groups referred to in Article 5 of this Agreement.

. . .

# APPENDIX E-3
## CACM: Agreement on the System of Integrated Industries
### (June 10, 1958)

**Article II** The contracting States declare their interest in the development of industries with access to a common Central American market. These shall be designated Central American integrated industries and shall be so declared jointly by the contracting States, through the agency of the Central American Industrial Integration Commission established in conformity with Article VIII of this Agreement.

The contracting States shall regard as Central American integrated industries those industries which, in the judgment of the Central American Industrial Integration Commission, comprise one or more plants which require access to the Central American market in order to operate under reasonably economic and competitive conditions even at minimum capacity.

**Article III** The application of the present System of Central American Integrated Industries is subject to signature by the contracting States, in respect of each of the said industries, of an additional protocol stipulating:
  a) The country or countries in which the industrial plants covered by this System are to be initially situated, the minimum capacity of the said plants and the conditions under which additional plants are to be subsequently admitted into the same or other countries;
  b) The quality standards for the products of the said industries and any other requirements that may be deemed convenient for the protection of the consumer;
  c) The regulations that may be advisable as regards the participation of Central American capital in the enterprises owning the plants;
  d) The common Central American tariffs which shall be applied to the products of Central American integrated industries; and
  e) Any other provisions designed to ensure the attainment of the objectives of this Agreement.

**Article IV** The products of plants which form part of a Central American integrated industry and which are covered by the present System, shall enjoy the benefits of free trade between the territories of the contracting States.

The products of plants which form part of the same industry but which are not covered by the System, shall enjoy in the contracting States successive annual reductions of ten percent in the applicable uniform Central American

Reprinted from Inter-American Institute of International Legal Studies, *Instruments Relating to the Economic Integration of Latin America*, vol. 2 (Dobbs Ferry, New York: Oceana, 1975), p. 451.

tariff, from the date specified in the relevant additional protocol. As from the tenth year, such products shall enjoy the full benefits of free trade.

Except as provided in the preceding paragraph and in any other provisions of this Agreement or of the additional protocols, all trade in commodities produced by the Central American integrated industries shall be governed by the provisions of the Multilateral Treaty of Free Trade and Central American Economic Integration.

. . .

**Article VII**  Except in cases of emergency, the governments of the contracting States shall not grant customs duty exemptions or reductions below the Central American common tariff on any imports from countries outside Central America of goods which are equal or similar to or substitutes for goods manufactured in any of the Central American countries by plants of industrial integrated industries, nor shall they apply to such imports preferential exchange rates equivalent to such exemptions or reductions.

The governments and other state bodies shall also give preference in their official imports to the products of the Central American integrated industries.

. . .

**Article IX**  Individuals or legal entities desiring the incorporation of a given plant into the present System shall present an application to that effect to the Secretariat of the Central American Industrial Integration Commission and accompany it with the required information.

When the Secretariat has sufficient information available, it shall advise the Commission of the application. If the Commission finds that the project meets the aims of this Agreement, the application shall be referred for an opinion to the Central American Institute for Industrial Research and Technology or to any other person or body that the Commission considers competent. Such opinion shall take into account the technological and economic aspects of the project and, in particular, the market prospects, and the costs incurred shall be borne by the interested parties.

The Commission shall decide on the project on the basis of the said opinion, and if it finds the project capable of being realized, shall make whatever recommendations it considers pertinent to the governments of the contracting States on the conclusion of the protocol covering the industry concerned and on the conditions to be stipulated.

. . .

**Transitional Article**  In order to promote an equitable distribution of the

Central American industrial integrated plants, the contracting States shall not award a second plant to any one country until all of the Central American countries have each been assigned a plant in conformity with the protocols specified in Article III.

.  .  .

# APPENDIX F-1
## CARICOM: Treaty Establishing the Caribbean Community (1973), Annex Establishing the Caribbean Common Market

### Article 11

### Disputes Procedure Within the Common Market

1. If any Member State considers that any benefit conferred upon it by this Annex or any objective of the Common Market is being or may be frustrated and if no satisfactory settlement is reached between the Member States concerned any of those Member States may refer the matter to the Council.

2. The Council shall promptly make arrangements for examining the matter. Such arrangements may include a reference to a Tribunal constituted in accordance with Article 12 of this Annex. The Council shall refer the matter at the request of any Member State concerned to the Tribunal. Member States shall furnish all information which may be required by the Tribunal or the Council in order that the facts may be established and the issue determined.

· · ·

### Article 12

### Reference to Tribunal

1. The establishment and composition of the Tribunal referred to in Article 11 of this Annex shall be governed by the following provisions of this Article.

2. For the purposes of establishing an *ad hoc* tribunal referred to in Article 11 of this Annex, a list of arbitrators consisting of qualified jurists shall be drawn up and maintained by the Secretary-General. To this end, every Member State shall be invited to nominate two persons, and the names of the persons so nominated shall constitute the list. The term of an arbitrator, including that of any arbitrator nominated to fill a vacancy, shall be five years and may be renewed.

· · ·

Reprinted from Inter-American Institute of International Legal Studies, *Instruments Relating to the Economic Integration of Latin America*, vol. 2 (Dobbs Ferry, New York, 1975), p. 665.

## Article 13

### Exclusion from the Annex

1. Subject to the provisions of this Article, nothing in this Annex shall be taken to prevent the Member State concerned from imposing import duties or quantitative restrictions on the products listed in Schedule I to this Annex for such periods as are specified therein for the purpose of giving effect to any undertaking by such Member State respecting import duties or quantitative restrictions.

· · ·

## Article 14

### Common Market Origin*

1. Subject to Schedule II of this Annex, in this Annex goods shall be treated as being of Common Market origin if they are consigned from a Member State to a consignee in another Member State and comply with any one of the following conditions, that is to say, the goods must—
   a) have been wholly produced within the Common Market;
   b) fall within a description of goods listed in a Process List to be established by the decision of Council and have been produced within the Common Market by the appropriate qualifying process described in that List, or
   c) have been produced within the Common Market and the value of any materials imported from outside the Common Market or of undedetermined origin which have been used at any stage of the production of the goods does not exceed
      i) in a Less Developed Member Country 60 per cent of the export price of the goods;
      ii) in any other Member State 50 per cent of the export price of the goods.

2. For the purpose of sub-paragraphs (a) to (c) of paragraph 1 of this Article, materials listed in the Basic Materials List which forms the Appendix to Schedule II to this Annex which have been used in the state described in that List in a process of production within the Common Market shall be deemed to contain no element from outside the Common Market.

· · ·

---

*Note: these rules have been changed. See p. 23, *supra*.

## Article 15

### Import Duties

1. Except as provided in Article 52 and Schedule III to this Annex Member States shall not apply any import duties on goods of Common Market origin.

2. Nothing in paragraph 1 of this Article shall be construed to extend to the imposition of non-discriminatory internal charges on any products or a substitute not produced in the importing Member State.

3. For the purposes of this Article and Schedule III to this Annex the term "import duties" means any tax or surtax of customs and any other charges of equivalent effect whether fiscal, monetary or exchange, which are levied on imports except duties notified under Article 17 of this Annex and other charges which fall within that Article.

. . .

## Article 19

### Dumped and Subsidised Imports

1. Nothing in this Annex shall prevent any Member State from taking action against dumped or subsidised imports that conforms with any other international obligations.

. . .

## Article 20

### Freedom of Transit

1. Products imported into, or exported from, a Member State shall enjoy freedom of transit within the Common Market and shall only be subject to the payment of the normal rates for services rendered.

2. For the purposes of paragraph 1 of this Article, 'transit' means transit within the meaning of Article V of the General Agreement on Tariffs and Trade.

## Article 21

### Quantitative Import Restrictions

1. Except where otherwise provided in this Annex, and particularly in Articles 13, 23, 24, 28, 29 and 56 and in Schedules VII, VIII, IX, X and XI, a Member State shall not apply any quantitative restrictions on the import of goods which are of Common Market origin.

2. "Quantitative restrictions" means prohibitions or restrictions on imports into, or exports from, any other Member State, as the case may be, whether made effective through quotas, import licences or other measures with equivalent effect, including administrative measures and requirements restricting imports or exports.

. . .

## Article 22

### Quantitative Export Restrictions

1. Except where otherwise provided in this Annex, and particularly in Articles 23 and 24 and in Schedules VIII, IX and XI, a Member State shall not apply any quantitative restrictions on exports to any other Member State.

2. This Article shall not prevent any Member State from taking such measures as are necessary to prevent evasion of any prohibitions or restrictions which it applies to exports outside the Common Market, provided that less favourable treatment is not granted to Member States than to countries outside the Common Market.

. . .

## Article 25

### Government Aids

1. Except as provided in this Annex, a Member State shall not maintain or introduce—
   a) the forms of aid to export of goods to any other part of the Common Market of the kinds which are described in Schedule VI to this Annex; or

b) any other forms of aid, the main purpose or effect of which is to frustrate the benefits expected from such removal or absence of duties and quantitative restrictions as is required by this Annex.

. . .

## Article 28

### Import Restrictions Arising from Balance of Payments Difficulties

1. Notwithstanding Article 21 of this Annex a Member State may, consistently with any international obligations to which it is subject, introduce quantitative restrictions on imports for the purpose of safeguarding its balance of payments.

. . .

## Article 29

### Difficulties in Particular Industries

1. If, in a Member State—

a) any industry or particular sector of an industry experiences serious difficulties due to a substantial decrease in internal demand for a domestic product; and

b) this decrease in demand is due to an increase in imports consigned from other Member States as a result of the establishment of the Common Market, that Member State may, notwithstanding any other provisions of this Annex

    i) limit those imports by means of quantitative restrictions to a rate not less than the rate of such imports during any period of 12 months which ended within 12 months of the date on which the restrictions came into force; the restrictions shall not be continued for a period longer than 18 months, unless the Council, by majority vote, authorises their continuance for such further period and on such conditions as the Council considers appropriate; and. . . .

## Article 30

### Restrictive Business Practices

1. Member States recognise that the following practices are incompatible

with this Annex in so far as they frustrate the benefits expected from such removal or absence of duties and quantitative restrictions as is required by this Annex—

    a) agreements between enterprises, decisions by associations of enterprises and concerted practices between enterprises which have as their object or result the prevention, restriction or distortion of competition within the Common Market;

    b) actions by which one or more enterprises take unfair advantage of a dominant position within the Common Market or a substantial part of it.

2. If any practice of the kind described in paragraph 1 of this Article is referred to the Council in accordance with Article 11 of this Annex the Council may, in any recommendation in accordance with paragraph 3 or in any decision in accordance with paragraph 4 of that Article, make provision for publication of a report on the circumstances of the matter.

3. a) In the light of experience, the Council shall, as soon as practicable, consider whether further or different provisions are necessary to deal with the effect of restrictive business practices or dominant enterprises on trade within the Common Market.

    b) Such review shall include consideration of the following matters—

        i) specification of restrictive business practices or dominant enterprises with which the Council should be concerned;

        ii) methods of securing information about restrictive business practices or dominant enterprises;

        iii) procedures for investigation;

        iv) whether the right to initiate inquires should be conferred on the Council.

. . .

## Article 31

### Establishment of Common External Tariff

Member States agree to establish and maintain a common external tariff in respect of all commodities imported from third countries in accordance with a plan and schedule to be adopted immediately upon the entry into force of this Annex, provided that—

    a) In so far as the Less Developed Countries, except Belize and Montserrat, are concerned, their existing Tariffs under the East Caribbean Common Market Agreement shall be deemed as fulfilling their initial obligations in relation to the Common External Tariff of the Caribbean Common Market.

b) Wherever the Plan and Schedule of rates in the existing Customs Tariff of the East Caribbean Common Market differ from those in the Common External Tariff of the Caribbean Common Market, the Plans and Schedules of rates in both the East Caribbean Common Market and the Caribbean Common Market Tariffs will be subject to annual review in the light of the prevailing economic situation of the Less Developed Countries for the purpose of determining the appropriate Plan and Schedule that will be introduced provided that the introduction of such a Plan and Schedule will commence not later than 1st August, 1977 and the phasing period will end not later than 1st August, 1981.

c) In so far as Belize and Montserrat are concerned, their existing Tariffs on 1st May, 1974, shall be deemed as fulfilling their initial obligations in relation to the Common External Tariff of the Caribbean Common Market. They shall progressively phase their tariffs in accordance with the annual reviews mentioned in paragraph (b) of this proviso; provided that, in the case of Montserrat, the introduction of the Plan and Schedule will commence not later than 1st August, 1981, and the phasing period will end not later than 1st August, 1985.

. . .

## Article 35

### Establishment

1. Each Member State recognises that restrictions on the establishment and operation of economic enterprises therein by nationals of other Member States should not be applied, through accord to such persons of treatment which is less favourable than that accorded in such matters to nationals of that Member State, in such a way as to frustrate the benefits expected from such removal or absence of duties and quantitative restrictions as is required by this Annex.

. . .

## Article 36

### Right to Provide Services

1. Each Member State agrees as far as practicable to extend to persons belonging to other Member States preferential treatment over persons belonging to States outside the Common Market with regard to the provision of services.

. . .

## Article 38

### Saving in Respect of Movement of Persons

Nothing in this Treaty shall be construed as requiring, or imposing any obligation on, a Member State to grant freedom of movement to persons into its territory whether or not such persons are nationals of other Member States.

. . .

## Article 56

### Promotion of Industrial Development
### in the Less Developed Countries

1. Upon any application made in that behalf by the Less Developed Countries the Council may, if necessary, as a temporary measure in order to promote the development of an industry in any of these States, authorise by majority decision such States to suspend Common Market tariff treatment of any description of imports eligible therefor on grounds of production in the other Member States.

2. Upon any application made in that behalf by the Less Developed Countries the Council may, if necessary, as a temporary measure in order to promote the development of an industry in any of those States, authorise by majority decision such states to impose quantitative restrictions on like imports from the other Member States.

3. In the light of the special position of Barbados that State may, in relation to trade with the Less Developed Countries, during the period for which the authorisations referred to in paragraphs 1 and 2 of this Article are in force, suspend Common Market tariff treatment of, or apply quantitative restrictions on, the like description of imports from the Less Developed Countries.

. . .

## Article 67

### Recognition of Existing Integration Arrangements
### Within the Common Market

Nothing in this Annex shall affect any decisions or things done under the East Caribbean Common Market Agreement immediately before the coming into force of this Annex or the continued application and development of that Agreement to the extent that the objectives of the Agreement are not achieved in the application of the objectives of this Annex, provided such application or development does not conflict with obligations under this Annex of the Member States which are Parties to that Agreement.

. . .

# CARICOM: Agreement on Harmonization of Fiscal Incentives To Industry
## (June 1, 1973)

ARTICLE 5: Classification of Approved Enterprises

. . .

4. Where an enterprise is engaged in a highly capital intensive industry—
(a) Nothing in the foregoing provisions of this Article shall apply thereto for the purpose of this Agreement; and
(b) a Member State may grant any benefit thereto for a period not exceeding that for which the benefit may be granted to Enclave Enterprises in accordance with Appendix I to this Agreement.

5. In paragraph 4 of this Article a "highly capital intensive industry" is one, the capital investment in which is not less than—
(a) $25 million in the currency of the Eastern Caribbean Territories in any Less Developed Country;
(b) $50 million in the currency of the Eastern Caribbean Territories in any More Developed Country.

ARTICLE 6: Relief from Tonnage Tax and Customs Duty on Plant, Equipment, Machinery, Spare Parts and Raw Materials

Member States must not grant to an approved enterprise relief from customs duties (including tonnage tax) on plant, equipment, machinery, spare parts, raw materials and components imported from outside the Member States for use in the manufacture of approved products for a period in excess of that respectively specified in Appendix I to this Agreement, so, however, that if the relevant authority of the Member State is satisfied that raw materials of a comparable price and quality and in adequate quantities are available from Member States for import and the approved enterprise continues to import raw materials from States other than Member States, the relevant authority must impose tariff and quota restrictions on the importation of such raw materials from States other than Member States provided that no restrictions shall apply to any relief from customs duty on imported raw materials or components used in Enclave Enterprises.

---

Reprinted from Inter-American Institute of International Legal Studies, *Instruments Relating to the Economic Integration of Latin America*, vol. 2 (Dobbs Ferry, New York: Oceana, 1975), p. 569.

ARTICLE 6: Relief from Tonnage Tax and Customs
Duty on Plant, Equipment, Machinery, Spare Parts
and Raw Materials

Member States must not grant to an approved enterprise relief from customs duties (including tonnage tax) on plant, equipment, machinery, spare parts, raw materials and components imported from outside the Member States for use in the manufactured of approved products for a period in excess of that respectively specified in Appendix I to this Agreement, so, however, that if the relevant authority of the Member State is satisfied that raw materials of a comparable price and quality and in adequate quantities are available from Member States for import and the approved enterprise continues to import raw materials from States other than Member States, the relevant authority must impose tariff and quota restrictions on the importation of such raw materials from States other than Member States provided that no restrictions shall apply to any relief from customs duty on imported raw materials or components used in Enclave Enterprises.

## ARTICLE 7: Relief from Income Tax

1. Member States must not grant to an approved enterprise relief from income tax in respect of profits or gains derived from the manufacture of the approved product for a period in excess of that respectively specified in Appendix I to this Agreement.

2. Subject to the provisions of this Agreement any relief from income tax shall be granted only in respect of profits accruing from the production date of an approved enterprise.

## ARTICLE 8: Relief from Income Tax Liability on Export Profits

1. Member States must grant relief from income tax on export profits only in accordance with this Article.

2. Member States must provide that if relief is granted under this Article to an approved enterprise, such relief may not be enjoyed by that enterprise during any period for which relief is granted under Article 6 or 7 or both.

3. The relief which may be granted to an approved enterprise under this Article shall be by way of a tax credit and must not be in excess of the percentage of income tax liability on the full amount of export profits of the approved enterprise from the manufacture of the approved product specified in the Second Column of the Table below, where the amount of export profit expressed

as a percentage of the full amount of the profits of the approved enterprise from the manufacture of the approved product is as respectively specified in the first column of the Table.

## TABLE

| First Column | Second Column |
|---|---|
| Percentage of Export Profits | Maximum Percentage of Income Tax Relief |
| 10 or more but less than 21 | 25 |
| 21 or more but less than 41 | 35 |
| 41 or more but less that 61 | 45 |
| 61 or more | 50 |

4. For the purpose of paragraph 3 of this Article export profits shall be taken to be the profits produced by the following formula:

$$\frac{E \times P}{S}$$

Where: E is the proceeds from export sales for the year;

P is the profits of the approved enterprise from all sales of the approved product for the year;

and S is the proceeds of all sales for the year.

5. No relief under this Article may be granted by a Member State to an enterprise engaged in a traditionally export-oriented industry in respect of a product of that industry that is traditionally exported by that Member State.

6. Subject to paragraphs 7 and 8 of this Article, relief under this Article may be granted only in respect of the export of an approved product to a State other than a Member State.

7. Less Developed Countries may grant relief under this Article to an approved enterprise for export to More Developed Countries, other than Barbados, for a period not exceeding five years next following the expiration of any period of relief granted under Article 6 or 7 or both of this Agreement.

8. During the period of five years after the commencement of this Agreement, a Less Developed Country may, notwithstanding paragraph 6, grant relief under this Article in respect of the exports to More Developed Countries,

other than Barbados, by an approved enterprise to which no relief under Articles 6 and 7 of this Agreement is granted.

## ARTICLE 9: Depreciation Allowances

Member States must provide that in computing the profits of an approved enterprise for the purposes of any relief from income tax under Article 7 of this Agreement, there shall be allowed and made

a) as from the production date of the approved enterprise, a deduction on account of any depreciation allowance which would, but for that relief, be claimable in the year;

b) such further deduction as an initial allowance for capital expenditure or plant, machinery and equipment incurred by the approved enterprise in the manufacture of the approved product after the expiration of the period of relief from income tax granted in accordance with Article 7 of this Agreement as the Member State may determine, but so that such deduction does not exceed 20% of the capital expenditure.

## ARTICLE 10: Carry Forward of Losses

1. Member States must provide that, upon the cessation of any relief from income tax under Article 7 of this Agreement, the net losses made during the period of such relief may, notwithstanding the grant of that relief in accordance with this Agreement, be carried forward for the purpose of set off in computing the profits of an enterprise for the period of five years next following the cessation of the relief.

. . .

## ARTICLE 11: Dividends and Other Distributions

. . .

2. Subject to paragraph 3, such dividends and other distributions made by an approved enterprise out of profits or gains accruing during the period of relief from income tax under Article 7 of this Agreement, or made by a recipient of such a dividend or other distribution may be exempt from income tax in the hands of a recipient.

. . .

## ARTICLE 12: Interest

Interest (in any form) on loan capital and any other borrowings of an approved enterprise (whether in the form of overdraft, debenture or otherwise) must not be exempt from income tax in the hands of the recipient.

. . .

## APPENDIX F-3
## CARICOM: Agreement for the Avoidance of Double Taxation and the Prevention of Fiscal Evasion With Respect to Taxes on Income and For the Encouragement of International Trade and Investment (June 1, 1973)

. . .

Agreement between the Governments of Barbados, Guyana, Jamaica and Trinidad and Tobago ON THE ONE HAND and Antigua, Belize, Dominica, Grenada, Montserrat, St. Kitts-Nevis-Anguilla, St. Lucia and St. Vincent ON THE OTHER HAND for the avoidance of Double Taxation and the prevention of fiscal evasion with respect to taxes on income and profits and for the encouragement of International Trade and Investment

. . .

### ARTICLE 2: Taxes Covered

1. The taxes which are the subject of this Agreement are
a)  i)  in Jamaica:
       the income tax, the company profits tax,
       the additional company profits tax and
       the investment company profits tax.
   ii)  in Barbados:
       the income tax
       the petroleum winning operations tax
       and the trade tax.
  iii)  in Guyana:
       the income tax and the corporation tax.
   iv)  in Trinidad and Tobago:
       the corporation tax, the income tax and
       the employment levy.

b)  in Antigua, Belize, Dominica, Grenada, Montserrat, St. Lucia, St. Vincent, St. Kitts, Nevis and Anguilla:
       the income tax.

2. This Agreement shall also apply to any identical or substantially similar taxes which are subsequently imposed in addition to, or in place of, those referred to in paragraph 1 of this Article.

Reprinted from Inter-American Institute of International Legal Studies, *Instruments Relating to the Economic Integration of Latin America*, vol. 2 (Dobbs Ferry, New York: Oceana, 1975), p. 587.

3. The competent authorities of the Contracting States shall notify each other of any change in the laws relating to the taxes which are the subject of this Agreement as soon as possible thereafter.

. . .

## ARTICLE 6: Income from Immovable Property

1. Subject to this Article any income from immovable property may be taxed in the Contracting State in which such property is situated, according to the laws of that State.

. . .

## ARTICLE 7: Business Profits

1. The industrial or commercial profits of an enterprise of a Schedule 1 State shall not be subject to tax in a Schedule 2 State unless the enterprise carried on a trade or business in the Schedule 2 State through a permanent establishment situated therein. If it carries on a trade or business as aforesaid tax may be imposed on those profits by the Schedule 2 State but only on so much of them as is attributable to that permanent establishment.

2. Notwithstanding the provisions of paragraph 1 where an enterprise of a Schedule 1 State which has a permanent establishment in a Schedule 2 State carries on business activities in the Schedule 2 State otherwise than through the permanent establishment, such business activities being of the same or similar kind as the business activities carried on through the permanent establishment then the profit of such activities shall, nevertheless, be attributed to the permanent establishment in that Schedule 2 State and taxed accordingly.

3. Where an enterprise of a Schedule 1 State is engaged in trade or business in a Schedule 2 State through a permanent establishment situated therein there shall be attributed to such permanent establishment the industrial or commercial profits which would be attributable to such permanent establishment if such permanent establishment were an independent enterprise engaged in the same or similar activities under the same or similar conditions and dealing at arm's length with the enterprises of which it is a permanent establishment.

. . .

## ARTICLE 10: Dividends

1. Dividends beneficially owned by a resident of a Schedule 1 State and derived from a company which is a resident of a Schedule 2 State may be taxed in the Schedule 1 State.

2. However, such dividends may be taxed in the State of which the Company paying the dividends is a resident and according to the law of that State, but the tax so charged shall not exceed:

a) In Barbados—
   The rate of tax chargeable in respect of the profits or income of the company paying the dividend;

b) In Guyana—
   25% of the gross dividend;

c) In Jamaica—
   i) 22 1/2 per cent of the gross amount of the dividends if the beneficial owner is a company which controls directly or indirectly at least 10% of the voting power of the company paying the dividends;
   ii) 15 per cent of the gross amount of the dividends in all other cases.

d) In Trinidad and Tobago—
   i) nil, where the beneficial owner of the dividend is a company which controls directly or indirectly at least 10% of the voting power of the company paying the dividend, or on remittances or deemed remittances of a permanent establishment;
   ii) 10% of the gross dividend, in all other cases;

e) In the Schedule 2 States—
   The rate of tax chargeable in respect of the profits or income of the company paying the dividend.

3. The provisions of paragraphs (1) and (2) of this Article shall not apply if the recipient of the dividends, being a resident of a Schedule 1 State, has in a Schedule 2 State, of which the company paying the dividends is a resident, a permanent establishment with which the holding by virtue of which the dividends are paid, is effectively connected. In such a case, the provisions of Article 7 of this Agreement shall apply.

. . .

## ARTICLE 11: Interest

1. Interest arising in a Schedule 1 State that accrues to and is beneficially owned by a resident of a Schedule 2 State may be taxed in the Schedule 2 State.

2. However, such interest may be taxed in the State in which it arises, and according to the law of that State, but, if that State is a Schedule 1 State, the tax so charged shall not exceed 10 percent of the gross amount of the interest.

3. The provisions of paragraph 1 and 2 of this Article shall not apply if the beneficial owner of the interest, being a resident of a Schedule 2 State, has in a

Schedule 1 State in which the interest arises a permanent establishment with which the indebtedness from which the interest arises is effectively connected. In such a case, the provisions of Article 7 of this Agreement shall apply.

. . .

## ARTICLE 12: Royalties

1. Royalties arising in a Schedule 1 State that accrue to and are beneficially owned by a resident of a Schedule 2 State may be taxed in that Schedule 2 State.

2. However, such royalties may be taxed in the State in which they arise and according to the law of that State, but if that State is a Schedule 1 State the tax so charged shall not exceed 5 percent of the gross amount of the royalties.

. . .

## ARTICLE 13: Management Charges

1. Management Charges arising in a Schedule 1 State and paid to a resident of a Schedule 2 State may be taxed in the Schedule 2 State.

2. However, such management charges may be taxed in the State in which they arise and according to the law of that State, but if that State is a Schedule 1 State the tax so charged shall not exceed 10 percent of the gross amount of such management charges.

. . .

# APPENDIX G
## ECCM: Agreement Establishing the East Caribbean Common Market (1968, as amended through 1981), Annex I to the Treaty Establishing the Organization of East Caribbean States (1981)

### ARTICLE 5: Import Duties

1. Member States shall not apply any import duties on goods which are eligible for Market Area tariff treatment in accordance with Article 6.

. . .

### ARTICLE 6: Market Area Origin for Tariff Purposes

1. For the purposes of Article 5 goods shall, subject to Annex A, be accepted as eligible for Market Area tariff treatment if they are consigned from a Member State to a consignee in the importing Member State and if they are of Market Area origin under any one of the following conditions:
   (a) that they have been wholly produced within the Market Area;
   (b) that they fall within a description of goods listed in a Process List to be established by decision of the Council of Ministers and have been produced within the Market Area by the appropriate qualifying process described in such List;
   (c) that they have been produced within the Market Area and that the value of any materials imported from outside the Market Area or of undetermined origin which have been used at any stage of the production of such goods does not exceed 50 per centum of the export price of such goods.

2. For the purposes of sub-paragraphs (a), (b) and (c) of paragraph 1 of this Article, materials listed on the Basic Materials List which forms the Schedule to Annex A, which have been used in the state described in such List in a process of production within the Market Area, shall be deemed to contain no element imported from outside the Market Area.

### ARTICLE 7: The Common Custom Tariff

Member States agree to work progressively towards the establishment of a common customs tariff on goods originating in non-member territories and countries. For this purpose Member States shall amend their tariffs applicable

Reprinted from *International Legal Materials* 20 (Washington, D.C.: American Society of International Law, 1981): 1166, 1176.

to non-member territories and countries to bring them to a mutually agreed level in such time not exceeding three years as the Council of Ministers may, by majority vote, decide.

. . .

## Article 10: Dumped and Subsidised Imports

1. Nothing in this Agreement shall prevent any Member State from taking action against dumped or subsidised imports consistent with any international obligations to which it is subject.

. . .

## ANCOM: Cartagena Agreement on Andean Subregional Integration (1969)

*Article 32.* The Member States pledge themselves to undertake a process of industrial development of the Subregion through joint programming to achieve the following goals, among others:
  a) Greater expansion, specialization and diversification of industrial production;
  b) Maximum utilization of available resources of the area;
  c) Stimulation of greater productivity and more efficient utilization of production factors;
  d) Utilization of large industry; and
  e) Equitable distribution of benefits.

*Article 33.* For the above enumerated goals, the Commission, at the proposal of the Board, shall approve Sectorial Programs of Industrial Development, to be jointly implemented by the Member States.

*Article 34.* The Sectorial Programs of Industrial Development must include stipulations on the following aspects:
  a) Identification of products to be subjected to the Program;
  b) Joint programming of new investment on a subregional scale, and of measures to insure their financing;
  c) Location of industries in the Subregional countries;
  d) Unification of policies on aspects directly influencing the Program;
  e) Programs for Exemptions which shall provide a different pace, by country and by product and, which in any case, shall permit free access to the subregional;
  f) A common External Customs Tariff; and
  g) The periods of time during which the rights and duties related to the Program must be continued in the case of denunciation of the Agreement.

• • •

*Article 45.* The Liberalization Program shall be automatic and irrevocable, and shall include all products, in order to attain total liberalization not later than 31 December 1980. The various aspects of this Program shall be applied:

Reprinted from *International Legal Materials* 8 (Washington, D.C.: American Society of International Law, 1969): 910.

a) To goods which are subject to Sectorial Programs of Industrial Development;
b) To goods included, or to be included, in the Common Schedule defined in Article 4 of the Montevideo Treaty;
c) To commodities not being produced in any country of the Subregion, which are included on the corresponding schedule; and
d) To goods not comprised in any of the above section.

*Article 46.* Restraints of all kinds shall be eliminated not later than 31 December 1970.

Exceptions to the above rule shall be made for restraints applied to goods reserved to the Sectorial Programs of Industrial Development, which restraints shall be eliminated whenever liberalization is effected pursuant to the respective program, or to the provisions of Article 53.

Bolivia and Ecuador shall eliminate restraints of all kinds at the time that they initiate compliance with the Liberalization Program for each product, pursuant to the rules established in Article 100, but they may substitute charges not to exceed the lowest level fixed by Section a) of Article 52, in which case application shall affect both the imports proceeding from the Subregion as well as those from outside the area.

. . .

*Article 49.* Goods that are included in the first stage of the Common Schedule described in Article 4 of the Montevideo Treaty shall be totally liberated from all charges and restraints within one hundred and eighty (180) days following the date that this Agreement becomes effective.

. . .

*Article 50.* Prior to 31 December 1970 the Commission, at the proposal of the Board, shall prepare a schedule of goods not being produced within any of the Subregional countries, nor reserved for any Sectorial Program of Industrial Development, and shall select those to be reserved for production in Bolivia or Ecuador, establishing with respect to the latter the conditions and terms of such reservation.

The charges on the goods included on such a schedule shall be totally eliminated by 28 February 1971. The liberalization of goods reserved for production in Bolivia or Ecuador shall be for the exclusive benefit of these countries.

. . .

*Article 52.* Goods not included under Articles 47, 49 and 50 shall be liberated from charges in the following manner:

a) The point of departure shall be calculated on the minimum charge on each product listed on the national customs tariffs of Colombia, Chile and Peru, or in their respective National Schedules in effect on the date of signature of the present Agreement. Said point of departure may not exceed the *ad valorem* percentage of the CIF value of the merchandise;

b) On 31 December 1970, all charges in excess of the level stipulated in the preceding section shall be reduced to said level; and

c) The remaining charges shall be gradually eliminated through annual reductions of ten percent each until total liberalization is achieved by 31 December 1980.

. . .

## Common External Tariff

*Article 61.* The Member States shall pledge themselves to make the Common External Tariff fully operative by 31 December 1980 at the latest.

*Article 62.* Prior to 31 December 1973 the Board shall prepare a Draft Common External Tariff, to be submitted for consideration of the Commission for approval within the following two years.

On 31 December 1976, the Member States shall commence a process directed toward adoption of a Common External Tariff by reconciling the charges levied by their domestic tariffs on imports from outside the Subregion, to be effected on an annual, automatic and parallel basis, and in a manner to make it fully operative by 31 December 1980.

*Article 63.* Prior to 31 December 1970, the Commission, at the proposal of the Board, shall approve a Minimum Common External Tariff, whose basic aims shall be:

a) To establish adequate protection for subregional production;

b) To create progressively a subregional preference margin;

c) To expedite the adoption of a Common External Tariff; and

d) To stimulate effective exploitation of subregional production.

*Article 64.* On 31 December 1971, the Member States shall initiate a reconciliation of the charges levied on imports from outside the Subregion with those established in the Minimum Common External Tariff, in those cases where the former are lower than the latter, and this procedure shall be effected by an annual horizontal and automatic progression, enabling it to become fully operative by 31 December 1975.

. . .

*Article 97.* As indicated in the preceding article, products originating in Bolivia and Ecuador shall be governed by the following criteria:

a) By 31 December 1973, at the latest, those products described under Section d) of Article 45 shall be granted free and definite access to the Subregional market. To this end, the charges shall be automatically eliminated in three annual and successive reductions of forty, thirty and thirty percent, respectively, the first reduction to be instituted on 31 December 1971, using as a point of departure those levels defined in Section a) of Article 52;

b) The Commission, at the proposal of the Board and prior to 31 December 1970, shall approve schedules of goods to be liberated for the benefit of Bolivia and Ecuador on 1 January 1971;

c) Charges on the products referred to in Article 53 shall be totally eliminated to the benefit of Bolivia and Ecuador on 1 January 1974, or 1 January 1976, depending upon whether or not these were subject to extension under terms of Article 47;

d) Prior to 31 March 1971, the Commission, at the proposal of the Board, shall fix preferential margins favoring a number of items of production of special interest to Bolivia and Ecuador, and shall fix the periods of time during which said margins, effective on 1 April 1971, shall be maintained at that level.

   The schedule referred to in this section shall incorporate those products covered by Section d) of Article 45; and

e) The same procedure indicated in Section c) shall be applied to the schedule of goods selected from among those which had been reserved to Sectorial Programs of Industrial Development, but not incorported therein within the time limits set by Article 47.

*Article 98.* The non-extendible concessions to Bolivia and Ecuador, granted by Member States in the liberalization of products on the Common Schedule, shall govern exclusively to their benefit. This exclusiveness shall be limited to the State which is granting the concession.

· · ·

*Article 100.* Bolivia and Ecuador shall comply with the Liberalization Program in the following form:

a) Liberation of products incorporated in Sectorial Programs of Industrial Development in the manner established for each;

b) Liberation of products which, although reserved to said programs, were not in fact included therein in the manner or within time limits set by the Commission, at the proposal of the Board. The Commission and the Board, upon making such decision, shall weigh basically those benefits to be derived from the programming and the placement of industry referred to in Article 93;

c) The period set by the Commission may not exceed by more than five (5) years, that stipulated in Article 52, Section C);

d) Products incorporated or to be incorporated in the Common Schedule shall be liberated in the manner and time limits provided in the Montevideo Treaty and in the pertinent Conference Resolutions;

e) Commodities not as yet being produced within the Subregion, and not forming part of the reserve set aside for their benefit under Article 50, shall be liberated within sixty days after such reserve has received Commission approval.

Nevertheless, exceptions may be made from this treatment with respect for those goods which the Board, upon its own initiative or as petitioned by Bolivia or Ecuador, may qualify for this purpose as being luxuries or non-essential.

These commodities shall be governed by procedures established in Section f) of the present Article, for their subsequent liberalization; and

f) The commodities not included in the preceding sections shall be eliminated from the national tariffs through annual and successive reductions of ten (10) percent each, the first to be made on 31 December 1976. Nevertheless, Bolivia and Ecuador may initiate the liberalization of these products during the course of the first six (6) years that this Agreement is in force.

•  •  •

*Article 104.* On 31 December 1976, Bolivia and Ecuador shall initiate the process directed toward adoption of the Common External Tariff through annual, automatic and lineal reductions, and they must complete liberalization by 31 December 1985.

Bolivia and Ecuador shall be compelled to adopt the Minimum Common External Tariff only in application to commodities not being produced within the Subregion, defined in Article 50. With respect to such products, minimum charges shall be adopted through a lineal and automatic process to be completed within three years computed from the date on which the production of these goods has been initiated within the Subregion.

•  •  •

# ANCOM: Final Act of the Negotiations Between the Commission of the Cartagena Agreement and the Government of Venezuela for the Adherence of that Country to the Agreement (February 13, 1973)

. . .

*Article 1.*  Within 120 days following the date on which Venezuela deposits in the Secretariat of the Commission the instrument of its adherence to the Cartagena Agreement, that country shall begin to totally eliminate all tariffs and trade restrictions of every nature applied against the importation of the following products originating in the member countries:

a) Those included in the first round of the Common List as defined in Article 4 of the Treaty of Montevideo, in conformity with the provisions of Articles 49 and 98 of the Agreement;

b) Those included in the list defined by Article 50 of the Cartagena Agreement, approved by Decision No. 26 of the Commission;

c) Those included in Annex I of Decision No. 28 of the Commission, in favor of Bolivia;

d) Those included in Annex II of Decision No. 28 of the Commission, in favor of Ecuador;

e) Those included in Annex I of Decision No. 29 of the Commission, in favor of Bolivia; and

f) Those included in Annex II of Decision No. 29 of the Commission, in favor of Ecuador.

In the cases of paragraphs (c) and (d) of this Article, the conditions established in Decision No. 28 of the Commission shall be fulfilled.

*Article 2.*  Within the same period of time established in the preceding Article, Venezuela shall adopt the measures established in Decision No. 34 with respect to the products included in the Annex thereto, in order to establish and maintain the margins of preference for Bolivia and Ecuador established in that Decision.

. . .

*Article 4.*  With respect to the products referred to in Article 52 of the Cartagena Agreement, which list was approved by Decision No. 27 of the Commission, Venezuela shall proceed in the following manner:

. . .

Reprinted from Inter-American Institute of International Legal Studies, *Instruments Relating to the Economic Integration of Latin America,* vol. 1 (Dobbs Ferry, New York: Oceana, 1975), p. 219.

## THE MINIMUM COMMON EXTERNAL TARIFF

*Article 8.* As the starting point for the fulfillment, by Venezuela, of the minimum common external tariff, the tariffs established in the Decision of the Commission in accordance with Article 6 of this Decision shall be taken.

Starting from these levels, Venezuela shall initiate the process of approximating those of the minimum common external tariff beginning on December 31, 1973 and it shall complete this process in an annual, lineal and automatic manner so that the minimum common external tariff will be in full effect for that country by December 31, 1975.

## APPENDIX H-3
## ANCOM: Lima Protocol Amending Cartagena Agreement
### (October 30, 1976)

. . .

*Article 1.* To extend for three years the term stipulated in Article 47 of the Agreement for the close of the reservation period and in Article 45, the third, fourth and fifth paragraphs of Article 55, the final paragraph of Article 57, Article 61, Section c) of Article 97, the second paragraph of Article 102, Article 104, the second paragraph of Article 105 and Article 112 of the Agreement for completion of the liberalization program and the Common External Tariff. Also, to extend for three years the terms stipulated in Article 8 of the Additional Instrument for the Adherence of Venezuela.

*Article 2.* To replace Article 62 of the Agreement with the following:

The Commission, at the proposal of the Board, and by December 1978, shall approve the Common External Tariff that must provide levels of maximum and minimum protection to subregional production, taking into account the objective of the Agreement to harmonize the economic policies of the member states and the present existence of different economic policies which include *inter alia*, monetary, exchange and paratariff policies.

On December 31, 1979, the member states shall commence a process directed toward adoption of a Common External Tariff by harmonizing the charges levied by their domestic tariffs on imports from outside the Subregion, to be effected on an annual, automatic and parallel basis, and in a manner to make it fully operative by December 1988 in Bolivia and Ecuador.

*Article 3.* Prior to October 31, 1977, the Commission, at the proposal of the Board, shall approve a list of products which shall be excluded from the reserve list for programming and shall reserve from among those not produced, a separate list of the products to be produced in Bolivia and Ecuador, indicating the conditions and terms of the reservation.

On December 31, 1977, the member states shall adopt for the products of this list the point of departure referred to in Section a) of Article 52 on the Agreement and shall eliminate all charges levied on imports of those products.

The remaining charges shall be eliminated through six annual reductions of five, ten, fifteen, twenty, twenty-five percent, the first of which shall be made on December 31, 1978.

---

Reprinted from *International Legal Materials* 16 (Washington, D.C.: American Society of International Law, 1977): 235.

227

Colombia, Peru and Venezuela shall eliminate by December 31, 1977 the charges levied on imports originating from Bolivia and Ecuador.

Bolivia and Ecuador shall liberate the importation of these products in the form indicated in Section b) of Article 100 of the Agreement.

*Article 4.* To replace Article 53 of the Agreement with the following:

With respect to products which had been selected for Sectoral Programs of Industrial Development but were not included therein within the time periods stipulated in Article 47, the member states shall comply with the Liberalization Program in the following manner:

a) The Commission, at the proposal of the Board, shall select lists of commodities not produced, to be produced in Bolivia and Ecuador, and shall establish the conditions and terms of the reservation;

b) On December 31, 1978, the member states shall adopt for the remaining countries the point of departure referred to in Section a) of Article 52 of the Agreement and shall eliminate all charges levied on imports of those products;

c) The remaining charges shall be eliminated through five annual successive reductions of five, ten, fifteen, thirty and forty percent, the first of which shall be made on December 31, 1979;

d) Colombia, Peru and Venezuela shall eliminate by December 31, 1978 all charges levied on imports originating from Bolivia and Ecuador.

*Article 5.* To delete item 2 of Annex II of the Agreement and add the following paragraphs to Article 11:

The Sectoral Programs of Industrial Development must be adopted by affirmative vote cast by two-thirds of the member states, with no negative vote.

The proposals receiving an affirmative vote of two-thirds of the member states, but which are subject of a negative vote, must be returned to the Board for consideration of the reasons originating the said negative vote.

Within a period of not less than one nor more than three months, the Board may renew its proposal for Commission consideration with amendments deemed desirable and in such event, the amended proposal shall be considered as approved if it receives an affirmative vote of two-thirds of the member states.

*Article 6.* The country or countries that have cast a negative vote may abstain from participating in the program, in which case it shall enter into force under the following conditions:

a) At least four member states must participate;

b) The country which does not participate shall include the products which are subject of the program in its schedule of exceptions, if they are not already there. The Commission, at the proposal of the Board, shall determine the period and conditions for liberalization and adoption of the Common External Tariff for these products. In its proposals the Board shall consider the results of the negotiations held for this purpose between the countries participating in the program and the country not participating;

c) The member states participating in this type of program shall commit themselves not to encourage for two years the manufacture of products that have been assigned exclusively for inclusion for the benefit of the nonparticipating member state. When this period has expired, the countries participating in the program shall decide on the distribution of those products, at the proposal of the Board.

*Article 7.* A member state that does not participate initially in a sectoral program of this type may request its inclusion at any time. The Commission, at the proposal of the Board, shall approve the conditions for the inclusion through the voting method stipulated in Section b) of Article 11 of the Agreement. In its proposals the Board shall consider the results of the negotiations held for this purpose between the countries participating in the program and the country not participating.

*Article 8.* To replace Section c) of Article 52 of the Agreement with the following:

> After the reduction made on December 31, 1975, the remaining charges shall be eliminated through seven annual successive reductions of six percent each, the first to be made on December 31, 1976, and a final reduction of eight percent, to be made on December 31, 1983.

*Article 9.* To replace Section f) of Article 100 with the following:

> The commodities not included in the preceding sections shall be eliminated from the national tariffs through annual successive reductions, three of five percent each, beginning December 31, 1979; five of ten percent each, beginning December 31, 1982; one of fifteen percent on December 31, 1987, and a final reduction of twenty percent on December 31, 1988.

*Article 10.* Prior to December 31, 1977, Bolivia may present an additional schedule of exceptions comprising up to two hundred thirty six (236) items of NABALALC [the applicable system of tariff nomenclature] in order to complete, in the same terms as Ecuador, the schedule authorized by Article 102 of the Agreement.

*Article 11.* To add to Article 45 of the Agreement the following paragraph:

> Notwithstanding the provisions of the first paragraph of this Article, the Commission, at the proposal of the Board, may include in the Sectoral Programs of Industrial Development liberalization programs extending beyond December 31, 1983, thus establishing for the benefit of Bolivia and Ecuador terms additional to those of the other member states.

. . .

ANCOM: Decision 24 of the Commission of the Cartagena Agreement, Common Regime of Treatment of Foreign Capital and of Trademarks, Patents, Licenses and Royalties, as amended (1976)*

. . .

## CHAPTER I

Article 1.  For the purposes of this regime, the following definitions are understood:

Direct Foreign Investment: Contributions, coming from abroad and belonging to foreign natural or juridical persons, made to the capital of an enterprise, in freely convertible currency, or the physical or tangible goods indicated in II (b) of Annex No. 1, and having the right to repatriation of their value and the transfer of profits abroad.

Likewise, investments in national currency from funds which are entitled to be transferred abroad and the reinvestments which are made in accordance with this regime shall be considered to be foreign investments.

National investor: The State, national individuals, national non-profit entities, and the national enterprises defined in this Article.

Foreign nationals with consecutive residence in the recipient country of no less than one year, who renounce before the competent national authority the right to repatriate the capital and to transfer profits abroad, shall also be considered to be national investors. In cases when it may be justified, the national competent entity of the host country may exempt said persons from the requirement of uninterrupted residency for not less than one year.

Each Member Country may exempt foreign natural persons whose investments have been generated internally from the obligation to renounce established in the preceding paragraph.

Likewise, the investments of property of subregional investors shall be considered (equivalent to the investments of) national investors under the following conditions:

a)  The investment must be previously authorized by the country of origin of the investor, when the corresponding national legislation so provides;

Reprinted from International Legal Materials 16 (Washington, D.C.: American Society of International Law, 1977): 138. The earlier versions of Decision 24, adopted December 31, 1970, are reprinted in International Legal Materials 10 (1971): 152; International Legal Materials 10 (1971): 1065; and International Legal Materials 12 (1973): 349.

*Notes deleted.

b) The investment must be submitted for the prior approval of the host country and be registered by the national competent entity which shall request certification from the national competent entity of the country of origin notifying it of the investment made;

c) The repatriation of capital and the transfer of earnings shall be subject to the provisions of this Decision and the national competent entities shall not authorize such remissions except to the territory of the Member Country of origin of the capital;

d) The national competent entities shall not authorize subregional investments in enterprises which produce or exploit products assigned in an Industrial Sectoral. Development Program to a Member Country different from the host country, except in cases of programs of coproduction or complementation previously agreed upon.

Subregional Investor: The national investor of any Member Country different from the host country.

Foreign Investor: The owner of a direct foreign investment.

National Enterprises: An enterprise organized in the recipient country, more than 80% of whose capital belongs to national investors, provided that in the opinion of the competent national authority, that proportion is reflected in the technical, financial, administrative, and commercial management of the enterprise.

Mixed Enterprise: An enterprise organized in the recipient country and whose capital belongs to national investors in a proportion which may fluctuate between 51% and 80%, provided that in the opinion of the appropriate national authority, that proportion is reflected in the technical, financial, administrative, and commercial management of the enterprise.

Foreign Enterprise: An enterprise organized or established in the recipient country whose capital in the hands of national investors amounts to less than 51% or, if that percentage is higher, it is not reflected in the opinion of the proper national authority, in the technical, financial, administrative, and commercial management of the enterprise.

New Investment: Investment made after July 1, 1971, in either existing or new enterprises.

Reinvestment: Investment of all or part of undistributed profits resulting from a direct foreign investment, in the same enterprise which produced them.

Portfolio Development Bonds: These are titles or obligations issued for development purposes and publicly offered by the State, State entities, quasi-State entities, national and mixed enterprises or by the Andean Development Corporation the acquisition of which does not confer in any case, the right to participate in the technical, financial, administrative or commercial direction of the issuing entity and which must always be qualified, for this purpose, by the competent national authority.

Recipient Country: The country in which the direct foreign investment is made.

Commission: The Commission of the Cartagena Agreement.

Board: The Board of the Cartagena Agreement.

Member Country: One of the Member Countries of the Cartagena Agreement.

Article 2. All foreign investors who wish to invest in one of the Member Countries must submit an application to the competent national authority, which, after evaluating it, will authorize the investment when it corresponds to the development priorities of the recipient country. The application must follow the model indicated in Annex No. 1 of the regime.

Upon the proposal of the Board, the Commission may approve common criteria for the evaluation of direct foreign investments in the Member Countries.

Article 3. Member Countries shall not authorize any direct foreign investment in activities which they consider are adequately covered by existing enterprises.

Likewise, they shall not authorize any direct foreign investment of which the purpose is to acquire shares, participations, or rights owned by national or subregional investors.

Direct foreign investments made in a national enterprise to prevent its imminent bankruptcy are excepted from the provisions of the preceding paragraph, provided the following conditions are met:

a) That the agency in charge of supervising corporations in the respective country, or its equivalent, verifies that bankruptcy is imminent;

b) That the enterprise proves that it has granted an option to purchase preferably to national or subregional investors; and

c) That the foreign investor agrees to place on sale the shares, participations, or rights that he may acquire in the enterprise for purchase by national investors, in a percentage necessary to constitute a national enterprise, within a period not exceeding 15 years, which period will be established in each case according to the characteristics of the business sector. The authorization issued by the competent national authority shall specify the period of time and the conditions under which that obligation will be met, the way in which the value of the shares, participations, or rights will be determined at the time they are sold, and, if pertinent, the systems by which the transfer of the latter to national investors will be ensured.

Article 4. Authorization for foreign investors to participate in national or mixed enterprises may be given, provided that it signifies increasing the capital of the respective enterprise and that the enterprise at least maintains its mixed classification.

Article 5. All direct foreign investments shall be registered with the competent national authority, together with the agreement specifying the terms of the authorization. The amount of the investment shall be registered in freely convertible currency.

. . .

Article 7. Foreign investors shall be entitled to re-export the invested capital when they sell their shares, participations, or rights to national investors or when liquidation of the enterprise occurs.

The sale of shares, participations, or rights, of a foreign investor to another foreign investor must be previously authorized by the competent national authority and will not be considered as re-exportation of capital.

The subregional investor shall have the right to repatriate the capital invested when the shares, participations or other rights are sold to national or subregional investors, or when the enterprise is liquidated.

Article 8. Re-exportable capital is understood to be the capital formed by the total of the original direct foreign investment which is registered and actually made, plus the reinvestments made in the same enterprise in accordance with the provisions of this regime and minus the net losses, if any.

In cases of participation of national investors, the foregoing provisions shall be understood to be limited to the percentage of direct foreign investment in connection with the reinvestments made and with the net losses.

Article 12. Reinvestment of profits earned by foreign enterprises shall be considered to be new investment and may not be made without previous authorization and registration.

. . .

Article 13. Governments of the Member Countries may permit reinvestment of the profits received by a foreign enterprise without any special authorization, up to an amount not exceeding 7% per year of the company's capital. In these cases, the obligation to register is still in force.

The governments of the Member Countries may allow foreign enterprises, without the necessity of special authorization, to apply their undistributed earnings to the acquisition of Portfolio Development Bonds when the total of these purchases plus reinvested earnings, in conformity with the preceding paragraph, does not exceed, when considered together, 70% of the capital of the particular enterprise. In these cases, the purchase of such bonds shall be considered to be a reinvestment and the obligation to register them shall continue to prevail.

The foreign enterprise may apply its other undistributed earnings to the acquisition of Portfolio Development Bonds, but in such cases they will not benefit from the treatment referred to in the preceding paragraph.

. . .

Article 15. Governments of the Member Countries shall refrain from endorsing or guaranteeing in any form, either directly or through official or semi-official institutions, external credit transactions carried out by foreign enterprises in which the State does not participate.

Article 16. . . . For foreign credit contracts concluded between the parent company and its affiliates or between affiliates of the same foreign enterprise, the real rate of annual interest may not exceed by more than three points the rate of interest of first-class securities prevailing in the financial market of the country of origin of the currency in which the transaction is registered. . . .

Article 17. In regard to domestic credit, foreign enterprises shall not have access to long-term credit. The terms and conditions of access to short- and medium-term credit shall be those established in the respective national legislation covering this matter, with medium-term credit considered as that which does not exceed three years.

Article 18. All contracts on the importation of technology and on patents and trademarks must be examined and submitted for the approval of the competent authority of the Member Country, which must appraise the effective contribution of the goods incorporating the technology, or other specific forms of measuring the effects of the imported technology.

<u>Article 19</u>. Contracts on importation of technology must contain, at least, clauses on the following subjects:
a) Identification of the terms of the transfer of technology;
b) Contractual value of each of the elements concerned in the transfer of technology, expressed in a form similar to that followed in the registration of direct foreign investments; and
c) Determination of the time period involved.

<u>Article 20</u>. Member Countries shall not authorize the conclusion of contracts for the transfer of foreign technology or patents which contain;
a) Clauses by virtue of which the furnishing of technology imposes the obligation for the recipient country or enterprise to acquire from a specific source capital goods, intermediate products, raw materials, and other technologies or of permanently employing personnel indicated by the enterprise which supplies the technology. In exceptional cases, the recipient country may accept clauses of this nature for the acquisition of capital goods, intermediate products or raw materials, provided that their price corresponds to current levels in the international market;
b) Clauses pursuant to which the enterprise selling the technology reserves the right to fix the sale or resale prices of the products manufactured on the basis of the technology;
c) Clauses that contain restrictions regarding the volume and structure of production;
d) Clauses that prohibit the use of competitive technologies;
e) Clauses that establish a full or partial purchase option in favor of the supplier of the technology;
f) Clauses that obligate the purchaser of technology to transfer to the supplier the inventions or improvements that may be obtained through the use of the technology;
g) Clauses that require payments of royalties to the owners of patents for patents which are not used; and
h) Other clauses with equivalent effects.

Save in exceptional cases, duly appraised by the competent authority of the recipient country, no clauses shall be accepted in which exportation of the products manufactured on the basis of the technology is prohibited or limited in any way.

In no case shall clauses of this nature be accepted in connection with subregional trade or the exportation of similar products to third countries.

<u>Article 21</u>. Intangible technological contributions shall grant the right to payment of royalties, upon authorization by the competent national authority, but they may not be computed as capital contributions.

When these contributions are furnished to a foreign enterprise by its parent company or by another affiliate thereof, no payment of royalties shall be authorized and no deductions will be allowed in this connection for tax purposes.

. . .

Article 25.   Licensing contracts for the utilization of trademarks of foreign origin in the territory of the Member Countries may not contain certain restrictive clauses such as:

a) Prohibition or limitation on the exportation or sale in certain countries of the products manufactured under the trademark concerned, or similar products;

b) Obligation to use raw materials, intermediate goods, and equipment supplied by the owner of the trademark or his affiliates. In exceptional cases, the recipient country may accept clauses of this nature provided the prices correspond to current levels on the international market;

c) Fixing of sale or resale prices of the products manufactured under the trademark;

d) Obligation to pay royalties to the owner of the trademark for unused trademarks;

e) Obligation permanently to employ personnel supplied or indicated by the owner of the trademark; and

f) Other obligations of equivalent effect.

. . .

Article 27.   The advantages deriving from the duty-free program of the Cartagena Agreement shall be enjoyed only by products produced by national or mixed enterprises of the Member Countries, as well as by foreign enterprises which are in the process of being transformed into national or mixed enterprises, pursuant to the terms of this Chapter.

Article 28.   Foreign enterprises that currently exist in the territory of any Member Country and that wish to enjoy the advantages deriving from the duty-free program of the Cartagena Agreement for their products must agree with the competent authority of the recipient country, within three years following the date the present regime enters into force, to their gradual and progresssive transformation into national or mixed enterprises, in accordance with the provisions of Article 31.

At the end of the aforesaid three-year period, there must be in all cases a participation of national investors in the capital of the enterprises of no less than 15%.

The time period in which this transformation must be carried out may not exceed 15 years in Colombia, Peru, and Venezuela, nor 20 years in Bolivia and Ecuador, starting from January 1, 1974.

Upon completion of two-thirds of the time period agreed for the transformation, there must be a participation of national investors in the capital of the said enterprise of no less than 45%.

Foreign enterprises that currently exist will be understood to be those that are legally organized or established in the territory of the respective country on January 1, 1974.

Article 29. The national authorities responsible for issuing certificates of origin of merchandise shall grant such certificates to products produced by currently existing foreign enterprises which, within the period of three years referred to in the first paragraph of Article 28, formally express to the government of the recipient country their intention to transform into national or mixed enterprises.

The products of currently existing foreign enterprises which do not enter into the agreement to transform themselves into national or mixed enterprises within the aforesaid three-year period may not enjoy the advantages deriving from the duty-free program of the Agreement, and consequently they shall not be issued a certificate of origin by the competent authority.

Article 30. Foreign enterprises that may be established in the territory of any Member Country after July 1, 1971, shall agree, in representation of their shareholders, to place on sale for purchase by national investors, gradually and progressively, in accordance with the provisions of Article 31, the percentage of their shares participations or rights necessary for the transformation of such enterprises into mixed enterprises, within a period which may not exceed 15 years in Colombia, Venezuela and Peru, and 20 years in Bolivia and Ecuador.

In the case of Colombia, Venezuela, and Peru, the agreement must stipulate a participation of national investors in the capital of the enterprises of no less than 15% at the time production begins, no less than 30% upon completion of one-third of the agreed period, and no less than 45% upon completion of two-thirds of that period.

In the case of Bolivia and Ecuador, the progressive participation of national investors in the capital of the enterprise must be no less than 5% three years after production begins, no less than 10% upon completion of one-third and no less than 35% upon completion of two-thirds of the agreed period.

[In figuring the percentages referred to in this Article, any participation of subregional investors or of the Andean Development Corporation shall be counted as national investors.]*

---

*Notes deleted.

In all cases the period of 20 years with respect to Bolivia and Ecuador shall start to be counted two years after production begins.

Article 31. Agreements on the transformation of foreign enterprises into mixed enterprises must stipulate the following items, among others:
  a) The period of time for compliance with the obligation to transform the foreign enterprise into a mixed enterprise;
  b) The gradual scale for the transfer of shares, participations, or rights to national investors, including in that gradual scale, at least, the rules on minimum percentage referred to in Articles 28 and 30;
  c) Regulations that will ensure the progressive participation of national investors or their representatives in the technical, financial, commercial, and administrative management of the enterprise, at least as of the date on which the enterprise begins production;
  d) The method of determining the value of the shares, participations, or rights at the time of their sale; and
  e) The systems that will ensure the transfer of shares, participations, or rights to national investors.

The transformation of a foreign enterprise to national or mixed, in the terms of this Decision, may also occur as a result of an increase of capital.

. . .

Article 34. Foreign enterprises or whose production 80% or more goes into exports to the markets of third countries shall not be obligated to abide by the provisions of this Chapter. In that case, the products of such enterprises may not enjoy in any way the advantages deriving from the duty-free program of the Cartagena Agreement.

In the same manner as foreign enterprises of whose production 80% or more is for exportation to third country markets, foreign or mixed enterprises in the tourism sector shall not be subject to the norms of Chapter II of Decision 24.

. . .

Article 36. Mixed enterprises shall be considered to be those in which the State or State enterprises participate, even if the participation is less than 51% of the capital, provided that the State representation has a determining capacity in the decisions of the enterprise. It shall be the duty of the Commission, on recommendation of the Board, to establish the minimum percentage of participation of the State or of the State enterprises referred to in this article, within three months following the date on which the present regime enters into force.

Article 37. Upon authorization by the competent national authority, the owners of a direct foreign investment shall have the right to transfer abroad, in freely convertible currency, the verified net profits resulting from the direct foreign investment, but not in excess of 20% of that investment annually.

However, each Member Country may authorize greater percentages and shall communicate to the Commission the provisions or decisions taken in this respect.

The national competent entity may also authorize the investment of excess distributed earnings, in which case (such investments) shall be considered (to be) direct foreign investment.

## CHAPTER III

## SPECIAL REGULATIONS BY SECTORS

Article 38. Each Member Country may reserve sectors of economic activity for national, public, or private enterprises and determine whether the participation of mixed enterprises in those sectors shall be admitted.

Without prejudice to the provisions of other articles of this Chapter, the Commission, on the recommendation of the Board, may determine the sectors which all the Member Countries shall reserve for national, public, or private enterprises, and determine whether participation of mixed enterprises shall be admitted in them.

Article 39. Foreign enterprises in the sectors referred to in this Chapter shall not be obligated to abide by the provisions of the previous Chapter regarding the transformation of foreign enterprises into national or mixed enterprises. However, they shall be subject to the other provisions of the common regime and to special provisions specified in Articles 40 to 43, inclusive.

Article 40. During the first ten years of the life of this regime, the activities of foreign enterprises in the sector of basic products under the concession system may be authorized, provided the duration of the contract does not exceed 20 years.

For purposes of this regime, the basic-products sector is understood to mean the one comprising the primary activities of exploration and exploitation of minerals of any kind, including liquid and gaseous hydrocarbons, gas pipelines, oil pipelines, and exploitation of forests. For Bolivia and Ecuador, this sector also includes primary agricultural and livestock activities.

Member countries shall not authorize deductions on account of depletion to be made for tax purposes by enterprises investing in this sector.

The participation of foreign enterprises in the exploration and exploitation of liquid and gaseous hydrocarbons shall tbe authorized preferably in the form of contracts of association with State enterprises of the recipient country.

Member Countries may grant foreign enterprises established in this sector treatment different from that provided in Article 37.

Article 41.  The establishment of foreign enterprises or new direct foreign investment shall not be permitted in the sector of public services. Investments which had to be made by currently existing foreign enterprises in order to operate under technically and economically efficient conditions are excepted from this rule.

For these purposes, public services are considered to be those that provide drinking water, sewers, electric power and lighting, cleaning and sanitary, telephone, postal and telecommunications services.

Article 42.  New direct foreign investment shall not be permitted in the sector of insurance, commercial banking, and other financing institutions.

Foreign banks which currently exist in the territory of the Member Countries shall cease receiving local deposits in current accounts, savings accounts, or time deposits within a period of three years from the date on which this regime enters into force.

Currently existing foreign banks which desire to continue accepting local deposits of any kind must convert into national enterprises, for which purpose they must place on sale shares representing at least 80% of their capital to be purchased by national investors within the period of time indicated in the previous paragraph.

Article 43.  New direct foreign investment shall not be permitted in domestic transportation enterprises, advertising enterprises, commercial radio stations, television stations, newspapers, magazines, or enterprises engaged in domestic marketing enterprises of products of any kind.

Foreign enterprises which currently operate in these sectors must convert into national enterprises, for which purpose they must place on sale at least 80% of their shares for purchase by national investors within a period not exceeding three years from the date on which this regime enters into force.

Article 44.  When, in the opinion of the recipient country, special circumstances exist, that country may apply other regulations than those provided in Articles 40 to 43 inclusive.

The products of foreign enterprises included in the sectors of the Chapter which do not agree to convert into national or mixed enterprises, or with respect to which the Member Countries apply different regulations than those referred to in the previous paragraph, shall not enjoy the advantages of the duty-free program of the Cartagena Agreement.

## CHAPTER IV

Article 45. The capital of stock companies must be represented in registered shares.

Bearer shares that currently exist must be converted into registered shares within a period of one year from the date on which this regime enters into force.

Article 46. When projects are concerned that pertain to products reserved for Bolivia or Ecuador by application of Article 50 of the Cartagena Agreement, the four remaining countries agree not to authorize direct foreign investment in their territories, except as stipulated in contracts signed before December 31, 1970.

. . .

Article 51. In no instrument relating to investments or the transfer of technology shall there be clauses that remove possible conflicts or controversies from the national jurisdiction and competence on the recipient country to allow the subrogation by States to the rights and actions of their national investors.

Differences between Member Countries of this regime in regard to its interpretation or implementation shall be resolved by following the procedure indicated in Chapter II, Section D, "on the settlement of controversies" of the Cartagena Agreement.

# ANCOM: Decision 169 on Andean Multinational Enterprises
## (As amended through 1982)

. . .

Article 1. For the purpose of this code an Andean multinational enterprise shall be one that fulfills the following conditions:

a) The principal domicile is located in the territory of one of the member countries;

b) There are capital subscriptions by national investors from two or more member countries that in total account for over eighty percent of the capital of the company;

c) When established with investments by investors from only two member countries, the total investment from each member country may not be less than fifteen percent of the total capital of the company. If there are investors from more than two member countries, the investments originating in at least two of the countries shall each fulfill the referred to percentage. In both cases the investors of the country which is the principal domicile of the company shall represent not less than fifteen percent of the capital of the company.

d) The majority subregional capital must be reflected in the technical, administrative, financial and commercial management of the company, in the judgment of the corresponding competent national entity referred to in Article 6 of Decision 24.

Article 2. For a period of ten years from the date of their constitution the Andean multinational enterprises established in Bolivia or Ecuador may exist with the capital subscriptions referred to in letter b) of the preceding article for an amount not less than sixty percent of their capital. The termination of the period may not exceed fifteen years from the date of entering into force of this Decision. While these companies continue to exist under this exception they may not establish branches in Colombia, Peru or Venezuela in the terms and conditions of the Decision.

Article 3. The capital of an Andean multinational enterprise shall be represented by nominative shares of equal value which shall confer on the shareholders equal rights and obligations.

. . .

Reprinted from *International Legal Materials* 21 (Washington, D.C.: American Society of International Law, 1982): 542.

## CONSTITUTION OF ANDEAN MULTINATIONAL ENTERPRISES

Article 9. Andean multinational enterprises must be constituted as corporations subject to the procedure established by the corresponding national legislation, and they must add to their name the words "Andean Multinational Enterprise" or the letters "E.M.A."

. . .

Article 15. The principal domicile of the Andean multinational enterprise shall be in the member country where it was constituted or where the transformation referred to in Article 10 occurred.

### Section 2—Administration

Article 16. The composition, functioning, powers and responsibilities of the administrative structure, as well as the dissolution and liquidation of the company, and the resolution of conflicts that arise between shareholders or between shareholders and the company shall be governed by the legislation of the member country of principal domicile, without prejudice to the following provisions.

1. The principal domicile shall be the site of the shareholders meetings and of the executive offices of the company;
2. The articles of incorporation must contemplate terms and provisions that assure the shareholders the exercise of their preferential right, as well as other rights, as contemplated in the respective legislation or that have been provided in the articles of incorporation; and
3. At least one director must be contemplated for each member country whose nationals have an equity participation of not less than fifteen percent in the capital of the enterprise.

. . .

Article 19. In regard to national internal taxation Andean multinational enterprises shall be entitled to the same treatment established, or that may be established for national companies in the economic activity in which they are engaged, provided that they fulfill the obligations required by the corresponding legislation.

Article 20. Andean multinational enterprises shall have access to internal credit and, in general, to the financial treatment established, or that may be established for national companies in the economic activities in which they are engaged, provided that they fulfill the obligations required by the respective credit legislation and policies.

. . .

Article 23. Without prejudice to that provided in Articles 2, 21 and 22, Andean multinational enterprises shall have the right to establish branches in the member countries distinct from the country of principal domicile. Their legal representation, assigned capital and operations shall be subject to that provided in the pertinent national legislation of the member country in which they are established.

Article 24. The branches of Andean multinational enterprises shall have the right, upon the prior authorization of the national competent entity, to transfer to the principal domicile, in freely convertible currency, the whole of their proven net earnings, after the payment of the corresponding taxes.

. . .

Article 26. In order to avoid situations of double taxation, neither income nor remittance tax shall be levied [on]:

a) In the member country of principal domicile of the Andean multinational enterprise: the portion of the dividends distributed by it which corresponds to earnings previously taxed in the member country of the domicile of a branch, as well as the income derived from the redistribution of this portion of the dividends paid by investor enterprises in the same country;

b) In the remaining member countries: the income derived from the redistribution of dividends previously taxed that is received by investor enterprises in an Andean multinational enterprise.

. . .

# APPENDIX H-6
## ANCOM: Decision 85 on the Application of Rules on Industrial Property
### (June 5, 1975)

Article 5.  Patents shall not be granted for:
a) Inventions which contravene public order or good morals;
b) Vegetable varieties or animal races, and essentially biological processes for obtaining vegetables or animals;
c) Pharmaceutical products, medications, active therapeutic substances, beverages and food for human, animal or vegetable consumption;
d) Foreign inventions, the patent for which is requested one year after the date of the filing for patent registration in the first country in which it was sought. Upon expiration of this term, no rights may be asserted deriving from said application.
e) Inventions which affect the development of the respective Member Nations or the procedures, products or groups of products, the patentability of which has been excluded by the Governments.

. . .

Article 10.  The first application for an invention patent initially filed in any Member Nation shall give its owner a priority right for a term of one year, computed from the date of said application, to request a patent on the same invention in the other Member Nations.

. . .

Article 24.  In the area of inventions of interest to national security or related to processes, products, or groups or products reserved to the Government, or when so determined by law, the granting of a patent may be subjected to conditions as to its exploitation. In such event, the administrative act granting it shall be duly supported or founded.

. . .

Article 29.  A patent shall be granted for a maximum term of ten years, computed from the date of the administrative resolution granting it. Initially it shall be granted for five years and in order to obtain an extension, the owner must prove to the competent national office that the patent is being adequately exploited.

---

Reprinted from F. V. Garcia-Amador, *The Andean Legal Order: A New Community Law* (Dobbs Ferry, New York: Oceana, 1978), p. 368.

A patent for an improvement shall expire with the original patent.

Article 30. The patent owner is under duty:
a) To communicate to the competent national organs, within a term of three years computed from the date of the granting of the patent, that exploitation has been initiated. Omission of such communication shall give rise to the presumption that the exploitation has not been commenced for purposes of the concession of compulsory licenses, as stipulated in Article 34.

. . .

Article 34. Upon expiration of three years, computed from the date of concession of the patent, any person may apply to the competent national office for a grant of a compulsory license to exploit that patent if, at the time of the request and with the exception of a justifiable, legitimate excuse by said office, one of the following acts has ocurred;
a) That the patented invention has not been exploited within the country;
b) That the exploitation of said invention has been suspended for more than one year;
c) That the exploitation does not satisfy reasonable conditions of quantity, quality, or price as demanded by the national market;
d) That the patent owner has not granted any contractual licenses under reasonable conditions in such manner that the holder thereof can satisfy the demands of the national market, under reasonable conditions of quantity, quality or prices.

The term of five years having expired, as computed from the date of concession of the patent, a compulsory license may be granted by the competent national office without need to prove the existence of any of the above listed acts of paragraphs b), c) and d) of this Article.

The holder of a compulsory license must pay an adequate compensation of the patent owner.

. . .

Article 39. In the case of patents of interest to public health, or based on national development needs, the Government of the respective Member Nation may submit the patent to compulsory licensing at any time, and in such cases, the competent national office may grant the licenses requested to it.

. . .

## TRADEMARKS

. . .

Article 70. In order to enjoy the right of renewal, the interested party must prove to the respective competent national office that the mark in question is being utilized in any Member Nation.

. . .

Article 72. The exclusive right to a trademark shall be acquired by registration of same in the competent national office.

Article 73. Acceptance of the application for registration of a trademark in a Member Nation shall give the applicant a priority right for a term of six months in order that he may, within that specified time, apply for registration in the remaining Member Nations.

. . .

Article 75. The owner of a trademark may not object to the importation or entry of merchandise or products originating in another Member Nation, which carry the same trademark. The competent national authorities shall require that the imported goods be clearly and adequately distinguished with an indication of the Member Nation where they were produced.

. . .

# APPENDIX H-7
## ANCOM: Decision 45 on Standards on Competition
### (December 18, 1971)

Article 2. The following, among others, are considered practices that distort competition:

a) Dumping;
b) Improper manipulation of prices;
c) Practices intended to disturb the normal supply of raw materials;
d) Other practices with equivalent results.

. . .

Article 8. In conformance with the procedure indicated in Articles 5 and 7, the Board (*Junta*) may, among other measures, authorize the affected member countries to impose duties and/or restrictions of a discriminatory nature on imports of the commodities affected by the distortion of competition.

Also, the Board (*Junta*) shall request the member country from which or in whose territory the practices involved in the complaint emanate to adopt the necessary measures to eliminate the distortion.

. . .

Reprinted from F. V. Garcia-Amador, *The Andean Legal Order: A New Community Law* (Dobbs Ferry, New York: Oceana, 1978), p. 406.

# APPENDIX H-8
## ANCOM: Decision 146 on the Metal Working Sectorial Program

Article 9.   Within 90 days following the approval of this Decision, member countries other than those favored with an assignment shall eliminate any duties against assigned products originating from the favored country.

· · ·

Article 11.   For products whose production in the assigned country has been verified as of the date of approval of this Decision, member countries other than the one favored with the assignment shall apply the duties set forth in Annex VI until December 31, 1983 on such products when they come from another non-favored member country. In the case of an assignment to Bolivia or Ecuador, the foregoing date shall be December 31, 1989. [Annex VI is the Common External Tariffs.]

For products whose production has not been verified in accordance with the prior paragraph, the member countries other than the one favored with an assignment shall apply the duties set forth in Annex VI until December 31, 1987 on assigned products originating from another non-favored country. In the case of products assigned to Bolivia or Ecuador, the corresponding dates shall be December 31, 1992.

Article 12.   For products whose production has been verified as of the date of approval of this Decision, member countries favored with an assignment shall apply to such products coming from non-favored member countries the same duties applicable to such products when imported from outside the Subregion [i.e., the common external tariff]; and, if the favored nation is Colombia, Peru or Venezuela, it will eliminate such duties by December 31, 1983; if Bolivia or Ecuador is the favored nation, it will eliminate them by December 31, 1989.

For products whose production has not been verified in accord with the previous paragraph, member countries favored with an assignment shall apply to such products coming from non-favored member countries the same duties applicable to such products where imported from outside the Subregion; and if the favored nation is Colombia, Peru or Venezuela, it will eliminate such duties by December 31, 1987; if the favored nation is Bolivia or Ecuador, it will eliminate them by December 31, 1992.

*Notes:* Decision 57 was replaced by Decision 146, which provided for Venezuela to share in the metalworking sector.

Reprinted from Spanish original in Junta del Acuerdo de Cartagena, *Orde namiento Juridico del Acuerdo de Cartagena: Decisiones 146-159.* Tomo 4, (1982), p. 1 (translated by Beverly May Carl).

. . .

Article 14. Member countries that share an assignment of the same product shall reciprocally eliminate the duties on such goods coming from one another, in accord with the following:
  a) For products whose production have been verified . . . as in existence at the date of this Decision, such duties shall be eliminated within 90 days . . . .
  b) For products whose production is not verified as being in existence as of the date of the approval of this Decision, the duties set forth in Annex V shall be adopted, which duties in turn shall be eliminated by two equal, annual and successive reductions, the first of which shall take place not later than December 31, 1986.

. . .

Article 16. In the case of assignments shared between Bolivia or Ecuador and another member country, they shall reciprocally eliminate the duties on such goods coming from one another, in accord with the following:
  a) Within 60 days from the approval of this Decision, the countries which share an assignment with Bolivia or Ecuador shall totally eliminate duties on such products originating in the latter favored nation;
  b) Bolivia or Ecuador may apply to such goods coming from the other favored nation the same duty as applicable when the goods come from another non-favored country;
  c) Bolivia or Ecuador shall eliminate the duties referred to in the prior paragraph by means of three annual successive reductions of 40, 30 and 30 percent respectively, which shall take effect starting from December 31 of the year in which the initiation of production of the goods in its own territory is verified. If such initiation of production is not verified, such duties must be eliminated not later than December 31, 1992.

Article 17. In the case of an assignment shared between Bolivia and Ecuador, they shall reciprocally reduce the duties on such products from each other in the following way:
  a. Within 60 days following the approval of this Decision they shall adopt the duties set forth in Annex V.
  b. The duty indicated in the above paragraph shall be reduced by means of three annual, successive reductions of 40, 30 and 30 percent respectively, which shall take effect starting from December 31 of the year in which the initiation of production in one of said countries has been verified. If such initiation of production is not verified, such duties must be eliminated no later than December 31, 1992.

. . .

Article 19. The duties on unassigned products [i.e., products reserved for this Sectorial Program, but not assigned] shall be eliminated for all member countries as follows:

a) Colombia, Peru and Venezuela shall eliminate such duties completely within 90 days following the approval of this Decision;

b) Bolivia and Ecuador shall eliminate such duties in accord with Decision 57 by means of annual, successive reductions which shall consist of three reductions of five percent each, starting on December 31, 1981; five of 10 percent each starting from December 31, 1984; one of 15 percent for December 31, 1989 and one of 20 percent for December 31, 1990.

Article 20. Without prejudice to any provision in the present Chapter, the member countries may not apply duty rates any higher than the common external tariff to any products originating from the other members.

. . .

Article 23. Not later than 60 days after notification of verification that [production has started in the assigned country], . . . the member countries shall adopt the rates established for the common external tariffs in Annex VI for the importation of such products from outside the Subregion.

In the case of products whose production has been verified . . . as of the date of approval of this Decision, member countries shall completely adopt the tariffs set forth in Annex VI, not later than 90 days from that date.

. . .

Article 30. In order to ensure the effectiveness of the assignments made under this Program . . . and prevent the installation of factories which would injure or prejudice the assigned productions, member countries, not later than 90 days after the date . . . of this Decision, shall adopt the necessary measures and internal regulations, such as prohibiting competing production or the registration thereof, as well as the prohibition of imports of specified capital equipment therefor, or the concession of governmental assistance, credits, tax incentives, or customs relief or letters of credit therefor.

. . .

Article 31. Member Countries shall not increase production in products assigned to others . . . . This same rule shall apply to production facilities which may already exist in the Subregion . . . .

Article 32. Member Countries promise to not authorize foreign direct investment in . . . their territories not to contract for the importation of technology when such transactions would involve products assigned to another country or countries. . . .

# APPENDIX H-9
## ANCOM: Treaty Creating the Court of Justice (May 28, 1979)

Article 17.   It shall correspond to the Court to decide the nullification of Decisions of the Commission and Resolutions of the Junta adopted in violation of the norms which comprise the juridical structure of the Cartagena Agreement, including ultra vires acts, when these are impugned by any member country, by the Commission, by the Junta, or by natural or juridical persons as provided in Article 19 of this Treaty.

Article 18.   The member countries may only bring an action of nullification against the Decisions approved without their affirmative vote.

Article 19.   Natural and juridical persons may bring actions of nullification against Decisions of the Commission or Resolutions of the Junta which are applicable to them and cause them harm.

Article 20.   An action of nullification must be presented to the Court within one year following the date of entry into force of the Decision of the Commission or the Resolution of the Junta.

Article 21.   The bringing of an action of nullification shall not affect the applicability or enforceability of the norm impugned.

Article 22.   In the event that the Court rules the total or partial nullification of a Decision or Resolution, it shall indicate the effects of its ruling over such period of time as may be deemed appropriate under the circumstances.

The body of the Cartagena Agreement whose act has been nullified must adopt the measures required to assure the effective fulfillment of the decision of the Court.

Article 23.   Whenever the Junta considers that a member country is not complying with its obligations under the norms which comprise the juridical structure of the Cartagena Agreement, it shall present its written observations to said country. The member country must respond to them within a period compatible with the urgency of the matter, which in no case may exceed two months. Upon the receipt of the response, or once the referred to period has terminated, the Junta shall issue its considered opinion.

---

Reprinted from *International Legal Materials* 18 (Washington, D.C.: American Society of International Law, 1979): 1203.

If the Junta finds that there is noncompliance, and the member country persists in the action which was the object of the observations, then the Junta may present the matter to the Court for its decision.

Article 24. Whenever a member country considers that another member country is not complying with its obligations under the norms which comprise the juridical structure of the Cartagena Agreement, it may present its complaint, together with the facts on which the complaint is based, to the Junta which shall issue its considered opinion, after completing the procedure referred to in the first paragraph of Article 23.

If the Junta finds that there is noncompliance and the accused member country persists in the action which was the object of the complaint, the Junta must present the matter to the Court. In the event that the Junta has not brought the action within the period of two months following the date of its opinion, the complainant country may present the matter directly to the Court.

In the event that the Junta has not issued its opinion within three months following the date on which the complaint is presented, or the finding is that there has not been noncompliance, then the complainant country may present the matter directly to the Court.

Article 25. In the event that the ruling of the Court is of noncompliance, the member country whose action is the object of the complaint is obligated to adopt the measures necessary for complying with the decision within three months following notification.

In the event that said member country does not comply with the obligation referred to in the preceding paragraph, the Court, summarily and after hearing the opinion of the Junta, shall determine the limits within which the complainant country, or any other member country, may restrict or suspend, totally or partially, the advantages deriving from the Cartagena Agreement which benefit the noncomplying member country. The Court, through the Junta, shall notify the member countries of its decision.

Article 26. The rulings issued in actions of noncompliance may be reviewed by the Court, upon the petition of an interested party, if such petition is based on a fact which could have decisively influenced the outcome of the proceeding, provided that such fact was unknown to the party petitioning for review as of the date on which the ruling was handed down.

The petition for review must be presented within two months from the date of discovery of the fact and, in all cases, within one year following the date of the ruling.

Article 27.  Natural and juridical persons shall have the right to bring causes of action in the competent national courts, in accordance with the provisions of domestic law, when the member countries do not comply with that provided in Article 5 of this Treaty and the rights of such persons are affected by this noncompliance.

## Third Section

## Advisory Opinions

Article 28.  It shall correspond to the Court to interpret, through prior advisory opinions, the norms which comprise the juridical structure of the Cartagena Agreement, in order to assure uniform application in the territories of the member countries.

Article 29.  National judges who have before them a case in which any of the norms which comprise the juridical structure of the Cartagena Agreement must be applied may petition the Court for its interpretation of such norms, but provided that the ruling is subject to appeal within the national judicial system. In the event that it is necessary for the national court to issue its ruling before receiving the interpretation of the court, the judge must proceed to decide the case.

In the event that the ruling is not subject to appeal within the national judicial system, the judge shall suspend the proceeding and petition the interpretation of the Court, ex officio in all cases, or upon the petition of an interested party, if so required by law.

Article 30.  The Court shall restrict its interpretation to defining the content and scope of the norms of the juridical structure of the Cartagena Agreement. The Court may not interpret the content and scope of domestic law nor judge the substantive facts of the case.

Article 31.  The judge hearing the case must adopt the interpretation of the Court.

## CHAPTER IV

## GENERAL PROVISIONS

Article 32.  To be enforceable, the rulings of the Court shall not require homologation or exequatur in any of the member countries.

Article 33. The member countries shall not submit any controversy which may arise from the application of the norms which comprise the juridical structure of the Cartagena Agreement to any court, arbitration system or any other procedure not contemplated by this Treaty.

The member countries agree to recur to the procedure established in Article 23 of the Cartagena Agreement only in the event of controversies which arise between any of them and another contracting party of the Treaty of Montevideo which is not a member of the Cartagena Agreement.

. . .

# LAIA: Montevideo Treaty Establishing Latin American Intergration Association (August 12, 1980)

## Mechanisms

Article 4.   In order to fulfill the basic functions of the Association, as provided in Article 2 of this Treaty, the member countries hereby establish an area of economic preferences consisting of a regional tariff preference, agreements of regional scope and agreements of partial scope.

## First Section—Regional Tariff Preference

Article 5.   The member countries shall reciprocally grant a regional tariff preference, which shall be applied in relation to the level set for third countries and be subject to corresponding regulations.

## Second Section—Agreements of Regional Scope

Article 6.   Agreements of regional scope are those in which all of the member countries participate.

These shall be agreed upon within the framework of the objectives and provisions of this Treaty, and they may refer to areas and encompass the measures contemplated for the agreements of partial scope, as provided in the Third Section of this Chapter.

## Third Section—Agreements of Partial Scope

Article 7.   Agreements of partial scope are those in which all of the member countries do not participate, and they shall tend to create the conditions necessary to advance the regional integration process by means of their progressive multilateralization.

The rights and obligations established in the agreements of partial scope shall apply exclusively for the subscribing, or subsequently adhering, countries.

Article 8.   Agreements of partial scope may refer to commerce, economic complementation, agriculture, the promotion of commerce, or they may adopt other forms in accordance with Article 14 of this Treaty.

---

Reprinted from *International Legal Materials* 20 (Washington, D.C.: American Society of International Law, 1981): 672.

Article 9. Agreements of partial scope shall be governed by the following general norms:

a) They must be open to the adherence of the other member countries, following negotiation;

b) They must contain provisions which tend to stimulate convergence so that their benefits extend to all the member countries;

c) They may contain provisions which tend toward convergence with other Latin American countries, in accordance with the mechanisms established by this Treaty;

d) They shall contain differential treatment for the three categories of countries contemplated by this Treaty, the application of which shall be determined in each agreement, as well as negotiating procedures for their periodic review upon the request of any member country which considers it is being harmed thereby;

e) The reduction of tariffs may be for the same products or tariff subdivisions and based on a percentage reduction with respect to the duties applied to the imports originating in non-participating countries;

f) They shall have a minimum duration of one year; and

g) They may contain, among others, specific norms regarding origin requirements, safeguard clauses, nontariff barriers, the withdrawal of concessions, the renegotiation of concessions, denouncement, and the coordination and harmonization of policies. In the event that such specific norms were not adopted, the provisions of a general nature established by the member countries in these areas shall be taken into account.

Article 10. Commercial agreements are exclusively intended to promote trade among the member countries, and they shall be subject to the specific norms which are established for this purpose.

Article 11. The objectives of economic complementation agreements are, among others, to promote the maximum utilization of factors of production, stimulate economic complementation, assure equitable conditions of competition, facilitate the export of the products to the international market, and promote the balanced and harmonious development of the member countries.

These agreements shall be subject to the specific norms which are established for this purpose.

Article 12. The object of agricultural agreements is to develop and regulate intraregional agricultural trade. They must contain elements of flexibility which take into account the socioeconomic characteristics of production of the participating countries. These agreements may refer to specific products or groups of products, and may be based on temporary or seasonal concessions, by quotas or under a mixed system, or in contracts between state or quasi-state entities. They shall be subject to the specific norms which are established for this purpose.

Article 13. Promotion agreements shall refer to nontariff matters and they shall tend to promote intraregional commercial flows. They shall be subject to the specific norms which are established for this purpose.

Article 14. The member countries may establish, by corresponding regulations, specific norms for other types of agreements of partial scope.

In this sense, they shall consider, among other areas, scientific and technological cooperation, the promotion of tourism and the preservation of the environment.


## CHAPTER III

### System of Support for the Relatively Less Economically Developed Countries

Article 15. The member countries shall establish favorable conditions for the participation of the relatively less economically developed countries in the economic integration process, based on the principles of nonreciprocity and communitarian cooperation.

Article 16. In order to assure for them an effective preferential treatment, the member countries shall provide the opening of their markets, as well as approve programs and other specific forms of cooperation.

Article 17. The measures in favor of the relatively less economically developed countries shall be established in agreements of regional scope and in agreements of partial scope.

In order to assure the efficacy of these agreements, the member countries shall formalize negotiated norms related to the preservation of the preferences the elimination of the nontariff barrier restrictions and the application of safeguard clauses in justified cases.

### First Section—Agreements of Regional Scope

Article 18. The member countries shall each approve negotiated lists of products, preferably industrial, that originate in each of the relatively less economically developed countries for which all of the remaining countries of the Association shall agree to, without reciprocity, the complete elimination of customs duties and other restrictions.

The member countries shall establish the procedures necessary to achieve the progressive expansion of the respective free trade lists, indertaking the corresponding negotiations when it is deemed appropriate.

Likewise, they shall endeavor to establish efficacious compensation mechanisms for the negative effects arising from the intraregional trade of the landlocked relatively less economically developed countries.

### Second Section—Agreements of Partial Scope

Article 19. The agreements of partial scope which the relatively less economically developed countries negotiate with the other member countries shall conform, insofar as may be relevant, to the provisions contemplated in Articles 8 and 9 of this Treaty.

Article 20. In the interest of promoting an effective collective cooperation in favor of the relatively less economically developed countries, the member countries shall negotiate with each of them Special Programs of Cooperation.

Article 21. The member countries may establish programs and cooperation measures in the areas of preinvestment, financing and technology primarily intended to provide support for the relatively less economically developed countries and, among them, especially for the landlocked countries, to facilitate their benefiting from the tariff reductions.

Article 22. Notwithstanding that provided in the preceding Articles, as part of the treatment in favor of the relatively less economically developed countries, collective and partial cooperation measures may be established which contemplate efficacious mechanisms intended to compensate the disadvantageous situation faced by Bolivia and Paraguay due to their landlocked status.

Provided that with regard to the regional tariff preference, referred to in Article 5 of this Treaty, criteria of graduality over time are adopted, it shall be endeavored to preserve the margins granted in favor of the landlocked countries, by means of accumulative reductions.

Likewise, it shall be endeavored to establish compensation formulas both with respect to the regional tariff preference, when this is extended, as well as in the agreements of regional and partial scope.

Article 23. The member countries shall endeavor to grant facilities for the establishing in their territories of free zones, deposit areas or ports, and other international transit administrative facilities, in favor of the landlocked countries.

## CHAPTER IV

### Convergence and Cooperation with Other Countries and Economic Integration Areas of Latin America

Article 24. The member countries may establish systems of association or multilateral ties which tend toward the convergence with other countries and economic integration areas of Latin America, including the possibility of agreeing with said countries or areas on the establishing of a Latin American tariff preference.

The member countries shall opportunely regulate the characteristics these systems must have.

Article 25. Likewise, the member countries may enter into agreements of partial scope with other countries and economic integration areas of Latin America in accordance with the diverse forms contemplated in the third section of Chapter II of this Treaty, and with the terms of the respective regulatory provisions.

Notwithstanding the foregoing, these agreements shall be subject to the following norms:

a) The concessions granted by the participating member countries shall not be made extensive to the rest, except to the relatively less economically developed countries;

b) When a member country includes products already negotiated in partial agreements with other member countries, the concessions it grants may be superior to those extended to the latter in which case the member country shall consult with the affected member countries in the interest of finding mutually satisfactory solutions, except in the case of the respective partial agreements in which there are included clauses for the automatic extension or the denouncing of the preferences granted in the partial agreements referred to in this Article; and

c) They must be reviewed multilaterally by the member countries in a meeting of the Committee in regard to the scope of the commitments undertaken and to facilitate the participation of the other member countries in such agreements.

## CHAPTER V

### Cooperation with Other Economic Integration Areas

Article 26. The member countries shall undertake the efforts necessary to establish and develop bonds of solidarity and cooperation with other integration areas outside of Latin America through the participation of the Association in the horizontal cooperation programs carried out at the international level, in fulfillment of the normative principles and commitments assumed in the context of the Declaration and Action Plan for achieving the New International Economic Order and the Charter of the Economic Rights and Duties of States.

The Committee shall decide the measures appropriate to facilitate the fulfillment of these objectives.

Article 27. Likewise, the member countries may enter into partial agreements with other developing countries or respective economic integration areas outside Latin America in accordance with the diverse forms contemplated in the third section of Chapter II of this Treaty, and in the terms of their respective regulatory provisions.

Notwithstanding the foregoing, these agreements shall be subject to the following norms:

a) The concessions which the member countries participating in them grant shall not be extensive to the rest, except to the relatively less economically developed countries;

b) When products already negotiated with other member countries are included in agreements of partial scope, the concessions granted may not be superior to those extended to them, but if they are, they shall automatically be extended to these countries; and

c) They must be declared to be compatible with the contractual commitments of the member countries in the context of this Treaty and in conformity with clauses a) and b) of this Article.

. . .

Article 48. Investment capital originating in the member countries of the Association shall enjoy in the territory of the other member countries a treatment no less favorable than that granted to investments originating in any other non-member country, without prejudice to the provisions of the agreements which the member countries may enter into in this area, in the terms of the Treaty.

. . .

Article 51. The products imported or exported by a member country shall enjoy freedom of transit within the territories of the other member countries and shall solely be subject to the payment of the rates normally applied for the providing of services.

. . .

# APPENDIX I-2
## LAIA: Latin American Integration Association Agreement
## on the Regional Preference

Art. 3. The regional tariff preference shall apply to the importation of all kinds of products coming from the member states.

Products contained in lists of exceptions to be established in accordance with Chapter VI of this Agreement shall be excluded from such preferences. . . .

.  .  .

Art. 5. The regional tariff preference is as follows depending on the category of the nations involved . . .

| Nation Granting the Preference | Nation Receiving Preference* | | |
|---|---|---|---|
| | Relatively Least Developed Countries | Countries of Intermediate Development | Other Countries |
| Relatively Least Developed Countries | 5 | 3 | 2 |
| Countries of Intermediate Development | 7 | 5 | 3 |
| Other Countries | 10 | 7 | 5 |

.  .  .

*The least developed nations are Ecuador, Bolivia and Paraguay. The intermediate nations are Colombia, Chile, Peru, Uruguay and Venezuela. The "others" are Argentina, Mexico and Brazil.

Reprinted from Latin American Integration Association Agreement on the Regional Preference (ALADI/AR.PAR/4), April 27, 1984 (translated by Beverly May Carl). The Spanish text is reprinted in *Integracion Latinoamericana* (Buenos Aires: INTAL, May 1984), no. 80, pp. 77–9.

# APPENDIX J-1
## The COMECON Charter

## Article III: Functions and Attributes

1. In conformity with the purposes and principles set forth in Article I of the present Charter, the Council for Mutual Economic Assistance shall:

   a. Organize comprehensive economic, scientific, and technical coopera-tion among the member countries of the Council, in order to achieve the most rational use of their natural resources and more rapid development of their productive forces, as well as to promote socialist economic integration;

   b. Contribute to improving the international socialist division of labor through organizing mutual consultations on the most important questions of economic policy, through coordinating national economic development plans, through establishing programs for long-term association, through fostering production specialization and cooperation among the member countries of the Council, taking into consideration the worldwide division of labor;

   c. Adopt measures for studying economic, scientific, and technical problems of interest to the member countries of the Council;

   d. Assist the member countries of the Council in the preparation, coor-dination and execution of joint measures regarding:

      • the development of transport, for the primary purpose of ensuring the conveyance of the increasing volume of export-import and transit freight among member countries of the Council;

      • the most effective use of investments by member countries of the Council to develop extractive and refining industries, as well as to assist in the construction of high priority projects of interest to two or more countries;

      • the development of the exchange of goods and services between member countries of the Council and with other countries;

      • the exchange of information concerning scientific and technical achievements, as well as advanced methods of production;

   e. Assist the member countries of the Council in bringing their bilateral ventures under the framework of the Council to achieve long-term

---

"Estatutos del Consejo de Ayuda Mutua Ecoñomica" (as amended through 1979), reprinted in Junta Central de Planificación de Cuba, *Cuestiones de la Economia Planificiada* (Havana), no. 7 (January–February 1981): 199ff. The 1960 version in English appears in U.N.T.S. vol. 368 (1960): 264. This reprint is translated by Dr. Teresa Genta Fons and Beverly May Carl.

multilateralization and to ensure complete exchange of information among countries about bilateral arrangements;

    f.  Undertake such other actions as may be required to achieve the aims of the Council.

2.  In conformity with the present Charter, the Council for Mutual Economic Assistance is authorized to:

    a.  Adopt recommendations and decisions through its agencies acting within their authority;

    b.  Conclude international agreements with the member countries of the Council, other countries and international organizations.

## Article IV: Recommendations and Decisions

1.  Recommendations shall be adopted on questions of economic, scientific, and technical cooperation. Such recommendations shall be communicated to the member countries of the Council for consideration. Recommendations adopted by member countries of the Council shall be implemented by them through decisions of the government or other authorized authorities of those countries, in conformity with their laws.

2.  Decisions shall be adopted on organizational and procedural questions. Such decisions shall take effect, unless specified otherwise, from the date on which the record of the meeting of the Council again is signed.

3.  All recommendations and decisions of the Council shall be adopted only with the consent of the member countries concerned; each country is entitled to state its views on any question under consideration by the Council.

The lack of participation of one or more member countries of the Council, in measures of interest to other member countries, will not prevent collaboration of the Council with the interested countries on these measures.

Recommendations and decisions shall not apply to countries which state that they have no interest in the question at issue. Nevertheless, any such country may subsequently adhere to the recommendations and decisions adopted by the remaining member countries of the Council.

4.  The member countries may conclude agreements to implement measures considered by the agencies of the Council concerning economic, scientific, and technical cooperation issues. Such agreements shall be valid and take effect in the participating countries in accord with their laws and regulations.

. . .

## Article XV: Languages

The official languages of the Council for Mutual Economic Assistance shall be the languages of all the member countries of the Council.

The working language of the Council shall be Russian.

.  .  .

# APPENDIX J-2
## COMECON: AGREEMENT ON THE ESTABLISHMENT OF THE INTERNATIONAL INVESTMENT BANK
### (January 1, 1971)

## Article II

The fundamental task of the Bank shall be to grant long-term and medium-term credits primarily for carrying out projects connected with the international socialist division of labour, specialization and cooperation of production, expenditures for expansion of raw materials and fuel resources for the members' collective interest, and the construction of enterprises of mutual concern to member-states in other branches of the economy, as well as construction of projects for development of national economies of the countries and for other purposes, established by the Council of the Bank and consistent with the aims of the Bank.

In its activities the Bank will proceed from the principle that efficient use must be made of resources, provision must be made to guarantee that all obligations can be met, and strict responsibility must be accepted for the return of credits granted by the Bank.

Credits will be provided to finance the construction only of such projects as conform to the advanced technological standards, and promise high quality output with minimum expenditures, while the prices of goods produced must be competitive on the world market.

The Bank shall grant credits for carrying out measures and constructing projects of common interest to several member-countries provided a long-term agreement or any other understanding is available on measures and constructing projects and realization of production in the interests of member-countries with due regard to the recommendations on coordination of national economic plans of member-countries.

. . .

The Bank's activities must be organically linked to other measures which promote the further development of socialist economic cooperation and the gradual elimination of disparities between levels of economic development among member-countries. At the same time the principle that the Bank's credits must be put to efficient use must remain in force. By agreement with the Council for Mutual Economic Assistance, the Bank will participate in the work

Reprinted from *International Legal Materials* 23 (Washington, D.C.: American Society of International Law, 1984): 641. Cuba joined in 1974 and Vietnam in 1977. Ibid. at p. 644, n.1.

of the Council for Mutual Economic Assistance organs examining questions connected with the coordination of its members' national economic development plans in the field of capital investment.

· · ·

## Article VI

The Bank may attract funds in transferable rubles, national currencies of interested countries, and convertible currencies by obtaining financial and bank credit and loans, accepting medium and long-term deposits, and also by other means.

The Bank's Council can take decisions on the issue of interest-bearing bond loans placed on international money markets.

The conditions of issuing bond loans shall be determined by the Council of the Bank.

## Article VII

1. The Bank shall grant long-term and medium-term credits for the purposes provided for in Article II of the present Agreement.

2. Credits shall be granted to:
(a) banks, economic organizations and enterprises of member-countries officially authorized to receive credits;
(b) international economic organization and enterprises of member-countries;
(c) banks and economic organizations of other countries. The procedure for this is established by the Bank's Council.

3. The Bank may issue guarantees. The procedure for this is established by the Council of the Bank.

## Article VIII

The way of credit planning, time limits, terms of granting, employment and repayment of credits, issuing guarantees as well as imposition of sanctions in case of violation of terms of credits or guarantees are regulated by the Statutes and decisions of the Council of the Bank.

## Article IX

The Bank can place surplus funds with other banks, and buy and sell currencies, gold and securities as well as conduct other banking operations appropriate to the aims and purposes of the Bank.

## Article X

The Bank's activities must be economically viable.

· · ·

## APPENDIX J-3
## COMECON: STATUTES (BYLAWS) OF THE
## INTERNATIONAL INVESTMENT BANK
### (January 1, 1971)

### Article 9

The authorized capital stock is 1,000 in transferable rubles.

It is formed in collective currency (transferable rubles) and in convertible currencies or gold.

The authorized capital shall be used for the purpose set out in the Agreement and the Statutes of the Bank and shall serve as security of Bank's obligations.

The authorized capital may be increased in accordance with provisions of the Agreement.

Contributions to the authorized capital shall be made in conformity with provisions of the Agreement and decisions of the Council of the Bank.

The country which paid its installment into the authorized capital receives a certificate from the Bank which serves as an acknowledgement and evidence of the payment made.

In case of withdrawal from the Bank the amount paid to the authorized capital shall be taken into account when regulating relations between that country and the Bank under their mutual obligations.

. . .

### Article 15

Long- and medium-term credits, whether representing a project's sole source of finance or being complemented by the borrower's own resources, are granted from the Bank's own capital, reserves and borrowings.

Each credit or guarantee granted by the Bank must be the subject of an agreement.

Economic criteria characterizing high efficiency of financed projects, terms of granting, using and repayment of credits are provided for in a credit contract.

Credits are provided primarily for carrying out projects of high efficiency.

Economic efficiency criteria are: the highest technical standards in construction; optimum volume of production and efficient use of capital for the industry concerned; optimum for a given branch of industry; timely returns of

Reprinted from *International Legal Materials* 23 (Washington, D.C.: American Society of International Law, 1984): 645.

the expenses made; conformity to world standards in respect of the product quality and price; availability of the appropriate raw materials and the market for the product; the duration of the construction of the enterprise and a number of other economic and financial considerations determined by the Council of the Bank and depending on the character and purpose of the investment.

The Bank at its discretion can carry out an appraisal or send the plan of a project, technical documentation and estimate for an appraisal to the competent national organizations or international groups of specialists. Data necessary for carrying out an appraisal are provided by the beneficiaries of the credits.

When giving credits and guarantees the Bank may require provision with appropriate security.

The manner of granting and repayment of credits, security, terms and conditions which are to be stipulated in credit contracts are determined by the Council of the Bank.

## Article 16

Medium-term credits are made as a rule for up to 5 years, long-term credits—for a maximum term of up to 15 years.

. . .

## Article 20

The Bank will charge interest on the credit it grants.

The Bank will pay interest on attracted funds, receive commission for providing guarantees and carrying out instructions from its clients and correspondents.

The basic principles of the Bank's policy with regard to interest rates, commission and other charges will be established by the Council of the Bank.

Interest rates will vary according to the length of credit being provided and the currency in which it is made.

. . .

## APPENDIX J-4
## COMECON: AGREEMENT CONCERNING MULTILATERAL SETTLEMENTS IN TRANSFERABLE RUBLES AND THE ORGANIZATION OF THE INTERNATIONAL BANK FOR ECONOMIC COOPERATION.
### (May 19, 1964, as amended through November 23, 1977)

. . .

### Article I

Settlements stipulated in bilateral and multilateral agreements and separate contracts concerning mutual deliveries of goods as well as in agreements on other payments between the Contracting Parties shall, as of January 1, 1964, be effected in transferable rubles.

The gold content of the transferable ruble is set at 0.987412 gram of fine gold.

Each member-country of the Bank, possessing funds on its accounts in transferable rubles, may use them freely.

Each member-country of the Bank entering into trade agreements shall ensure the balance of collections and payments in transferable rubles with all other member-countries of the Bank as a whole within the calendar year or any other period, agreed upon by member-countries of the Bank. Creation or use of possible reserves in transferable rubles, as well as credit operations, shall then be taken into consideration.

Each member-country of the Bank shall assure full and timely discharge of its payment obligations in transferable rubles in relations with other member-countries of the Bank and with the International Bank for Economic Cooperation.

### Article II

In order to further economic cooperation and the development of the national economies of the Contracting Parties and to widen the cooperation of these Parties with other countries, it has been decided to establish the International Bank for Economic Cooperation, with its location in the city of Moscow.

The Founding Members of the Bank are the Contracting Parties.

The Bank shall:

(a) undertake multilateral settlements in transferable rubles;

(b) advance credits to finance foreign trade and other operations of the member-countries of the Bank:

(c) attract and keep non-committed funds in transferable rubles;

Reprinted from *International Legal Materials* 23 (Washington, D.C.: American Society of International Law, 1984): 650. Cuba joined both the multilateral settlements agreement and the bank for economic cooperation in 1974. Vietnam did so in 1977. Ibid. at p. 653, n. 3.

(d) attract gold, free convertible and other currencies from other countries, and perform other operations with gold, free convertible and other currencies.

The Council of the Bank will examine the possibility for the Bank to carry out transactions in exchanging transferable rubles for gold and free convertible currencies;

(e) perform other banking operations corresponding to the aims and tasks of the Bank resulting from its Statutes.

In addition to the above functions, the Bank may effect crediting of international production organizations, banks and other organizations created by the member-countries of the Bank, as well as banks of other countries, out of its own and borrowed funds, in accordance with principles and basic provisions set forth by the Council of the Bank.

The Bank may effect the financing of international economic and other organizations created by the member-countries of the Bank out of funds allocated by interested countries.

The activities of the Bank are regulated by the present Agreement, by the Statutes of the Bank which constitute an integral part to the present Agreement, and by Instructions and Regulations issued by the Bank within its competence.

. . .

## Article VI

The International Bank for Economic Cooperation may grant credits in transferable rubles, as follows:

(a) settlement credit—to satisfy requirements for funds of the authorized banks during short-term excesses in payments over collections. This credit is of a revolving type. It is advanced immediately, when needed, up to a limit determined by the Council of the Bank. The term for its repayment is not set. Credit received outstanding may be carried over to the following year;

(b) term credit—to cover requirements for funds of the authorized banks for longer periods. The credit is made available for arrangements relating to specialization and cooperation of production, for the expansion of trade turnover, for bringing the balance of payments into equilibrium, for seasonal needs, etc. The Bank advances this credit on the basis of well-grounded applications of the authorized banks for fixed terms within one year, and, in certain cases, according to the decision of the Council of the Bank, for a period of up to two or three years.

Interest is charged on credits granted. Rates of interest for credits in transferable rubles are set by the Council of the Bank, with the view of stimulating economical use of funds and ensuring the Bank's profitability.

Countries with a pronounced seasonal type of export receive term credit for seasonal needs according to procedure established by the Council of the Bank on favourable terms (as concerns interest rates).

. . .

## Article XI

The International Bank for Economic Cooperation possesses full juridical personality. The Bank enjoys the legal capacity required for the performance of its functions and the realization of its aims in accordance with the provisions of the present Agreement and the Statutes of the Bank.

As an international organization the Bank may conclude international agreements.

The Bank, as well as representatives of the member-countries in the Council of the Bank and officials of the Bank enjoy in the territory of each member-country of the Bank privileges and immunities required for the performance of the functions and the realization of the aims stipulated by the present Agreement and the Statutes of the Bank. The above privileges and immunities are determined by the Statutes of the Bank.

The Bank may open branches, agencies and representative offices in the territory of the country in which the Bank is located, as well as in the territory of other countries. The relations between the Bank and the country in which the Bank or its branches, agencies and representations are located, are determined by appropriate agreements.

# APPENDIX J-5
## COMECON: STATUTES (BYLAWS) OF THE INTERNATIONAL BANK FOR ECONOMIC COOPERATION
### (as amended through November 23, 1977)

### Article 2

1. The Bank possesses full juridical personality known as the "International Bank for Economic Cooperation."

2. The Bank has the right to:
(a) conclude agreements and sign any contracts within the limits of its competence;
(b) acquire, rent or alienate property;
(c) institute legal proceedings and be sued in courts and at arbitration;
(d) establish branches and agencies in the country where the Bank is located and in the territory of other countries, as well as have its representatives;
(e) issue instructions and regulations in matters within its competence;
(f) take other actions with the aim of fulfilling tasks vested in the Bank by the present Statutes.

. . .

### Article 5

The nominal capital of the Bank is established at 300 million transferable rubles and is built up by subscription payments in transferable rubles. A part of this nominal capital is created in gold and in free convertible currencies by the decision of the Council of the Bank.

Each member-country of the Bank has the right to pay up its share of the nominal capital of the Bank (in transferable rubles) also in free convertible currencies or in gold.

Subscription payments in the nominal capital are made on terms and within the periods established by the Council of the Bank.

The nominal capital of the Bank is a security for meeting its liabilities and is used for purposes envisaged by the Statutes of the Bank.

The amount of the nominal capital of the Bank can be increased in accordance with the provisions of Article III of the Agreement.

---

Reprinted from *International Legal Materials* 23 (Washington, D.C.: American Society of International Law, 1984): 653. Cuba joined both the multilateral settlements agreement and the bank for economic cooperation in 1974. Vietnam did so in 1977. Ibid. at p. 653, n. 3.

In case of a country's withdrawal from the Bank its subscription payments shall be refunded, less the indebtedness of this country to the Bank.

In the event of the liquidation of the Bank, subscriptions and other holdings of the Bank, after meeting claims of creditors on its liabilities, shall be refunded to the member-countries of the Bank and distributed among them, less amounts to cover indebtedness in settling mutual claims.

. . .

## Article 9

The Bank organizes and undertakes multilateral settlements in transferable rubles connected with trade and other transactions. Settlements are conducted through the transferable ruble accounts of the banks of the member-countries (hereinafter referred to as authorized banks) opened in their favour with the International Bank for Economic Cooperation or, with its consent, with other authorized banks.

Payments are effected by the Bank within the limits of holdings on transferable ruble accounts of each authorized bank.

. . .

## Article 13

The Bank may undertake the settlement operations resulting from the financing of capital investment and granting credits for the joint establishment, modernization and operation of industrial enterprises and other undertakings by the interested countries.

. . .

## CREDIT OPERATIONS OF THE BANK

### Article 19

The Bank grants credits to authorized banks. Credits are granted for specific purposes and on terms of repayment within agreed periods.

The purposes for which credits are granted, the methods of their allocation, security and repayment are determined by the Council of the Bank.

The Bank may also grant credits to international production organizations, banks and other organizations created by the member-countries of the Bank, as well as to banks of other countries in accordance with principles and basic provisions set forth by the Council of the Bank.

## Article 20

The Bank works out credit plans for its credit operations.

Credit plans of the Bank are drawn up on the basis of credit applications of the authorized banks, proceeding from data provided in their plans for development of national economies and foreign trade, as well as in trade agreements and contracts. Credit applications of the international production organizations, banks and other organizations, created by the member-countries of the Bank, as well as credit applications of banks of other countries are also included into credit plans of the Bank. When drawing up credit plans the Bank also makes use of its own data and estimates. Credit plans are endorsed by the Council of the Bank. If an authorized bank makes an application for credits surpassing the level envisaged by the credit plan, the Bank examines the application taking into account all data submitted by the bank concerning the fulfillment of trade agreements by that country, as well as other pertinent information.

. . .

## Article 24

The Bank may grant and receive credits and loans in convertible and other currencies on the basis of agreements concluded with banks and other organizations and institutions of the member-countries of the Bank and non-member countries, conduct deposit, arbitrage, bill of exchange, guarantee, settlement and other operations in these currencies accepted in international banking practice, as well as operations with gold.

# INDEX

Abidjan, Treaty of, 14
across the board tariff reductions, 12, 15, 18, 20, 102; ANCOM, 17; EEC 12, 15, 26; ECOWAS, 14, [protocol, 182]
Africa, Central (*see* ECCAS)
Africa, Eastern and Southern (*see* PTA)
Africa, West (*see* ECOWAS)
agreements to agree: ECOWAS, 14–15; ECCAS, 15; PTA, 15
agricultural production, 1, 109
ANCOM: 7; conventions on avoidance of double taxation, 52, 106; peso andino, 62; relation to LAFTA/LAIA, 5, 71, 76, 78, 107; trade relations with LAIA members, 16–17; basic treaties 220ff. (*see also* across the board tariff reductions; Andean Development Corporation; Andean Reserve Fund; common external tariffs; common list; competition; courts, supra-national; Decision 24; escape devices; goods not produced in the region; indigenous multinational enterprises; less economically developed countries; non-scheduled goods; non-tariff barriers; origin, rules of; quotas; sectorial programs; tax incentives; and technology transfer)
Andean Development Corporation, 59
Andean Foreign Investment Code (*see* Decision 24)
Andean Reserve Fund, 63
Antitrust (*see* competition)
Aragão, José Maria, 3
Argentina, 16–17, 21–22, 24, 46, 71, 75–76, 77, 83, 104, 112
ASEAN (Association for Southeast Asian Nations): 4; basic documents, 117; extraregional agreements, 76–77, 84, 111–112

(*see also*, "ASEAN Industrial Complementation Projects" (AIC): "ASEAN Industrial Projects" [AIP]; "ASEAN Industrial Joint Ventures" [AIJV]; complementation; indigenous multinational enterprises; origin, rules of; preferential trade associations; preferences, regional tariff; product by product negotiations)
"ASEAN Industrial Complementation Projects" (AIC): 49
"ASEAN Industrial Joint Ventures" (AIJV), 45, 50–51, 79, 88–89, 106, 128–132
"ASEAN Industrial Projects" (AIP), 48
assistance, public, 2

barter (*see* countertrade)
Bolivia, 1, 7, 18, 21–22, 24, 26, 37–38, 44, 48, 59, 64, 71, 72, 74, 76–78, 80, 84, 85, 111
Brazil, 1, 6, 16, 21, 24–25, 46, 71, 75–77, 82, 83–85, 104, 105, 106–107
Brunei, 4

CARICOM (Caribbean Common Market), 4, 71; common market treaty, 200 (*see also* clearinghouse facilities; common external tariffs, competition; court, supra-national; immediate free internal trade; movement, freedom of; non-tariff barriers; origin, rules of; tax incentives; taxation, treaties to avoid double; unit of account; and withdrawal, right of)
CARAFTA (Caribbean Free Trade Association), 4
CACM (Central American Common Market), 4, 13, 76, 83, 85; basic treaty 190 (*see also* clearinghouse facilities, immediate free internal trade, "integrated industries"; quotas; tax incentives; and unit of account)

279

# ABOUT THE AUTHOR

Beverly May Carl is a Professor of Law at Southern Methodist University, Dallas, Texas. During 1979 she was a visiting Fulbright Professor at the University of Padjadjaran in Bandung, Indonesia. Besides having taught courses in Venezuela, Taiwan, and the People's Republic of China, she has lectured throughout Latin America, Asia, the Indian subcontinent, and Australia.

Professor Carl entered teaching after ten years of service with the U.S. Department of Commerce, the U.S. Treasury Department, and the U.S. Agency for International Development. While with the latter agency, she served in Rio de Janeiro for two years as Chief of the Private Investment Division; subsequently she worked as a deputy administrator of the relief program during the Nigeria-Biafra War.

She has published widely in the field of international law and development. Her articles have appeared in the *Harvard International Law Journal*, the *Columbia Journal of Transnational Law*, the *Virginia Journal of International Law*, among others. From 1980 to 1983, she was the editor and contributor of a multivolume work, *Doing Business in Mexico* (Matthew Bender).

She holds a Juris Doctor degree from the University of Southern California and an LL.M. from Yale University, after which she attended the Law School at the National University of Chile as a Fulbright Scholar.